A Structural Theory of Social Influence

This book addresses a phenomenon that has been much studied in anthropology, sociology, and administrative science – the social structural foundations of coordinated activity and consensus in complexly differentiated communities and organizations. Such foundations are important because social differentiation makes coordination and agreement especially hard to achieve and maintain. Noah Friedkin examines the process of social influence and how this process, when it is played out in a network of interpersonal influence, may result in interpersonal agreements among actors who are located in different parts of a complexly differentiated organization. This work builds on structural role analysis, which provides a description of the pattern of social differentiation in a population. Interpreting the revealed social structures has long been a problem. Friedkin proposes new steps for structural analysis to deal with this problem. To explain the coordination of social positions, the author seeks to develop a structural social psychology that attends to both social structure and process.

Noah E. Friedkin is Professor of Sociology at the University of California, Santa Barbara. The author of numerous articles, Friedkin has served on the editorial boards of the *American Journal of Sociology, American Sociological Review*, and *Social Psychology Quarterly*. His work has been supported by grants from the National Science Foundation.

Structural Analysis in the Social Sciences

Mark Granovetter, editor

Other books in the series:

Mark S. Mizruchi and Michael Schwartz, eds., *Intercorporate Relations: The Structural Analysis of Business*
David Knoke, *Political Networks: The Structural Perspective*
John L. Campbell, J. Rogers Hollinsworth, and Leon N. Lindberg, eds., *Governance of the American Economy*
Kyriakos Kontopoulos, *The Logics of Social Structure*
Philippa Pattison, *Algebraic Models for Social Networks*
Stanley Wasserman and Katherine Faust, *Social Network Analysis: Methods and Applications*
Gary Herrigel, *Industrial Constructions: The Sources of German Industrial Power*
Philippe Bourgois, *In Search of Respect: Selling Crack in El Barrio*
Per Hage and Frank Harary, *Island Networks: Communication, Kinship, and Classification Structures in Oceania*
Thomas Schweizer and Douglas R. White, *Kinship, Networks and Exchange*
David Wank, *Commodifying Communism: Business, Trust, and a South China City*

The series Structural Analysis in the Social Sciences presents approaches that explain social behavior and institutions by reference to *relations* among such concrete entities as persons and organizations. This contrasts with at least four other popular strategies: (a) reductionist attempts to explain by a focus on individuals alone; (b) explanations stressing the causal primacy of such abstract concepts as ideas, values, mental harmonies, and cognitive maps (thus, "structuralism" on the Continent should be distinguished from structural analysis in the present sense); (c) technological and material determinism; (d) explanations using "variables" as the main analytic concepts (as in the "structural equation" models that dominated much of the sociology of the 1970s), where structure is that which connects variables rather than actual social entities.

The social network approach is an important example of the strategy of structural analysis; the series also draws on social science theory and research that is not framed explicitly in network terms but stresses the importance of relations rather than the atomization of reductionism or the determinism of ideas, technology, or material conditions. Though the structural perspective has become extremely popular and influential in all the social sciences, it does not have a coherent identity, and no series yet pulls together such work under a single rubric. By bringing the achievements of structurally oriented scholars to a wider public, the *Structural Analysis* series hopes to encourage the use of this very fruitful approach.

A Structural Theory of Social Influence

NOAH E. FRIEDKIN

PUBLISHED BY THE PRESS SYNDICATE OF THE UNIVERSITY OF CAMBRIDGE
The Pitt Building, Trumpington Street, Cambridge CB2 1RP, United Kingdom

CAMBRIDGE UNIVERSITY PRESS
The Edinburgh Building, Cambridge CB2 2RU, UK http://www.cup.cam.ac.uk
40 West 20th Street, New York, NY 10011-4211, USA http://www.cup.org
10 Stamford Road, Oakleigh, Melbourne 3166, Australia

First published 1998

Printed in the United States of America

Typeset in Sabon 10/12 pt, in Penta [RF]

Library of Congress Cataloging-in-Publication Data

Friedkin, Noah E., 1947–
A structural theory of social influence / Noah E. Friedkin.
p. cm.
Includes bibliographical references and index.
ISBN 0-521-45482-4 (hardback)
1. Social influence. 2. Social structure. I. Title.
HM259.F74 1998
303.3'4 – DC21 97–31998
CIP

A catalog record for this book is available from the British Library

ISBN 0 521 45482 4 hardback

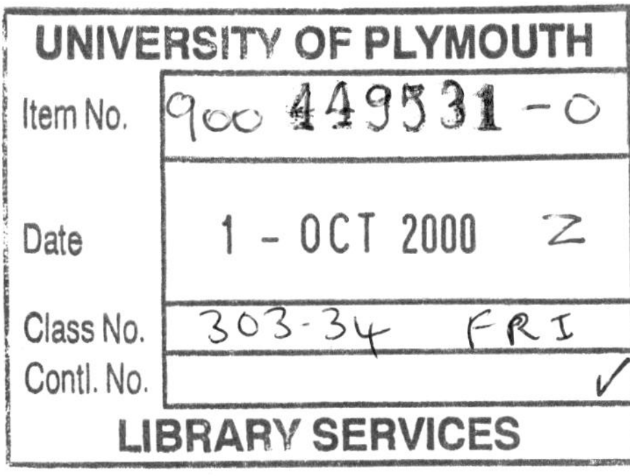

Contents

Part B. Measures of the Theoretical Constructs

Part C. Analysis

Tables and Figures

Tables

Figures

Preface

In this book I address a phenomenon that has been much studied in anthropology, sociology, and administrative science – the social structural foundations of coordinated activity and consensus in complexly differentiated communities and organizations. Such foundations are important because social differentiation makes coordination and agreement especially hard to achieve and maintain; Laumann and Knoke (1986) describe the problem in this way:

> The structural differentiation of large-scale complex social systems has two fundamental implications for the integrative problems that such systems confront. First, structural differentiation is the basis of the objective differentiation of interests – i.e., claims for scarce goods, services, and facilities that component actors make on the larger social system, and for the differentiation of means (or relative power) by which they assert these claims with greater or lesser effect. Second, structural differentiation is also likely to lead to the differentiation of evaluative standards (values) that are used by various system elements to specify and establish the priorities among competing ends or goals that the system as a whole should collectively seek to achieve.

Emile Durkheim's (1933) treatise, *The Division of Labor in Society,* is the point of departure for this field of work. Durkheim's insight was that social differentiation does not necessarily lead to discordant activities and opinions, that there are different forms of social differentiation, and that one of the possible forms of social differentiation entails an integrative social structure – an organic solidarity – in which interpersonal discord is limited. Durkheim did not provide a clear definition of organic solidarity, and the problem with which he was so passionately engaged is still being researched.

It is useful to conceptualize Durkheim's problem in *Division of Labor* as a problem of social control that arises not only in the large-scale societies with which Durkheim was concerned, but also in smaller-scale civic and professional communities and formal organizations. Janowitz (1975) reminds us that in classical sociological studies the concept of social control refers to the occurrence and effectiveness of ongoing efforts in a group to formulate, agree upon, and implement collective courses of action. Janowitz argues that the "problem of social control" is not only to elucidate social control mechanisms, but also (taking the reduction of mechanisms based on coercion as a desirable goal) to discover conditions under which noncoercive mechanisms provide an effective basis of social control. Thus, the classical approach to the study of social control has emphasized voluntary mechanisms of coordination and control that are based on networks of interpersonal communication (social influence), legitimized decision-making procedures (social choice), and bargaining (markets).

My interest focuses on the process of social influence and how this process, when played out in a network of interpersonal influence, may result in interpersonal agreements among actors who are located in different parts of a complexly differentiated organization. In Durkheim's terms, I am concerned with the social structure and processes that constitute organic solidarity. My work builds on structural role analysis (White, Boorman, and Breiger 1976; Laumann and Pappi 1976; Burt 1982), which provides a description of the pattern of social differentiation in a population. Interpretation of the revealed social structures has been a problem, and the new steps for structural analysis that I propose are addressed to this problem. These new steps include (a) a more elaborate description of social structures, which entails not only the social positions that actors occupy, but also the network of interpersonal influences among the positions, (b) the specification of a social influence process by which the predispositions (initial preferences and opinions) of actors in the various social positions may be modified, and (c) an analysis of the systemic implications of the influence process. In short, to explain the coordination of social positions, I pursue the development of a structural social psychology that attends to both social structure and process.

The merits of the proposed new steps can be assessed on at least three different levels. First, a critic might question how much, if any, social process we need to take into account to elucidate the structural bases of coordination and control. Second, a critic might grant the usefulness of employing a social process model to elucidate such bases, but reject the particular model that I have employed. Third, a critic might accept the social process model, but find flaws in my measures of the model's constructs. Chapters 1–3 of this book address the importance of a process-oriented approach to social structure and describe a network theory of social influence. Chapters 4–7 deal with the measurement of the theoretical constructs and describe a structural approach to these constructs. Chapters 8–10 deal with the structure of influence systems in differentiated populations, and they address the consequences of such systems for the production of dominant social positions and agreements between actors in different social positions. Chapter 11 concludes the book with a discussion of Durkheim's vision of a sociology that would help to mitigate anomy. My approach is formal. I work with a particular mathematical model of the opinion-formation process that has been under development by social psychologists and mathematicians since the late 1950s (French 1956; Harary 1959; DeGroot 1974; Friedkin 1986; Friedkin and Cook 1990; Friedkin and Johnsen 1990; Friedkin 1990b; Friedkin 1991; Friedkin and Johnsen 1997).

I will not be upset if the present work encourages a substantial refinement or rejection of my theory or methods so long as they are replaced by an alternative *equally comprehensive* formal scheme. Science operates under the assumption that the architect of reality is a mathematician whose works are elegant. Even if this assumption is incorrect, the process of constructing, rejecting, and reconstructing formal theories of events has an important heuristic value, for science also assumes that events are intelligible, and formal theories have a demonstrated utility in stimulating the accumulation of knowledge. Formal theories shift attention from discrete propositions to schema (entailing general viewpoints and assumptions) from which a large number of propositions are deduced. While providing plentiful matter for hypothesis testing, they transform such testing from an end to a means of evaluating approaches from which we might deduce substantial segments of reality. Although formal theories generally do not withstand disinterested scrutiny, they often make an enduring contribution to understanding as a by-product of the structured speculation and empirical work that occurs when attention is focused on them. The main aim of this book is the initiation of such structured speculation and empirical work on the interface of social structure and social psychological process.

My theoretical agenda is pursued in tandem with an empirical analysis of science faculties at The University of Chicago and Columbia University. I selected scientists in university settings for several reasons. Universities are modern manifestations of the type of medieval corporate organization that Durkheim believed must be restored throughout modern society in order to establish the coordinative structures of organic solidarity. At the same time, Durkheim illustrated his concept of anomy in an analysis of the scientific community. Hence, it seemed to me that the social structure of the professoriate in research universities would be a theoretically strategic focus for a study of the Durkheimian problem of social control.

The data for this book were collected in 1977–78, while I was a Research Associate in the Educational Finance and Productivity Center at The University of Chicago. The initial analysis of the social networks was not a pleasant experience. The networks were cumbersome and expensive to analyze because of their large size and because a theoretical focus on detailed structural features required the development of custom-written FORTRAN programs. I published several papers that drew on these data and then moved on to related inquiries, especially the development of the formal theory of social influence that enters into the present study. Although I had put the work on these science faculty networks aside, I felt that several of the findings I had obtained on the relationship between communication structure and interpersonal visibility were unusually beautiful and ought to be pursued (Friedkin 1982, 1983). Moreover, in light of developments in network theory that have occurred during the past several decades, I realized that my arguments and results could be usefully elaborated and that I might more forcefully make certain theoretical points. However, the initial experience of analyzing these data dampened my desire to pursue this project.

The circumstances that had impeded my work on these science faculties were dramatically altered several years ago. I had developed computer software – SNAPs – that facilitated the analysis of the type of detailed structural features of networks that were of especial interest to me; but, because this software was based on the GAUSS programming language, I could not address networks of more than ninety members. When this limitation in GAUSS was removed, I was in a position to analyze the science faculty networks with little difficulty, and I immediately began to consider and plan the present volume. Although the data are old, they are suited to my theoretical concerns. If I had not collected such data previously, I would want to collect them now.

I am indebted to my teachers at The University of Chicago: Charles Bidwell, who supported the data collection on which this book is based and my early interest in social networks; James Coleman, who gave me valuable advice and encouragement during the data-collection phase of this project; and Edward Laumann, whose research program on structural analysis was important in initiating and defining the line of my own work. I also am indebted to my colleagues in Santa Barbara, especially Dorwin Cartwright and Eugene Johnsen, with whom I have met, virtually every Monday afternoon for several hours since 1978, in a faculty seminar devoted to discussions of network phenomena. I have no doubt that these discussions have sustained my passion for the study of social networks. Finally, I thank my father, a biochemist, whose deep skepticism of social science and high expectations for his son have served to create a powerful pressure on me to pursue fundamental inquiries with the most rigorous methods at my disposal. I dedicate this book to my parents, my wife, and my children.

Part A

Theory and Setting

1

Social Structure and Social Control

Abstract. Elucidating mechanisms by which actors in differentiated social positions come to be coordinated remains a key theoretical problem for structural analysis. The strength of structural analysis has been its success in describing complex patterns of social differentiation; its weakness has been that it is not wedded to a structural social psychology that elucidates how interpersonal agreements are formed in a complexly differentiated group. Hence, interpreting the revealed social structures has been difficult, especially with regard to their implications for social control.

Analysis of social structure has been advanced by the idea that social differentiation is defined by networks of social relations. Prior to the network approach to social structure, analysts relied on nominal classifications of actors (based on gender, race, ethnicity, religion, or occupation among other variables) to describe the social differentiation of groups, communities, and organizations. In the network approach to social structure, the positions of actors are revealed by their patterns of relations with other actors, and a differentiated social structure is defined by the existence of actors who occupy different positions in networks of social relations.[1] The approach has been widely applied. For instance, it has been used to describe the social structure of elite families in Florence circa 1430, monks in a present-day monastery, major corporate actors in national markets and policy communities, and researchers in scientific specialties.

I build on this line of structural analysis. Social differentiation is my *start point.* I focus on the consequences of social structure for patterns of interpersonal influence and agreement among actors in different social positions. In the present chapter I describe the theoretical concerns of

1 A social network exists in a population of actors whenever we can say that "actor *i* is related to actor *j*" or that "actor *i* is not related to actor *j*" for each ordered pair of actors. Thus, networks of kinship, friendship, advice seeking, and discussion (among other relations) may be defined. Wasserman and Faust (1994), a useful reference book on social networks, contains a thorough review of the methods that have been developed in this field to describe social positions.

the inquiry. First, I describe the network approach to mapping differentiated social structures. Second, I describe pertinent theoretical work on the importance of informal social processes versus institutionalized features of social structure in elucidating a population's opinions and actions. Third, I describe the bearing of structural analysis on the classical problem of social control – the development of interpersonal agreement and coordinated action in complexly differentiated social structures.

I argue that a structural analysis which is restricted to a description of social differentiation does not address the problem of social control, and that the social influence process which links the occupants of different social positions must be taken into account to address this problem. If social control refers to the occurrence and effectiveness of ongoing efforts in a group to formulate, agree upon, and implement coordinated lines of action, then the process of interpersonal influence is a key foundation of social control. This viewpoint on social control stems from George Herbert Mead (1925), who argued that social control depends on "the degree to which individuals in society are able to assume attitudes of others who are involved with them in common endeavors." Interpersonal influence affects actors' attitudes and opinions and is, therefore, a foundation of actors' socialization, identity, and decisions. Interpersonal influence also is a foundation of actors' efforts to control their social environment by modifying the attitudes and opinions of significant others with whom they interact. In groups, communities, and organizations, this influence process can produce agreements that define the culture of the group and that frame the collective activities of its members.

Interpersonal influence typically occurs in a larger network of influences wherein the attitudes and opinions of actors reflect those of their significant others, whose attitudes and opinions reflect those of their significant others, and so forth. Because of this concatenation of reflections (based on the flows of interpersonal influence among actors), there is not always a simple relationship between the particular social position that is occupied by an actor and his or her attitudes and opinions. Structural analysis has not attended to this concatenation of reflections and has focused only on the proximate conditions of actors for an explanation of their attitudes and opinions. However, a characteristic feature of interpersonal influence is that actors' attitudes and opinions may reflect the preferences of others who occupy *different* social positions than their own (hence, children may reflect the attitudes of their parents and ancestors, adolescents may reflect the attitudes of friends and friends-of-friends who have a different socioeconomic status than their own, and workers may reflect the attitudes of supervisors and owners). Hence, unless we take into account the process of interpersonal influence that connects the occupants of different social positions, we are not likely to understand the opinions and attitudes that are expressed by the occupants of particular social positions. By the same token, we are not likely to understand how agreements and shared understandings come to be formed that include occupants of different social positions and that reduce their conflicts and coordinate their collective activities. Such agreements either emerge directly from the social influence process or are the result of social choice mechanisms that are supported by agreements that have emerged from this influence process.

In this argument, which I elaborate in the present chapter, I reject the brand of structuralism advocated by Robert Merton (1957) and others in which the individual's response to conflicting interpersonal influences does not appear as a key theoretical issue. Instead, I propose a structural social psychology in which the individual is the key site at which the integration of conflicting influences occurs, because it is this *ongoing repetitive integration by individuals* that sets in motion the flows of influence that, in turn, can result in interpersonal agreement and coordinated action in complexly differentiated social structures. Social structural constraints do not disappear in this approach. They are present in the social differentiation which is the origin of the different attitudes and opinions upon which the social influence process operates, and they are present in the network of interpersonal influence which is the context for the social influence process.

1.1 Social Differentiation

In the seminal work on a network approach to describing social structures, the definition of social positions went hand in hand with the definition of a *framework of relations among social positions* (Breiger, Boorman, and Arabie 1975; White, Boorman, and Breiger 1976; Boorman and White 1976; Arabie, Boorman, and Levitt 1978). I will consider this seminal work in some detail, because the theoretical problems that are my main concern spring from a close analysis of it.

Most investigators who work with a network definition of social positions describe positions in terms of the similarity of actors' relations to other actors (or types of actors) in one or more concrete social networks; however, this was not precisely the approach taken by Harrison White and his colleagues. Their approach – blockmodeling – is based on an analysis of contrasting densities of interpersonal ties among and between subsets of actors.[2] There are three steps involved in the analysis.

First, a partitioning of a population is sought that reveals *zeroblocks* or low-density submatrices in one or more social networks. The goal is to find a blockmodel (i.e., a partitioning of the population) that reveals a contrast between submatrices of low and high density. An example of a blockmodel for two hypothetical social relations is:

$$
\mathbf{P} = \begin{array}{c} \begin{array}{ccccccc} 1 & 4 & 5 & 7 & 2 & 3 & 6 \end{array} \\ \left[\begin{array}{cccc|ccc} 0 & 1 & 0 & 0 & 0 & 0 & 0 \\ 1 & 0 & 1 & 0 & 0 & 0 & 0 \\ 0 & 1 & 0 & 1 & 0 & 0 & 0 \\ 0 & 1 & 0 & 0 & 0 & 0 & 0 \\ \hline 0 & 0 & 0 & 0 & 0 & 1 & 1 \\ 0 & 0 & 0 & 0 & 1 & 0 & 0 \\ 0 & 0 & 0 & 0 & 1 & 1 & 0 \end{array}\right] \end{array}
\qquad
\mathbf{N} = \begin{array}{c} \begin{array}{ccccccc} 1 & 4 & 5 & 7 & 2 & 3 & 6 \end{array} \\ \left[\begin{array}{cccc|ccc} 0 & 0 & 0 & 0 & 0 & 1 & 0 \\ 0 & 0 & 0 & 0 & 1 & 0 & 0 \\ 0 & 0 & 0 & 0 & 0 & 1 & 0 \\ 0 & 0 & 0 & 0 & 0 & 1 & 0 \\ \hline 0 & 1 & 0 & 1 & 0 & 0 & 0 \\ 0 & 1 & 0 & 0 & 0 & 0 & 0 \\ 0 & 1 & 1 & 0 & 0 & 0 & 0 \end{array}\right] \end{array}
$$

where **P** indicates friendship and **N** indicates antagonism. The population has been partitioned into two subgroups; and the resulting blocks are submatrices that describe friendly or antagonistic ties from the members of one subgroup to the members of the same or different subgroup.

In the blockmodel approach, unlike previous cluster-detection approaches, the target is not a partition that maximizes the density of ties in the blocks on the main diagonal (i.e., within-group ties); instead, the target is a more general "block checkerboard" pattern that is based on a search for zeroblocks. Hence, "the blockmodel is given structure by the *absence* of ties in certain blocks instead of by the high density of blocks containing ties" (Arabie, Boorman, and Levitt 1978, p. 34). In a "block checkerboard" pattern, high-density blocks may appear off the main diagonal, and zeroblocks may appear on the main diagonal.

Actors are said to be *structurally equivalent* if they occupy the same block in the blockmodel. In comparison with more recent approaches to social positions, this blockmodel approach entails a subtle but enormously important difference of conceptualization: Actors are not located in the same block because they are structurally equivalent in their pattern of concrete relations with other actors; instead, they are structurally equivalent because they have been located in the same block as a consequence of a search for zeroblocks.[3] The CONCOR algorithm, which has

2 Network density is the proportion of ties that are present in a specified set of pairs of actors. For example, the density of a network $\mathbf{R}_{N \times N} = [\mathbf{r}_{ij}]$, where $\mathbf{r}_{ij} = 1$ if $i \rightarrow j$ and $r_{ij} = 0$ otherwise, is $(\Sigma_i \Sigma_j \mathbf{r}_{ij})/(N^2 - N)$ for $i \neq j$; similarly, the density of a submatrix (block) of **R** is obtained by dividing the number of ties in the submatrix by the number of possible ties.

3 This distinction disappears in the special case of a blockmodel composed of blocks that are either completely or vacuously dense.

been employed frequently in the construction of blockmodels, was not perceived originally as a method for isolating subsets of actors who are structurally equivalent in their networks of social ties; instead, the value of the algorithm was seen to rest on its empirically demonstrated ability to locate zeroblocks:

> The following empirical fact makes CONCOR a procedure which has been highly effective in the search for blockmodels: When a sufficiently sparse data matrix $\mathbf{M}_0$ is permuted to conform to CONCOR-derived blocks, the permutation will generally reveal zeroblocks or near-zeroblocks in the data. (Arabie, Boorman, and Levitt 1978, p. 36)

Thus, the social structure of a group is defined by the pattern of zeroblocks in the group.

Second, given a blockmodel of the group, an *image* of the macro-structure of the group is obtained. In this image, the social units are positions, and two positions are related if and only if the block that describes the ties between the two positions is not a zeroblock. The relations in the image matrix are described as *bonds*. For example, in the blockmodel illustrated earlier the image matrices are:

$$\hat{\mathbf{P}} = \begin{bmatrix} 1 & 0 \\ 0 & 1 \end{bmatrix} \quad \hat{\mathbf{N}} = \begin{bmatrix} 0 & 1 \\ 1 & 0 \end{bmatrix}$$

When strict zeroblocks do not arise, a generalization of this approach is employed: A bond is defined if the density of ties in the underlying block is above a threshold value. For a suitable threshold value, Arabie, Boorman, and Levitt (1978) suggest the density of ties in the population. It is the pattern of bonds that defines the structure of the blockmodel, and actors are said to be structurally equivalent with respect to these bonds, rather than with respect to the concrete (raw) social networks from which these bonds are derived.

Third, a further description of the macro-structure is obtained in terms of algebraic identities among compound relations, where a compound relation is based on Boolean multiplication of image matrices. A simple example of such an identification is $\hat{\mathbf{P}} \otimes \hat{\mathbf{P}} = \hat{\mathbf{P}}$, which states that "a friend of a friend is a friend." Another example is $\hat{\mathbf{N}} \otimes \hat{\mathbf{P}} = \hat{\mathbf{N}}$, which states that "an antagonist of a friend is an antagonist." The set of all such identifications describes the internal logic of the social structure and (with further formulation) also allows a comparison of social structures.

This blockmodel approach to macro-structure has the virtue of offering a coherent and elegant scheme for the description of social differentiation. It not only provides a description of the array of social positions in a population, but also provides a description of the macro-structure in which these positions are embedded.

The theoretical weakness of the blockmodel approach is the absence of a clear rationale for basing the description of social differentiation on an analysis of the density of social relations: The description of social structure (in terms of positions and bonds) stems from the pattern of "holes" (zeroblocks) in the underlying raw social networks. It is unclear why "holes" should be treated as decisive in the definition of social structure and override possibly marked variations in the densities within and among blocks. Obviously, "holes" define social structure when the areas of social structure that are not "holes" have a uniform density, just as a melody can result from playing a single note that is interrupted by silences of various lengths. However, the result of such an approach is a poor model for social structure (as it is for a symphony), which is based on highly variegated patterns of relations. To be sure, a blockmodel provides a summary description of the pattern of social ties in a population; but the social control implications of the revealed structure are unclear.[4]

Recent work on social positions has departed from the blockmodel approach in favor of grounding the definition of social position on a *direct analysis* of the profile similarity of actors in their concrete social networks. As part of this departure from the blockmodel approach, the heuristic value of CONCOR is reconceptualized: The product-moment correlations (upon which CONCOR is based) now appear as a plausible measure of profile similarity (among many possible alternative measures of such similarity), and the CONCOR algorithm itself now appears as one method (among alternative methods) for pursuing a cluster analysis of these profile similarities.[5]

However, the current direct approaches to social positions do no better than the blockmodel approach in elucidating the implications of the revealed social structures. These direct approaches obtain social positions from a hierarchical clustering or multidimensional scaling of profile similarities. It is expected, as in the blockmodel approach, that actors in the same or proximate social positions have more homogeneous status characteristics and predispositions, with respect to behavior and opinion,

4 It should also be noted that compound relations can be examined directly without the "smoothing" and loss of information that is entailed by image matrices (Pattison 1993). These compound identifications are statements about how concrete social relations hang together and, therefore, can be studied directly to assess the degree of fit of the hypothesized identification. Identifications based on image matrices do not reliably indicate the strength of the identification in the concrete networks.

5 CONCOR has been abandoned by its originators because of a lack of formal foundations for the partitions that the algorithm produces (Phipps Arabie, personal communication).

than actors in different or distant social positions. But can anything more be asserted about the implications of the revealed social structure, apart from this coupling of an actor's characteristics, predispositions, and social position? It is at this point, i.e., the analysis of the revealed social differentiation, that structural analysis runs into difficulty.

The definition of social positions does not describe the behavior of the system of social positions. Social positions entail conditions that have effects on opinions and behaviors, but the opinions and behaviors of actors that reflect their social positions may be modified by interpersonal influences. Actors in proximate (nonidentical) positions may be influenced by different subsets of actors who polarize the opinions of the actors; conversely, actors in distant social positions may come to an agreement as a consequence of interpersonal influences. Thus, without additional theory, there is no basis for concluding that the actors in proximate (nonidentical) social positions will have similar opinions and coordinated behaviors in the equilibrium state of the social influence process, or that actors who occupy certain markedly different social positions will have dissimilar equilibrium opinions or uncoordinated behaviors. A coordinative social structure that serves to maintain or form agreements between actors in different positions, including consensus, may or may not be present.

Structural analysis has sought to address the implications of social structure in three ways. (a) Qualitative analysis has been employed to describe the activities of actors who occupy particular positions in the social structure, and the collective outcomes of these activities. (b) Network analysis has been employed to describe the pattern of interpersonal ties within and between social positions.[6] (c) Statistical analysis of the distribution of status characteristics, opinions, and behaviors among and within social positions has been employed to describe any cleavages that may exist in the population. The studies of Edward Laumann and his colleagues show how these supplementary analyses may be combined in sophisticated ways to interpret a revealed social structure (Laumann and Pappi 1976; Heinz and Laumann 1982; Laumann and Knoke 1987; Heinz, Laumann, Nelson, and Salisbury 1993).

It is evident that structural analysis lacks a formal theory that predicts the consequences of the *system of social positions* for agreements and interpersonal influences; we do not have a theory that, building directly on the description of social positions, provides an analysis of the *sys-*

6 In these network analyses, heavy reliance is placed on tables that report network densities within and between distinguishable social positions (Marsden 1989). Obviously, such density tables raise the same theoretical issue that creates an interpretation problem in the original blockmodel approach; viz., why should network density be privileged with respect to the indication of linkages among social positions?

temic implications of the revealed set of positions, or the degree to which the opinions and behaviors of the actors who occupy different positions are coordinated. The closest approximation to such theory was achieved by the blockmodel approach in which social positions and the bonds between them are *simultaneously* generated by the pattern of zeroblocks. In contrast, the direct approach to social positions, when it severs the definition of a social structure from the pattern of zeroblocks, loses a grasp on the *structural basis of bonds between positions* that is the main virtue of the blockmodel approach.

A key aim of the present work is to place the analysis of interpositional connections on a more secure and formal footing. I will take a direct approach to describing social positions in multidimensional social space. I replace the inferences based on network density with inferences based on a formal model of social influence, and I show how the pattern of interpersonal influences among social positions affects the development of interpersonal agreements and dominant social positions.

1.2 Social Process and Institutions

Influence processes among social positions must be described in detail in order to elucidate the social control implications of a pattern of differentiation. This assertion may and should be questioned. I contrast two extreme viewpoints on the effects of social structure. According to one viewpoint, interpersonal influences simply reflect institutionalized elements of social organization and, therefore, the outcomes of such processes are obvious once the institutionalized features of the social structure are laid bare. According to the other viewpoint, institutionalized features of social structure weakly constrain outcomes, and the opinions and behaviors of actors can be understood only by taking into account the informal network of interpersonal influences that connects actors who occupy different social positions.

1.2.1 Strongly Constraining Structures

In a strongly constraining social structure the opinions and behaviors of actors are determined mainly by institutionalized status characteristics and power structures. The important agreements and disagreements among actors in different social positions are shaped by a population's history, culture, and governance structures and are affected mainly by macro-processes and events such as wars and revolutions, economic growth and decline, information and persuasion from mass media, social and political movements, and demographic trends. In a strongly constraining social structure, there is a clear set of material exigencies and normative expectations, and therefore little ambiguity or confusion about the appropriate opinions and actions in a domain of issues and situations. Interpersonal influences (based on coercion, authority, expertise, identification, or rewards) reflect and support institutionalized features of the social structure and, therefore, may be ignored in the explanation of the opinions and behavior of actors. It is the institutionalized situation that is important.

The prototypical strongly constrained social structure is a bureaucratic organization, in which many of the actions of the officeholders are entirely determined by formal regulations and authorities. To be sure, bureaucracies vary in the degree of constraint they exert on the behavior of actors; moreover, strongly constraining social structures are not found exclusively in bureaucracies. Two conditions appear especially important for the maintenance of a strongly constraining social structure, and they have been repeatedly emphasized in the literature.

First, there is a clear demarcation between the individual and positional (organizational) personality, so that a circumscribed domain of behavior and opinion is constrained. So-called greedy institutions and sects are special cases in which the whole individual is the object of constraint. Typically, however, there is segmentation of the actor so that only certain behaviors and attitudes are relevant. For example, the authority of a lieutenant over a sergeant should not depend on their relative ages, although broader societal norms – deference to age and experience – might encourage a respectful attitude of lieutenants toward those older and more experienced sergeants who are under their command. Socialization and selection serve to support the segmentation of actors by attenuating the importance of certain sources of variation in actors' behavior and opinions. In short, when social positions and interpersonal influences strongly constrain opinions and behavior, they usually do so within highly restricted domains of opinion and behavior, and it is likely that such restriction is a precondition of strong constraint.

Second, in strongly constraining social structures, agreements between occupants of different social positions arise either from unambiguous standards that specify appropriate behavior and opinions, from institutionalized channels of interpersonal influence (traditional or legal lines of authority) in which a consistent set of influential expectations are conveyed to the actors in different social positions, or from social choice mechanisms. Behavior may be coordinated either because the actors in each position independently adhere to norms and programs of activity that foster such coordination, or because they conform to the consistent dictates of higher authorities. Their opinions on issues may agree either because their opinions are molded by an identical set of conditions or because they conform to the opinion held by a higher authority.

Thus, formal organizations have been viewed as institutionalized arrangements of constraints, such that actors who are jointly located in the same part of an organization are likely to behave in expected ways. Herbert Simon (1976) has argued that the *rational* pursuit of organizational objectives depends crucially on the construction of microenvironments that strongly constrain the decisions of actors who are located in these environments. Simon argued that it is primarily through the construction of such social positions that organizations regulate individual decisions and surmount actors' limited abilities for rational calculation:

> The deliberate control of the environment of decision permits not only the integration of choice, but its socialization as well. Social institutions may be viewed as regularizations of the behavior of individuals through subjection of their behavior to stimulus-patterns socially imposed on them. It is in these patterns that an understanding of the meaning and function of organization is to be found. (Simon 1976, p. 109)

Cartwright (1965) refers to this type of constraint as "ecological control," where actors are influenced indirectly by a manipulation of the circumstances to which they are responding. In such a system, coordinated activity and interpersonal agreements are reflections of these institutionalized arrangements.

1.2.2 Weakly Constraining Structures

A prime agenda of the early Columbia School of structural analysis, led by Robert Merton, was the development of an argument concerning the problematic status of coordinated action and interpersonal agreements in many, even highly institutionalized, social structures. Other theorists have contributed analyses along the same lines. An important conclusion of this line of work is that, even among formal organizations, where strongly constraining structures are most frequent, social structure is often weakly constraining because the two key conditions of a strong constraint are usually absent.

First, Wrong (1961) pointed out that the model of a strongly constraining social structure entails an "oversocialized" view of individual action. Social positions do not subsume the whole individual; and the segmentation of personality into positional and nonpositional parts is often incomplete. Extraneous conditions seep into the determination of the behavior of actors in social positions and thereby introduce highly idiosyncratic and diverse responses to the circumstances of the position. Personal goals (power seeking, competitiveness), personal beliefs (ideological commitments), and personal circumstances enter into actors' opinions and behavior. Hence, while a stable set of institutionalized conditions may be influencing an actor, there also are more or less powerful idiosyncratic conditions that come into play. As a consequence of these idiosyncratic conditions, actors who are identical on some status characteristic (e.g., formal position in a bureaucratic hierarchy) are likely to occupy different social positions and, because of these different positions, are likely to have substantially different predispositions on issues. Wrong argued that an unrealistic degree of socialization and control must be assumed in order to dismiss such individual differences as unimportant in most circumstances.

Second, structuralists have argued that most institutionalized arrangements and power structures are not well integrated (i.e., they entail ambiguous and inconsistent expectations) and, therefore, do not adequately explain those instances of coordinated action or interpersonal agreements that occur among actors in different social positions:

> Structuralists hold that innovation, flexibility, and ingenuity are required in any interaction characterized by: a lack of consensus, incomplete instructions, role conflict, or role overload. And, it is an essential assumption of "modern" structuralism that the presence of one or more of these conditions is the rule. These conditions are not merely common – they are thought to be inherent in the nature of social structure. (Heiss 1981, p. 97)

With respect to institutionalized status characteristics, the actor typically encounters *inconsistency* (guidelines and norms point the actor in different directions), *conflict* (actors with some influence on the focal actor have conflicting opinions), and *ambiguity* (expectations are incomplete or insufficient so that the appropriate action is uncertain).

Merton and Barber (1976) argue that these features of the institutionalized components of social structures do not indicate an absence of social organization but are manifestations of a special type of social organization, which they refer to as *sociological ambivalence.* Merton and Barber start with the observation that an institutionalized status typically subjects those actors who occupy the status to conflicting or incompatible normative expectations. They argue that the inconsistency often takes the form of couplets of dominant norms and counter-norms and that:

> Since these norms cannot be simultaneously expressed in behavior, they come to be expressed in an oscillation of behaviors:

> of detachment and compassion, of discipline and permissiveness, of personal and impersonal treatment. (Merton and Barber 1976, p. 8)
>
> At issue is how we conceive the structure of social roles. From the perspective of sociological ambivalence, we see a social role as a dynamic organization of norms and counter-norms, not as a combination of dominant attributes (such as affective neutrality or functional specificity). We propose that the major and the minor counter-norms alternatively govern role-behavior to produce ambivalence. (Merton and Barber 1976, p. 17)

To be sure, conflicting guidelines are not always present in social structures; however, Merton argues that a unified and dominating set of guidelines is difficult to maintain. Hence, flexible guidelines are developed in many social structures that allow actors to deal with an array of complex circumstances in a way that minimizes interpersonal friction and individual stress:

> Dominant attributes alone would not be flexible enough to provide for the endlessly varying contingencies of social relations. Behavior oriented wholly to the dominant norms would defeat the functional objectives of the role. Instead, role-behavior is alternatively oriented to dominant norms and to subsidiary counter-norms in the role. This alternation of subroles evolves as a social device for helping people in designated statuses to cope with the contingencies they face in trying to fulfill their functions. (Merton and Barber 1976, p. 18)
>
> Action exclusively in terms of one component in the ambivalent pairs tends to be self-defeating, producing a lopsided development that undercuts the basic objectives of the complex activity. (Merton 1976, p. 63)

Merton's provocative argument concerning a *demand* for weak constraints should not distract attention from the observation that social structures rarely entail strong constraints on the opinions and behaviors of their occupants.

In short, according to this viewpoint, institutionalized social arrangements and power structures shape opinions and behavior, but such effects often do not reliably account for the observed opinions and behaviors of actors. Agreements among actors in different social positions arise mainly from informal (noninstitutionalized) conditions and processes. To be sure, institutionalized arrangements (such as a formal hierarchy of authority) affect both the social positions of actors and the network of interpersonal influences among actors. But if institutionalized arrangements are not the main determinant of actors' positions and influences, or if these institutions have complex effects on positions and influences, then we must examine the observed structure of social differentiation and interpersonal influences among actors and the process by which their opinions are formed.

1.3 Interpersonal Agreements and Social Control

Coordinated action and interpersonal agreements can occur in weakly constrained social structures. Even in circumstances where a massive consensus and a coherent system of coordinated action do not exist, there may be areas of the social structure in which interpersonal agreements and coordinated activity are maintained. The conclusion that interpersonal agreements are not mechanistically determined by institutionalized arrangements underscores the importance of a line of inquiry concerned with the question of how such agreements are established and maintained, and it justifies the importance of addressing possible structural conditions and social processes that have a bearing on the formation of interpersonal agreements.

In this section, I describe three main approaches to an account of mechanisms of interpersonal agreement in complexly differentiated social structures. These three avenues are (a) a structural approach suggested by Merton that attends to contextual conditions that foster and impede the development of interpersonal agreements, (b) an interactionist approach that attends to the influence processes that form interpersonal agreements, and (c) a social choice approach that attends to procedures through which collective decisions on issues are made in the absence of a preexisting consensus. The work on a structural theory of social influence developed in Chapter 2 will advance the interactionist approach, but it does so by taking into account contextual features of the social structure in which the influence process unfolds.

1.3.1 Structuralism

Merton (1957) initiated a research agenda concerned with the social mechanisms that articulate *role-sets*, where a role-set refers to the set of social relations with which an actor is involved as a consequence of the actor's social position. This agenda sought to identify social processes and structures that reduce conflicting influences among the actors who compose a role-set. The analytical focus is on the *social context* in which an actor operates:

> It is not primarily concerned with the familiar problem, of how the occupant of a status manages to cope with the many, and sometimes conflicting, demands made of him. It is thus a problem of social structure, not an exercise in the no doubt important but different problem of how individuals happen to deal with the complex structures of relations in which they find themselves. (Merton 1957, p. 112)

Six mechanisms are emphasized in Merton's analysis. For convenience, I will refer to the actor in a social position as "ego" or the "focal actor" and to the actors to whom the focal actor is related as "alters" or "significant others."

First, the number of conflicting influences from alters depends on the level of interest and concern among the alters in the opinions and behaviors of the focal actor. Given a large set of alters, conditions that lower the general level of interest, or that restrict interest to a few alters, may reduce the likelihood of importantly conflicting influences.

Second, the extent of conflict may be mitigated by a stratification of the importance of the persons who are influencing an actor. For example, if the conflicting influences involve a subset of highly influential and interested actors and a subset of less salient actors, with a less immediate involvement in ego's affairs, then the latter subset of actors may be discounted by the focal actor. Thus, the distribution of influence may affect the likelihood of importantly conflicting influences.

Closely related to this mechanism of weighting interpersonal influences is a mechanism of abridgment, whereby conflict is reduced by terminating relations with certain actors. Schachter (1951) and others have dealt with this process in terms of a cessation of interaction with "deviant" actors who hold highly divergent opinions from those of their peers. Similarly, Festinger's (1954) social comparison theory suggests that the amount of interpersonal influence between two actors is a negative function of their degree of opinion discrepancy.

Third, a conflict among actors who are each highly influential may have the effect of *neutralizing* each other. Merton puts it this way:

> To the extent that conflicting powers in his role-set neutralize one another, the status-occupant has relative freedom to proceed as he intended in the first place. . . . I do not say that the status-occupant subject to conflicting expectations among members of his role-set is in fact immune to control by them. I suggest only that the power and authority-structure of role-sets is often such that he has a larger measure of autonomy than he would have had if this structure of competing power did not obtain. (1957, p. 114)

Fourth, in a somewhat different vein, Merton suggests that ego, who is the focus of conflicting influences, may operate as the *tertius gaudens* by shifting the burden of conflict resolution from himself or herself to the conflicting alters. Conditions that reduce conflicts among the alters reduce the conflict for ego. A *tertius gardens* who promotes a negotiation of conflicting opinions and behaviors fosters the development of consensus.

Fifth, structural arrangements that increase an actor's insulation from observability may reduce conflicts. If actors are insulated from the observability of actors who differ from themselves, then conflict will be reduced: "To the extent that the social structure insulates the individual from having his activities known to members of his role-set, he is the less subject to competing pressures" (Merton 1957, pp. 114–15). Perfect insulation implies actor autonomy, i.e., no interpersonal influences upon the actor.

Sixth, the formation of associations among actors may serve to reduce the conflicting influences upon them. These associations may be informal groups or formal organizations that provide organizational and interpersonal resources for dealing with the conflicts in which actors find themselves. Merton writes:

> These organizations constitute a structural response to the problem of coping with the (potentially or actually) conflicting demands by those in the role-sets of the status. Whatever the intent, these constitute social formations serving to counter the power of the role-set; of being, not merely amenable to its demands, but of helping to shape them. Such organizations – so familiar a part of the social landscape of differentiated societies – also develop normative systems which are designed to anticipate and thereby mitigate such conflicting expectations. (1957, p. 117)

Merton's treatment of mechanisms was designed to open avenues of inquiry rather than to settle upon a set of conclusions about these mechanisms. It is the thrust of the approach, and what it does not deal with, that is most important to understand. The approach is not concerned with the manner in which an *actor weighs alternative demands, forms an opinion, or settles on a course of action.* Instead, the focus is on conditions under which problems of weighing alternative demands disappear or are markedly reduced. Consequently, the approach does not provide an account of the *content* of the opinions that are formed by actors in particular positions. Moreover, it is not concerned with the manner in which a consensus of opinion is produced among the set of alters of a focal actor or among actors in larger regions of the social structure.

Merton (1957, p. 117) recognized that the mechanisms to which he pointed might only slightly reduce the conflicting influences of alters upon a focal actor and that the residual conflict in the role-set might be considerable. Restrictions on interest, influence, and observability among alters will necessarily reduce conflict among alters only in the case of a focal actor whose active role-set has been reduced by these mechanisms to a *single alter* or to an *empty set.* In the special case of autonomy via a neutralization of influences, the number of interpersonal influences is reduced to zero.[7] Although an increase of autonomy reduces the social conflict problem, it leaves open the problem of how interpersonal agreements are formed.

Clearly, in the contextual approach described by Merton, the *social process* by which interpersonal agreements and consensus are formed remains crucial. (a) The role-set of a focal actor will not be in conflict when it is embedded in an influence hierarchy that is ruled by a leader or dominant coalition to whose preferences the occupants of different positions conform. However, such influence structures typically rest on broad agreements concerning personal and constitutional arrangements. (b) Given autonomous actors, the problem of social control appears in its most severe form, unless there are interpersonal agreements on procedural mechanisms of social choice and decision making that constrain actors. (c) Similarly, formal associations among actors rest fundamentally on the formation and maintenance of interpersonal agreements. Hence, in certain respects, the mechanisms that Merton describes are social structural derivatives of a consensus-formation process. Although it is useful to examine the direct effects of such derivative social arrangements, it also is important to keep a hold on the elementary prerequisites of these structural arrangements. Merton suggests that the process of interpersonal agreement formation is not sufficiently structural to qualify as a subject of sociological analysis. This suggestion is misleading, and I shall point to, and develop, a structural social psychology that both attends to and informs an analysis of social structures (Chapter 2).

7 The neutralization argument raises subtle and interesting questions. Given a pattern of equally balanced influences that pull an actor in different directions, the net effect of such influence will be an unchanged opinion. But this is a very special case of cross-pressure. Cross-pressures also may be unbalanced and give rise to change in the actor's opinion. However, if the existence of competing opinions diminishes the magnitudes of the interpersonal influences, then cross-pressures will always lead to autonomous and fixed opinions.

1.3.2 Interactionism

Heiss (1981, p. 101) argues that "structural theory lacks a systematic analysis of the mechanics of the interaction process" and that in order to understand how role conflicts are resolved, "a cogent analysis of structural effects requires a precise conceptualization of the details of the interaction process." Obviously, I agree with this assessment of the weakness of structural theory and the importance of social process. The process by which shared agreements are formed among actors has been investigated most vigorously by symbolic interactionists (Stryker and Statham 1985). A key contribution of this literature is its detailed documentation of the formation of various types of agreements: shared understandings, definitions of the situation, and interpersonal "contracts." As the symbolic interactionists make plain, agreements arise even in the absence of a formal demand for consensus (as in juries or committees); agreements are the ubiquitous outcome of the informal and voluntary efforts of actors to reduce their interpersonal friction and individual stress. Although symbolic interactionists have been the most active investigators of this viewpoint, they are not its only proponents (Wrong 1994, pp. 47–51).

However, this interactionist literature on agreement formation has several important limitations. First, it is fuzzy on the precise manner in which a focal actor integrates different interpersonal influences. Many studies in this tradition have concentrated on the development of agreements in dyads and, therefore, do not bear on the question of how multiple sources of conflicting influences are reconciled by an actor. Second, the implications of larger influence networks is not explicated. Dyads are embedded in a structure of interpersonal influences. Hence, actors are not simply adjusting their preferences to a set of fixed expectations, but rather are attending to a set of shifting expectations. In an interlocking structure of dyadic influences, the influence process may be conceived as an iterated sequence of interpersonal adjustments. Third, the consequences of the influence process for the development of agreements between actors in different social positions is unclear. If consensus arises via ongoing interpersonal influences, then what are the implications of different configurations of such influences (i.e., the structure of an influence network) for the development of agreements that may foster the coordination of a complexly differentiated group?

These limitations of the interactionist approach also are limitations of the large literature in social psychology concerned with social influence and interpersonal agreements. Much of social psychology is concerned with interpersonal influence:

> With few exceptions, social psychologists regard their discipline as an attempt to understand and explain how the thought, feeling, and behavior of individuals are influenced by the actual, imagined, or implied presence of others. The term "implied presence" refers to the many activities the individual carries out because of his position (role) in a complex social structure and because of his membership in a cultural group. (Allport 1985, p. 3)

For a time, social psychologists were interested in social influence *networks*. However, recent trends in social psychological research have turned away from research that might explain how a network of interpersonal influence enters into the formation of individual opinions and decisions. Recent lines of inquiry in social psychology concerned with the consequences of networks of interpersonal power deal mainly with *social exchange* networks. In these social exchange studies, agreements usually take the form of dyadic-level "contracts" about the division of available resources, and the outcomes of interest are the equilibrium distribution of resources, power imbalances, and patterns of exchange that emerge during the social exchange process.

One must look hard, in both the past and present literature in social psychology, for theoretical models of the social influence process that account for the emergence of collective decisions and opinions in natural settings and that take into account the network of interpersonal influences in this process (French 1956; Davis 1973; Latane 1981). Early studies of opinion formation dealt with special cases of influence networks in which an actor is faced with a fixed consensus of opinion that the actor must either conform to or reject (Asch 1951, 1956). More recent work has examined the influence of minority-group opinions on the majority (Moscovici 1985). Scant attention has been directed to the more general process of opinion formation – a network of interpersonal influences in which the influential opinions to which actors are responding may be in disagreement and changing in response to the influence of other actors.

1.3.3 Social Choice

Social choice mechanisms allow collective decisions in the absence of consensus. Groups often encounter difficulty in forging consensus on issues; although consensus is sought on important issues, it may not be achievable given a fixed set of preferences among actors, and it may not be practical (given time pressures) to pursue a consensus on every issue. Hence, most formal organizations rely heavily on social choice mechanisms. Typically these mechanisms involve a set of voting procedures that can be quite complex, with restrictions on who may vote on particular issues, the manner in which the vote is taken, the sequence of deliberative bodies through which the issue must be vetted, and so forth. Social choice mechanisms allow groups to behave *as if* a consensus is obtained on an issue. Rather than requiring actual consensus on an issue, social choice mechanisms achieve efficiency by requiring *one and only one area of agreement* – a procedural consensus – which stipulates that the decisions based on a particular set of procedures will be supported and taken as the group choice.

The procedural consensus upon which social choice mechanisms rest includes broad agreements on principles and structures of governance, on the legitimacy of the personnel who staff these structures and on their proper zones of authority, on the extent to which a consensus ought to be sought prior to implementing a collective choice mechanism, and on the appropriate sources of input that should be sought prior to decisions. Hence, social choice mechanisms do not render moot the theoretical problems that I have discussed. There must be mechanisms by which such procedural agreements are forged, and these agreements are likely to rest on a combination of historical precedent and informal processes of interpersonal influence. Once these procedural agreements are in place, social choice mechanisms may dovetail with social influences processes. When a social influence process generates consensus, social choice mechanisms become pro forma; when social influences eventuate in a settled pattern of fixed disagreements, social choice mechanisms serve to carry forward the group process toward a collective decision.

However, the conceptual relationship between the structural social psychology that I want to advance and social choice theory is not entirely comfortable, especially when the latter assumes autonomous actors. I will return to this relationship in the concluding chapter of the book, where I argue that recent rational choice approaches to the problem of coordination and control have vastly overestimated the effects of autonomous actors and bargaining mechanisms.

1.4 Concluding Remarks

Structural analysis lacks a formal theory that predicts the consequences of the *system of social positions* for agreements and interpersonal influences. We presently do not have a theory that, building directly on the definition of social positions, provides an analysis of the *systemic* implications of the revealed set of positions, or the degree to which the opinions and behaviors of the actors who occupy different positions are coordinated. The failure of structural role analysis to account for the coordination of social positions motivates the present work. My aim is to develop a structural social psychology that takes into account the structural context in which actors are situated and that describes the manner in which interpersonal agreements and influences arise.

2

Toward a Structural Social Psychology

Abstract. I describe new steps for structural analysis that are based on a structural theory of social influence. The theory describes a process in which a group of actors weigh and integrate the conflicting influences of significant others – within the context of social structural constraints. The social structure of the group defines the initial positions of actors, the network of interpersonal influences among the actors, and the weight of these interpersonal influences during the process of opinion formation.

While social structural analysis allows a description of complexly differentiated social structures, it has failed to develop a theory that elucidates the consequences of such structures for the production of interpersonal influences and agreements. This and other limitations of social structural analysis were noted by Komarovsky (1973) in her Presidential Address to the American Sociological Association. Boorman and White (1976) sought to address Komarovsky's concerns in their seminal paper on role structures. However, their efforts are only partially successful; in particular, they fail to present an account of the formation of agreements among actors in different social positions.

Komarovsky describes three limitations of social structural analysis. First, she suggests that social structural analysis "obscures and neglects the importance of individuality." How does the "self" or individuality enter into a conceptualization of social structure based on social positions? Second, she suggests that social structural analysis overemphasizes "conformity and stability" and neglects "deviation, malintegration and social change." How are the haphazard, informal, and unstable social structural contexts in which actors are situated taken into account in a theory of the behavior and opinions of actors? Third, she suggests that social structural analysis has not explained the formation of those interpersonal agreements that are important foci of social control processes (e.g., enforcement of agreed-upon standards) and points of reference in the development of subsequent opinions and behaviors.

In this chapter I describe a formal theory of social influence and outline the bearing of the theory on some of the outstanding theoretical problems in social structural analysis. The proposed new steps for structural analysis are based on a structural theory of social influence. This theory describes a process in which a group of actors weigh and integrate the conflicting influences of significant others – within the context of social structural constraints.

2.1 Social Influence Network Theory

There are four theoretical attractions of the theory that I will present. I introduce these features now and elaborate upon them later on. First, this theory relaxes the simplifying assumption of actors who must either conform to or deviate from a fixed consensus of others; it deals with the more complex situation in which influential opinions are in disagreement and liable to change. Second, this theory does *not* predict the ineluctable development of consensus; either a consensus or a stable pattern of disagreement may result from the influence process. Third, it is a multilevel theory in combining micro- and macro-phenomena. At the micro-level it is a cognitive theory concerned with how individuals weigh and combine divergent interpersonal influences. At the macro-level, it is a social structural theory concerned with how social structural arrangements enter into and constrain the opinion-formation process. Fourth, the theory allows an analysis of the systemic consequences of social structures.

2.1.1 Formal Theory

Social influence network theory has been under development by social psychologists and mathematicians since the 1950s (French 1956; Harary 1959; DeGroot 1974; Friedkin 1986; Friedkin and Cook 1990; Friedkin and Johnsen 1990; Friedkin 1990b; Friedkin 1991; Friedkin and Johnsen 1997). The theory can be described as an iterated two-stage weighted averaging of influential opinions. At each point in the social influence process, (a) a network "norm" is formed for each actor that is a weighted average of the influential opinions for the actor and (b) a modified opinion is formed for each actor that is a weighted average of the network "norm" and the initial opinion of the actor.

Two equations describe the theory. One concerns the origins of actors' initial opinions on an issue,

$$\mathbf{Y}^{(1)} = \mathbf{XB} \tag{2.1}$$

and the other concerns the subsequent transformation of these initial opinions

$$\mathbf{Y}^{(t)} = \mathbf{AWY}^{(t-1)} + (\mathbf{I} - \mathbf{A})\mathbf{Y}^{(1)} \tag{2.2}$$

for $t = 2, 3, \ldots,$ where $\mathbf{Y}^{(t)} = [y_{im}^{(t)}]$ is an $N \times M$ matrix of M-dimensional opinions for N actors at time t, $\mathbf{X} = [x_{ik}]$ is an $N \times K$ matrix of the K exogenous variables that affect the opinions of actors, $\mathbf{B} = [b_{km}]$ is a $K \times M$ matrix of coefficients for the exogenous variables, $\mathbf{A} = [a_{ii}]$ is a diagonal matrix of the weights of the endogenous interpersonal influences for each actor, and $\mathbf{W} = [w_{ij}]$ is an $N \times N$ matrix of endogenous interpersonal influences in which

$$\begin{Bmatrix} 0 \leqslant w_{ij} \leqslant 1 \\ \sum_j^N w_{ij} = 1 \\ w_{ii} = 1 - a_{ii} \end{Bmatrix} \tag{2.3}$$

for all i and j.

Flows of interpersonal influence are established by the *repeated* responses of actors to the (possibly changing) influential opinions on the issue. The influence network for the group, $\mathbf{W}$, describes the pattern and magnitude of these direct endogenous interpersonal responses. However, actors not only are influenced endogenously by the opinions of other actors; they also are influenced exogenously, at each point in the process, by the conditions that have formed their *initial* opinions. The balance of forces (relative weight) of the endogenous and exogenous influences is described by a_{ii}, the coefficient of social influence for each actor.

The balance of forces between exogenous and endogenous influences is a subtle but exceedingly important part of this model. Such a balance of forces was postulated by Festinger:

> When a person or a group attempts to influence someone, does that person or group produce a totally new force acting on the person, one which had not been present prior to the attempted influence? Our answer is No – an attempted influence does not produce any new motivation or force. Rather, what an influence attempt involves is the redirection of psychological forces which already exist. (1953, p. 237)

The assumption of such a balance was introduced (Friedkin and Johnsen 1990) as a constraint that confines equilibrium opinions to the range of initial opinions. Without this constraint, the social influence process can result in equilibrium opinions that "breach" the range or convex hull of initial opinions, a result that is grossly inconsistent with experimental evidence (Friedkin and Cook 1990).

For a viewpoint on the theory in scalar form, consider the special case of a $N \times 1$ opinion vector:

$$y_i^{(1)} = \sum_{k=1}^{K} b_k x_{ik} \tag{2.4}$$

and

$$y_i^{(t)} = a_{ii}\sum_{j=1}^{N} w_{ij}y_j^{(t-1)} + (1 - a_{ii})y_i^{(1)} \qquad (2.5)$$

for $t = 2, 3, \ldots$ The network "norm" at time t is the weighted average, $\sum_j w_{ij}y_j^{(t-1)}$, and the revised opinion of an actor at time t is a weighted average of this "norm" and the actor's initial opinion, $y_i^{(1)}$. The relative weights of the network "norm" and the initial opinion in the formation of the revised opinion are determined by the coefficient of social influence, a_{ii}, for each actor.

Beside the particular weight (w_{ij}) that an actor accords to the opinion of another actor, an actor also accords a more or less considerable weight to his or her own opinion. This self-weight (w_{ii}) enters into the formation of the network "norm" and coefficient of social influence, i.e., $a_{ii} = 1 - w_{ii}$ from Eq. (2.3). It follows that the larger the self-weight, the smaller the cumulative weight of the opinions of other actors,

$$1 - w_{ii} = \sum_{\substack{j=1 \\ j\neq 1}}^{N} w_{ij} \qquad (2.6)$$

and that this cumulative weight is equal to the weight of the endogenous interpersonal influences for each actor

$$a_{ii} = \sum_{\substack{j=1 \\ j\neq 1}}^{N} w_{ij} \qquad (2.7)$$

The first result is an implication of the stipulation that $\sum_j w_{ij} = 1$, and the second result is an implication of the stipulation that $w_{ii} = 1 - a_{ii}$.

The weights involved in the theory are *relative weights,*

$$(1 - a_{ii}) + a_{ii}\sum_{j=1}^{N} w_{ij} = 1 \qquad (2.8)$$

for all i, and, as such, they should not be interpreted as measures of the absolute magnitudes of the self and interpersonal influences for an actor. For example, suppose that an actor i is influenced equally by n_i actors, that actor j is influenced equally by n_j actors, that i is influenced by a larger number of actors than j ($n_i > n_j$), and that the two actors have identical self-weights ($w_{ii} = w_{jj}$). In such a case, the relative influence of some actor k, who influences both i and j, will be greater on actor j than on actor i: $w_{ik} < w_{jk}$ for all $k \neq \{i, j\}$. However, this set of circumstances does not imply that the interpersonal influences upon actor j are stronger in absolute magnitude than those on actor *i*. Of course, within the context of the bundle of interpersonal influences on an actor whose self-weight is not maximal (and therefore who is influenced by others), the stronger the influence of an actor *k* in this bundle, the stronger the relative weight of *k*.

2.1.2 Equilibrium Equations

Assuming equilibrium, under extreme conditions the model approaches the form of either (a) the classical linear model in which there are no endogenous interpersonal influences on opinions

$$\mathbf{Y}^{(\infty)} = \mathbf{XB} \tag{2.9}$$

or (b) the consensus model of French, Harary, and DeGroot in which there are no ongoing exogenous influences on opinions

$$\mathbf{Y}^{(\infty)} = \mathbf{W}^{\infty}\mathbf{Y}^{(1)} \tag{2.10}$$

In the first case ($\mathbf{A} = \mathbf{O}$), endogenous interpersonal influences are negligible and actors' equilibrium opinions are their initial opinions. In the second case ($\mathbf{A} = \mathbf{I}$), endogenous interpersonal influences are dominant and exogenous conditions have no direct impact on opinions other than forming the actors' initial opinions on an issue. Thus, apart from these extreme circumstances, the opinions that are formed at each point in the process reflect the *competing* influences of the personal circumstances of actors and the opinions (and, therefore, indirectly the circumstances) of their significant others.

Assuming $\mathbf{I} - \mathbf{AW}$ is nonsingular, actors' settled opinions may be described thus

$$\begin{aligned}\mathbf{Y}^{(\infty)} &= (\mathbf{I} - \mathbf{AW})^{-1}\,(\mathbf{I} - \mathbf{A})\mathbf{Y}^{(1)} \\ &= \mathbf{VY}^{(1)}\end{aligned} \tag{2.11}$$

where

$$\mathbf{V} = (\mathbf{I} - \mathbf{AW})^{-1}\,(\mathbf{I} - \mathbf{A}) \tag{2.12}$$

This equilibrium equation is useful in two regards.

First, this equilibrium equation establishes the formal relationship of the present theory with the statistical models of spatial econometrics (Doreian 1981; Anselin 1988; Marsden and Friedkin 1993; Lazer 1995). That is, we have

$$\begin{aligned}\mathbf{Y}^{(\infty)} &= (\mathbf{I} - \mathbf{AW})^{-1}\,(\mathbf{I} - \mathbf{A})\mathbf{Y}^{(1)} \\ &= \mathbf{AWY}^{(\infty)} + (\mathbf{I} - \mathbf{A})\,\mathbf{Y}^{(1)} \\ &= \mathbf{AWY}^{(\infty)} + (\mathbf{I} - \mathbf{A})\mathbf{XB}\end{aligned} \tag{2.13}$$

for which a special case is the mixed-regressive autoregressive model

$$\mathbf{Y}^{(\infty)} = \alpha\mathbf{W}\mathbf{Y}^{(\infty)} + \tilde{\mathbf{X}}\beta + \varepsilon \tag{2.14}$$

where $a_{ii} = \alpha$ for all i, $\mathbf{X}$ has been partitioned into observed $\tilde{\mathbf{X}}$ and unobserved subsets of variables that affect opinions, and $\beta = (1 - \alpha)\tilde{\mathbf{B}}$ is based on the subset of coefficients for the observed variables ($\mathbf{XB} = \tilde{\mathbf{X}}\beta + \varepsilon$). In this simplified model, the relative weight of the network "norm" is assumed to be the same for all actors, and actors' initial opinions are assumed to be a linear transformation of the observed exogenous conditions ($\tilde{\mathbf{X}}$). If the statistical assumptions of the model are met with respect to ε, then an estimate of the effects of the variables in $\tilde{\mathbf{X}}$ is obtained along with an estimate of α, the uniform coefficient of social influence.

Second, the equilibrium equation is useful in describing the systemic implications of the influence system. The coefficients in $\mathbf{V}$ describe the relative *total* interpersonal effect of the initial opinion (or social position) of actor j on the equilibrium opinion of actor i ($0 \leq v_{ij} \leq 1$, $\sum_j^N v_{ij} = 1$). These total effects arise as a cumulative summation of the direct and indirect flows of interpersonal influence in the system. More precisely, the total interpersonal effect of one actor on another is related to the number and length of the various paths and sequences that join them in the network of interpersonal influences.[1] This relationship has the following formal foundation:

$$\begin{aligned}\mathbf{V} &= (\mathbf{I} - \mathbf{AW})^{-1}(\mathbf{I} - \mathbf{A}) \\ &= [\mathbf{I} + \mathbf{AW} + (\mathbf{AW})^2 + (\mathbf{AW})^3 + \ldots](\mathbf{I} - \mathbf{A})\end{aligned} \tag{2.15}$$

Consider an arbitrary term, $(\mathbf{AW})^k$ in the infinite series $\mathbf{AW} + (\mathbf{AW})^2 + (\mathbf{AW})^3 + \ldots$. If all the nonzero entries in $\mathbf{AW}$ were converted to 1s, an entry in $(\mathbf{AW})^k$ would indicate the number of ways in which interpersonal influence flows in k-steps from one actor to another in the network; the greater the number of such k-step flows, the larger the expected impact of one actor on the other. The network model qualifies this expectation in two respects. First, the impact of a single k-step flow diminishes with the number of steps involved. Second, the impact of flows that traverse the same number of steps depends on the strengths ($a_{ii}w_{ij}$) of constituent links. In short, the total interpersonal effect of one actor upon another is a weighted sum of the number of different channels of interpersonal influence that join them in the network, where each channel is weighted according to its length and strength of constituent links.

1 In a path of interpersonal influences ($i \rightarrow j \rightarrow k \rightarrow l$), no actor appears more than once. In a sequence of interpersonal influences the same actor may appear more than once (e.g., $i \rightarrow j \rightarrow k \rightarrow j \rightarrow l$).

2.1.3 Social Positions

Actors have positions in **W**, the network of endogenous interpersonal influences, and in **X**, the matrix of exogenous variables that affect actors' opinions. These endogenous and exogenous positions have distinct roles in the development of the opinions of actors (Friedkin and Johnsen 1997). It is useful, for reasons outlined below, to assume a correspondence between these two types of positions; that is, I shall assume that actors who are structurally equivalent in **W** also have identical row vectors in **X** (and, therefore, identical initial opinions).

Exogenous social positions are defined by the variables in **X**, i.e., the exogenous determinants of the opinions of actors. As a theoretical construct, **X** contains all the conditions that affect the initial opinions of actors, and it also may contain a random component. These social positions may be based on individual attributes such as gender, age, and socioeconomic status; they also may be based on ubiquitous roles (physician, father, husband), local status (gang member, community leader), and locations in networks of social relations (friendship networks, authority structures). The social position of an actor is defined by the entire row vector for the actor in **X**.

Two actors are defined as *exogenously equivalent* if they have identical profiles of values across the K variables in **X**.[2] Thus, actors can be viewed as occupying more or less similar locations in a multidimensional space that is defined by the exogenous variables that affect their opinions. I refer to this multidimensional space as *social space* and to the distance between positions in this space as *social distance*. Close proximity in social space indicates an approximate equivalence of those exogenous conditions that affect the opinions of actors, and actors who occupy identical locations in social space must have identical initial opinions.

Whether or not actors who are exogenously equivalent also have identical *equilibrium* opinions depends upon the network of endogenous influences. *The influence network potentially disrupts the correspondence between the personal circumstances of actors and their settled opinions.* The notion that actors in similar circumstances have similar opinions follows from the classical assumption of actor independence. When this assumption of independence is relaxed to allow for actors who are responding, not only to their own circumstances, but also to the responses of other actors, then the "common fate" hypothesis falls to ground.

2 Social positions that are defined on the basis of concrete social networks (apart from the network of endogenous social influences) may be viewed in one of two ways. The resulting positions may be treated as variables within **X** (i.e., dummy variables) or they may serve as an empirical proxy of the profile similarity of actors in **X**.

I have pointed out that actors also have positions in the network of endogenous interpersonal influences; the position of an actor is defined by the row and column of values for the actor in **W**. Two actors are defined as *structurally equivalent* in **W** if they have identical effects to and from the other members of the network and on each other: $w_{ij} = w_{ji}$, $w_{ik} = w_{jk}$, and $w_{ki} = w_{kj}$ for $k \neq i, j$. Because $w_{ii} = 1 - a_{ii}$ and $\sum_j w_{ij} = 1$, the structural equivalence of actors i and j in **W** implies that $a_{ii} = a_{jj}$. It can be shown that if two actors i and j are structurally equivalent in **W**, then any initial difference of opinion between these two actors must be reduced by the process of opinion formation:

$$(\mathbf{y}_i^{(t)} - \mathbf{y}_j^{(t)}) = (\mathbf{y}_i^{(1)} - \mathbf{y}_j^{(1)})(1 - \alpha) \tag{2.16}$$

where $\alpha = a_{ii} = a_{jj}$.

It is useful to assume a *correspondence* between structural equivalence in **W** and the occurrence of identical row vectors in **X**. Such a correspondence will arise if the exogenous variables in **X** determine not only actors' initial opinions on issues but also their interpersonal influences on and from other actors. Hence, when I refer to a *social position* such a reference will imply a common endogenous and exogenous position. Under the assumption of this correspondence, a common position in **X** implies structural equivalence in **W**, and vice versa.

There are three important consequences of a correspondence between exogenous and endogenous social positions. (a) It justifies an empirical approach to social positions that bases social positions on the structural equivalence of actors in **W**. (b) Actors who are structurally equivalent in **W**, because they occupy the same positions in **X**, must have identical initial opinions. (c) The joint occupants of a social position must have identical equilibrium opinions. Social influences may increase initial differences of opinion between actors in proximate (nonidentical) social positions, but they cannot do so for actors in identical social positions. The joint occupants of a social position are "fellow travelers" so long as their structural circumstances remain the same.

2.1.4 Sources of Individuality

Individuality is not suppressed by the assumption that the joint occupants of a social position have identical opinions on issues. Individuality is preserved by a stringent criterion for joint occupancy of a position. Social positions are based on the full spectrum of variables that affect actors' opinions; hence, it is unlikely that two actors will occupy the same position. Issues of individuality arise when it is argued that institutionalized features of social structure (e.g., roles) determine the behavior of actors. In such arguments, actors appear "oversocialized" and Komarovsky asks, "Is there no man behind the mask?" (1973, pp. 650–1):

> Are men so programmed and passive that sociologists can afford to neglect the intrusion of self into the role or the individual innovations which may inaugurate social changes? (Bradbury et al. 1972)

> Are [roles] not played parts in a play that is partly being written in the act of being played? Do they not contain marks of individuality? (Naegele 1966)

The individuality of the "self" is manifested by the distinctive social positions of actors. Although proximity in social space suggests a subset of common conditions, such proximity (unless it is exact) does not necessarily imply identical *initial opinions* on issues. For example, although socioeconomic status has a powerful effect on opinions, there is very substantial variation in opinions among actors of the same socioeconomic status. Social positions may entail a combination of highly stable conditions into which individuals are distributed, but positions also entail conditions that are random and idiosyncratic. Moreover, given a relatively small number of important exogenous variables, a large number of distinctive combinations of statuses on these variables is implied. Unless the exogenous variables are strongly interrelated, a population is likely to be distributed across many distinctive social positions (Simmel 1955; Blau 1977), and although many actors may find themselves in proximate social positions, few social positions will be jointly occupied. Hence, initial disagreements and problems of coordination and control are ubiquitous, which brings us to the second criticism of structural analysis.

2.1.5 Social Organization

To what extent are actors' opinions in agreement and behavior coordinated as a consequence of their social positions? Under what conditions does a macro-structure of social positions imply consensus and coordinated action? What is the basis of social change? Komarovsky describes this problem as follows:

> The second criticism alleges that role conformity and stability have been overemphasized and, conversely, that deviation, malintegration and social change have been minimized or neglected. (1973, p. 651)

There are two parts to this issue: the extent to which social organization (consensus and coordination) is problematical, and the extent to which stability is assumed.

First, it should be clear from the discussion in Chapter 1 that structuralists following Merton do not assume that a role structure automatically implies consensus and coordinated behavior among actors who occupy *different* positions. Mechanisms for the articulation of role-sets and, more broadly, mechanisms for the formation of consensus and coordinated action have been a key concern of structural analysis for some time. Social distance generates differences of opinion: The greater the distance between two social positions, the larger the expected difference of initial opinion between the occupants of these positions.[3]

Moreover, similarity of opinion does not lessen social conflict. Although proximate (nonidentical) social positions imply similar initial opinions, even slight differences of opinion among actors are a potential source of concern and conflict for actors. Differences of opinion are no less meaningful when they involve actors in closely neighboring positions than when they occur between actors in distant positions. For instance, decisions concerning the allocation of resources – in which a governing committee divides resources among competing subunits that, in turn, have committees that divide resources among competing subunits, and so on – are usually meaningful to the parties involved regardless of the absolute amount of resources at stake. The occurrence and intensity of acrimonious disputes among actors in different social positions is not reliably associated with the distance between positions; such disputes may exist between actors whose positions on issues are both close and far apart. The field of opportunities for social conflict is uniform, so that differences of opinion of any magnitude may become salient to the actors involved.

In short, the theory permits a situation in which a population is partitioned into a small number of social positions that are each occupied by a large number of actors, and it also permits a situation in which each social position has only a single occupant. However, because few posi-

3 In this approach, interpersonal agreement on a particular issue is less theoretically important than the foundations that have determined the likelihood of such agreement. On a particular issue, actors in different positions may hold the same initial opinion; however, over a spectrum of issues in a particular domain, the probability of identical initial opinions should be associated with the distance between positions. Thus, two actors in distant social positions may have identical initial reactions to an issue; but such an event is unlikely when the distances between social positions correspond to expected differences of opinion. Theoretical attention is focused on the expected differences of opinion associated with conditions that affect the probability of interpersonal agreement.

tions are likely to be jointly occupied, the present theory describes a basis of social conflict and allows for ubiquitous disagreements.

Second, the theory currently assumes a stable set of parameters; i.e., the exogenous variables (**X**), effects (**B**), and interpersonal influences (**AW**) are fixed throughout the social influence process. The theory is concerned with the consequences of given social structural arrangements, and it presents an account of the transformation of opinions within these arrangements.[4] Social structural change is not precluded; it may arise via modifications of actors' locations in social space. Such modifications alter the social positions of actors and, potentially, the outcomes of the social system. However, this theory does not deal with such changes in the circumstances of actors, nor does it address the antecedents of social structure – ecology, culture, demographics, and politics.

The theory allows an investigation of the consequences of a social structure and a comparative analysis of structural *change,* but it is not a theory *of* social structure. Which type of theory is more important for sociology is not a useful question: both are important; however, there is a natural order in which the two sets of theoretical issues should be tackled. It is difficult to see how an adequate theory of the origins of social structure might be constructed in the absence of a thorough understanding of the consequences of social structural arrangements, because it is through the consequences of structures that theoretical attention is focused on relevant (as opposed to peripheral) structural conditions.

2.1.6 Consensus Formation

Finally, Komarovsky notes that, while structural analysis has sometimes relied on the assumption of consensus, it has failed to deliver an account of the formation of norms, shared values, and other interpersonal agreements:

> Beginning with *The Structure of Social Action,* Talcott Parsons challenged the assumption that enlightened self interest, con-

4 A careful reader will have noticed that when I have referred to the effects of social positions on opinions, I have referred to the effects on initial opinions. It is crucial to distinguish between (a) the initial opinions or predispositions of actors that are shaped directly by their social positions and (b) the equilibrium or settled opinions of actors that arise from the interactions of actors in different social positions. Generally, the initial and equilibrium opinions of an actor will differ as a consequence of the social influence process. Social positions also have effects on equilibrium opinions that arise from the flows of interpersonal influence among actors in different positions. However, these equilibrium effects of social positions can be described only if we have a model of the social influence process.

> tract, and exchange were enough to ensure social order (1937, pp. 89–102). Instead, he stressed internalized, shared values as the cement of society. (Komarovsky 1973, p. 651)

But the structural conditions and social processes by which such "cement" is produced and maintained have remained elusive. The burgeoning work on social exchange and rational choice among economists, political scientists, and sociologists has deflected attention away from the mechanisms that form interpersonal agreements. It is evident that exceedingly complex systems of coordinated behavior can rest on the mechanisms of social exchange and rational choice; however, these mechanisms, in turn, rest on interpersonal agreements among actors who are located in different social positions. Hence, the elucidation of consensus-formation processes remains a fundamental theoretical problem.

Social influence network theory addresses the structural conditions and mechanisms of consensus formation. The theory shows how interpersonal agreements may be formed between actors in particular social positions, and it describes the relative influence of different actors and social positions in forming these agreements. In this theory, consensus is not inevitable and various patterns of more or less marked disagreement are possible (cf. Abelson 1964). Horowitz (1962, p. 182) has commented that "any serious theory of agreements and decisions must at the same time be a theory of disagreements and the conditions under which decisions cannot be reached." The present theory satisfies Horowitz's criterion.

2.2 Concluding Remarks

In this chapter, I have introduced an approach to the analysis of social differentiation that builds on a formal model of the social influence process. I have shown how this approach addresses certain important theoretical issues concerning the effects of social structure on individual and collective outcomes. A structural social psychology begins with the understanding that an episode of interpersonal influence is not an isolated event, but one that occurs among many other interpersonal influences. In the context of such a system of interpersonal effects, one cannot understand how actors come to hold particular opinions or behave in particular ways without taking the system of effects into account.

3

A Setting in the Scientific Community

Abstract. To illustrate and develop my arguments, I analyze the faculties of science in the physical, biological, and social science divisions of two elite universities. In this chapter, I revisit the theoretical issues introduced in Chapters 1 and 2 and show how these issues are manifested in the scientific community. I argue that agreements formed among scientists in elite universities contribute to a nascent form of corporate organization that Durkheim argued was crucial for the coordination of a highly differentiated social structure.

3.1 Anomy in Science

In *The Division of Labor in Society*, Emile Durkheim (1933) illustrates his concept of anomy with an analysis of the scientific community. Anomic social organizations lack the system of rules and conventions – agreements between actors in different social positions – that permit the coordination of interdependent parts:

> Until very recent times, science, not being very divided, could be cultivated almost entirely by one and the same person. But as specialization is introduced into scientific work, each scholar becomes more and more enclosed, not only in a particular science, but in a special order of problems. Science, parceled out into a multitude of detailed studies which are not joined together, no longer forms a solidary whole. (Durkheim 1933, p. 356)
>
> There are hardly any disciplines which bring together the work of the different sciences in light of a common end. This is particularly true of the moral and social sciences, for the sciences of mathematics, physics, chemistry, and even biology, do not seem strangers to one another in this respect. But the jurist, the psychologist, the anthropologist, the economist, the statistician, the linguist, the historian, proceed with their investigations as if

> the different orders of fact they study constituted so many independent worlds. In reality, however, they penetrate one another from all sides; consequently, the case must be the same with their corresponding sciences. This is where the anarchical state of science in general comes from, a state that has been noted not without exaggeration, but which is particularly true of these specific sciences. They offer the spectacle of an aggregate of disjointed parts which do not concur. If they form a whole without unity, this is not because they do not have a sentiment of their likenesses; it is because they are not organized. If the division of labor does not produce solidarity it is because the relations of the organs are not regulated, they are in a state of anomy. (Durkheim 1933, pp. 367–8)

The issues that are raised in these passages parallel the theoretical issues that I raised in Chapter 1. What are the social positions that differentiate members of the scientific community? To what extent do institutionalized features of the social structure of science constrain its members? What are the foundations of interpersonal agreement and social control processes in the scientific community?

3.2 Social Differentiation

In Chapter 1, I made a distinction between an actor's social position and the bundle of institutionalized status characteristics: Actors who have an identical institutional status may occupy dramatically different social positions by virtue of their different abilities, personalities, other idiosyncratic factors, and circumstances. In the scientific community, the key institutionalized statuses are the corporate (e.g., university), disciplinary, and specialty affiliations of an actor; however, while these institutional affiliations are important, they do not entirely determine the social position of a scientist.

While the architecture of reality (the subject matter of science) places broad constraints on the pattern of social differentiation that occurs in the scientific community, the scientific community is a human enterprise and, therefore, the social differentiation that arises among its actors is importantly shaped by the actors' conceptualizations of reality, the traditions and ideologies that bear on these conceptualizations, and the organizational arrangements that have been set up to pursue scientific work. Hence, the intellectual and social structures of scientific work are not neatly arranged:

> [In the intellectual framework of science] there exist areas of inconsistency, not to say lacunae. It is as though a house consisted of many floors, on different levels, connected by rather ramshackle, ad hoc, ladders and staircases . . . the intellectual framework is somewhat less than monolithic, and [we] allow that in most periods it has been a somewhat crazy, rambling structure. (Hall 1963, p. 373)

At the same time, it is both possible and useful to conceptualize the differentiation of the scientific community as a hierarchy consisting of relatively stable clusters of social positions that subsume more unstable domains of scientific work (corresponding to specialties and subspecialties). A hierarchical perspective is useful because it provides a way of dealing with the volatility of the scientific enterprise – at the level at which the work of science is actually being done – while enabling a description of a more stable social structure in which such work is pursued.

3.2.1 Micro-Level Instability

Clearly, at the level of the specific problems that are addressed by scientists, there have been rapid changes in the social organization of the scientists who are pursuing research on particular problems. An implication of Kuhn's (1962) analysis of the cognitive development of scientific fields is that the social solidarity of the communities that are associated with these fields is being constantly formed and re-formed. Scientific social organization from this perspective is viewed as highly volatile because it is connected to the volatile development of scientific knowledge. Crane has described the typical pattern of change:

> The various stages of logistic growth of a research area are accompanied by a series of changes in the characteristics of scientific knowledge and of the scientific community that is studying the areas. Interesting discoveries that provide models for future work (paradigms) attract new scientists to the area during stage one. In stage two, a few highly productive scientists set priorities for research, recruit and train students who become their collaborators, and maintain informal contact with other members of the area. Their activities produce a period of exponential growth in publications and in new members in the area. (Crane 1972, p. 40)

As further development of a research area becomes increasingly difficult, one would expect the area to become less attractive to

> those outside it so that exponential growth in the expansion of the field is replaced by a period of linear growth. Kuhn has described such difficulties as anomalies that the paradigm is unable to explain. One would anticipate that this period of cognitive uncertainty would lead to increasing defensiveness on the part of different subgroups concerning their own interpretations of the intellectual problems of the area. This would be likely to produce increasing differentiation between groups of collaborators and a decline in the exchange of ideas among them. (Crane 1972, p. 37)

Such cycles of the formation, growth, and decline of scientific areas suggest instability at the level of subspecialties. Crane's model is based on a consideration of such subspecialties; she examines a field concerned with the diffusion of agricultural innovations, which is a subspecialty of rural sociology, and a field concerned with the theory of finite groups, which is a subspecialty of algebra.

Studies of the formation, growth, and decline of scientific fields and their associated social networks point to certain common patterns of professional relations. The elites that arise in scientific fields tend to be involved in a disproportionate number of the social connections existing between members of the field (Crawford 1970; Griffith, Jahn, and Miller 1971; Crane 1972; Breiger 1976). The rank and file are connected to various members of the elite and tend to be joined to other members of the rank and file primarily through relations with the elite (Price and Beaver 1966; Crawford 1970). The membership of the rank and file tends to be highly unstable: Few are consistent contributors to the field's literature or remain involved in the social network that is associated with the field's development. Price and Beaver (1966, p. 1017) describe the rank and file as a "large and weak transient population." Thus, research fields appear to be dominated by an elite, if only in the sense that it is the elite who are the consistent contributors to a field's development, and it is the elite who are in continuous interaction with whoever is contributing to the field along with them at a particular point in time.

Price suggests that the most active researchers in scientific fields are involved in a cohesive social organization based on their frequent informal interactions with one another:

> In each really active field of science today there is something which we call the "new Invisible Colleges" – the group of everybody who is anybody in the field at that segment of the research front; an official establishment based on fiercely competitive scientific excellence. They send each other duplicated

> preprints of papers yet to be published, and for big things they telephone and telegraph in advance. (1955, p. 236)

However, social network studies suggest that a highly cohesive elite or invisible college – in Price's sense of an establishment of scientists all of whom are in direct contact with one another – is not prevalent in science. More amorphous social networks in which members of a field's elite are joined to one another directly or indirectly through other members of the elite appear instead to be prevalent (Crawford 1970; Griffith and Miller 1970; Crane 1972).

Griffith and Miller (1970) speak of "loose, effective networks" as being the norm within scientific fields, and most investigators now appear to share this impression. Only rarely do high-density networks crystallize within scientific fields. Such networks tend to arise when a group is formed whose members "remain convinced, over a substantial period of time, that they are in process of formulating a radical conceptual reorganization" (1970, p. 139). "If we think of the highly coherent group in terms of a network, we can regard these groups as an extreme thickening in the network, with a resultant loss of some links to the remainder of the network" (Griffith and Mullins 1972, p. 961). Illustrating such groups, Griffith and Mullins point to the following: the phage researchers of molecular biology, the Skinnerians, the quantum physicists of Copenhagen, the Göttingen mathematicians, the audition researchers of psychology, and the ethnomethodologists. Griffith and Mullins estimate that the typical life span of such highly cohesive research clusters is somewhere between ten and fifteen years.

In the long run, even the social network in which the elite is involved is unstable. Research networks, write Mulkay, Gilbert, and Woolgar,

> are in a state of constant flux, partly due to overlapping personnel and to migration. At any one point in time, the research community as a whole, as well as particular disciplines or specialties, can be regarded as being composed of numerous networks at various stages of formation, growth or decline. (1975, p. 190)

In short, at the level of subspecializations and the research problems upon which scientists work, the social structure of science is unstable.

3.2.2 Macro-Level Stability

Typically, investigations of social networks among scientists focus on *one* among what may be several dimensions of a scientist, i.e., the dimension concerned with the scientist's research in a specified field. However, most active scientists are *multidimensional* professionals who have worked in and communicate about research in more than one field or subspecialty.[1] In studies of scientific fields, the theoretical focus is on a "partial" actor to the extent that the scientist has a larger bundle of professional relations that are ignored. Thus, studies of scientific fields, although they describe the social organization of these fields, do not necessarily describe the social organization of the scientists who practice research in those fields.

The linkage of social network structure to developments of scientific knowledge becomes less meaningful when broader areas of science are dealt with. A social network that joins the membership of a specialty may be maintained regardless of the developments in particular fields in the specialty. A network that joins the membership of a discipline may be maintained regardless of the developments in particular specialties in the discipline. And the network that joins the membership of a sector of science (biological, social, or physical sciences) may be maintained regardless of the developments in particular disciplines in the sector. In moving from micro - to macro-scientific areas, we move from the development of volatile fields to the consideration of networks of ties with relatively stable structural features that are based on scientists' continuing commitment to research within a *realm* of problems, and we move from the consideration of partial actors to the consideration of whole, multidimensional professionals. In so moving, I suggest that we move from issues concerned with the rise and growth of fields of scientific innovation (i.e., the sociology of knowledge) to issues concerned with social differentiation and social control in the scientific community.

3.3 Social Process and Institutions

In Chapter 1, I contrasted two extreme views on the effects of social structure. According to one view, interpersonal influences simply reflect the institutionalized characteristics of social structure, and, therefore, the systemic implications of a social structure are obvious once the institu-

1 Crane finds that nearly half of the social connections revealed by her survey of scientists in two specialties involve connections between the members of the two specialties and other scientists who never published in these areas (1972, p. 100). Given the narrowness of the subfields which are the subject of Crane's inquiry – the diffusion of agricultural innovations and the theory of finite groups – it is likely that most of the scientists in these areas also have professional interests in other areas and that the scientists are connected to other persons in their specialty and disciplines on the basis of these additional interests. See Ennis (1992) on the specialty affiliations of sociologists.

tionalized characteristics of the social structure are described. According to the other view, institutionalized characteristics only weakly constrain outcomes, and the opinions and behaviors of actors can be understood only by taking into account the social positions of actors that more fully reflect the spectrum of conditions that affect the actors.

I also marshaled arguments in Chapter 1 that most social structures are not strongly constraining. These arguments apply without qualification to the scientific community. Indeed the Mertonian school of structural analysis, in which the idea of structural ambivalence was developed, was informed by an analysis of the scientific community:

> Science appears as one of the great social institutions, coordinate with the other major institutions of society: the economy, education and religion, the family and the polity. Like other institutions, science has its corpus of shared and transmitted ideas, values and standards designed to govern the behavior of those connected with the institutions. The standards define the technically and morally allowable patterns of behavior, indicating what is prescribed, preferred, permitted or proscribed. The culture of science refers, then, to more than habitual behavior; its norms codify the values judged appropriate for the people engaged in doing science. (Merton 1976, p. 32)

Merton argues that in the scientific community, the opinions and behaviors of scientists are only roughly shaped by the institutionalized conditions. Hence, coordinated action and interpersonal agreements are *not* automatically entailed among actors who have an identical institutional status:

> In saying that the social institution of science is malintegrated, I mean that it incorporates potentially incompatible values: among them the value set upon originality, which leads scientists to want their priority to be recognized, and the value set upon humility, which leads them to insist on how little they have in fact been able to accomplish. These values are not real contradictories, of course – 'tis a poor thing, but my own – but they do call for opposed kinds of behavior. To blend these potential incompatibles into a single orientation and to reconcile them in practice is no easy matter. Rather, the tension between these kindred values creates an inner conflict among scientists who have internalized both of them. (Merton 1976, p. 36)

Merton described the value conflicts in science in terms of norms and counter-norms such as:

> The scientist must be ready to make his newfound knowledge available to his peers as soon as possible. *But:* He must avoid an undue tendency to rush into print.
>
> The scientist should not allow himself to be victimized by intellectual fads, those modish ideas that rise for a time and are doomed to disappear. *But:* He must remain flexible, receptive to the promising new idea and avoid becoming ossified under the guise of responsibly maintaining intellectual traditions.
>
> New scientific knowledge should be greatly esteemed by knowledgeable peers. *But:* The scientist should work without regard for the esteem of others.
>
> The scientist must not advance claims to new knowledge until they are beyond reasonable doubt. *But:* He should defend his new ideas and findings, no matter how great the opposition.
>
> The scientist should make every effort to know the work of predecessors and contemporaries in his field. *But:* Too much reading and erudition will only stultify creative work. (1976, pp. 33–4)

Differences of opinion among scientists about their professional work and conduct go far beyond the stylistic issues entailed in these norms and counter-norms. The differences of opinion penetrate into all aspects of scientific activity; for example, deep divisions occur among scientists with respect to their commitment to the Western Rationalistic Tradition (Searle 1993); their reliance on experimentation, statistical, and mathematical models; their emphasis on pursuing immediate applications versus basic research; their prioritization of teaching and student advising versus research; their perceptions of the overall quality and intrinsic worth of the subject matter of different fields; and their views on the proper distribution of professional rewards (symbolic honors, fellowships, research funding, and memberships in prestigious scientific societies).

As with other cultural systems, the culture of science is subject to diversification. Differentiation, Durkheim proposed (1933, p. 361), induces a cultural diversity that nothing can prevent. Durkheim (1933) argues that as a society becomes more differentiated, prevailing norms increasingly "rule only the most general forms of conduct and rule them in a very general way" (p. 289). In highly differentiated societies, nothing is left in *common* except a set of abstract guidelines that are open to different interpretations. So it is in the scientific community. The diversity of social and technical environments under which scientific work is conducted has increased with the advance of differentiation and has created a powerful strain toward divergent standards and practices.

Hence, we reach the same conclusion for the scientific community that we reached in the general exegesis of Chapter 1. Institutionalized social arrangements and power structures affect the pattern of actors' opinions, but do not reliably predict this pattern.

3.4 Interpersonal Agreements and Social Control

Although a massive consensus and coherent system of coordinated action do not exist in the scientific community, there are parts of the social structure of science in which interpersonal agreements and coordinated activity do occur. In this section, I address the origins of agreements between members of different scientific specialties and disciplines.

3.4.1 Formal Controls on Scientific Practices

In the scientific community, formal controls rest mainly on an inducement mechanism by which scientists are encouraged via rewards and punishments to work on certain problems, to employ certain types of methodologies, and to report their work in certain types of outlets (Cole and Cole 1973). The rewards and punishments take the form of positive and negative decisions on access to research funds, fellowships and awards for outstanding work, memberships in honorific societies, publication in prestigious journals and book presses, appointments to prestigious university departments or other research institutions, and career mobility and promotions. Although many scientists are motivated by the intrinsic satisfactions of scientific inquiry, the reward system of science also has an important effect on professional conduct and attitudes – reward systems channel activities and attitudes in directions that are consistent with the receipt of available rewards.

The scientific community is a punishing system as well as being a system of positive reinforcements. Although norms of academic freedom protect scientists' right to pursue problems of their choice, there are constraints on the choice of problems and the methods for pursuing them. An extreme illustration of such constraint is the case of a researcher who abandoned his study into the behavioral consequences of chromosomal aberration after heavy criticism of the study and himself. The opposition charged that the study was unethical and harmful. The researcher, who was the focus of this criticism, explained why he abandoned the study:

> I hope no one thinks I don't still believe in my research. I do. But this whole thing has been a terrible strain. My family has been threatened. I've been made to feel like a dirty person. And, even after I won with the faculty, it was clear that the opposition would go on. In fact, new groups were becoming involved. I was just too emotionally tired to go on. (Culliton 1975, p. 1284)

Although such extreme cases rarely occur in the scientific community, there is a general shaping of scientists' behavior that occurs via control over access to resources. Scientists who work on problems that are perceived to be trivial, or who work on their problems with unacceptable methods, may be denied access to professional employment that would allow them to pursue their work, denied funds to support their research, or denied visibility in prestigious publication outlets. Hence, there is some pressure on scientists to pursue, with approved methods, problems that are perceived to be important.

Formal decisions concerning the allocation of rewards and punishments to scientists may involve actors who are outside the specialty of the scientist who is being evaluated. A clear example of such outside control occurred in the American National Academy of Sciences:

> Scientists may be curious to know how the rest of the Academy feels about having social and behavioral sciences firmly in the nest instead of hanging on by their toenails. Handler (the Academy's president) explains that "the most remarkable aspect of why my colleagues who are natural scientists are not sneeringly distrustful of soft science is that we struck a bargain." They were welcome if they followed the rules. Under the NRC reorganization plan an Academy-wide review process was installed. The review board of 11 supervises the review of all reports with an eye towards ensuring that conclusions flow logically (and scientifically) from the information presented. Handler boasts that this is the only place where work of social scientists is passed on by physical scientists. Since the review board is and always will be dominated by hard scientists, there is little chance that the Academy will find itself throwing its immense prestige behind any pie in the sky from the vaporous fringes. (Holden 1978, pp. 1184–5)

Actually, there are many situations (especially in universities) where formal interdisciplinary evaluations on personnel issues, honors, and resources are made about scientists. However, these formal interdisciplinary controls do not appear to have important consequences for agreements among scientists. As scientific activity has enlarged and become more differentiated, rewards have become decentralized and tailored to the activities of specialties. Hence, many of the important rewards are controlled by peers rather than actors who are outside of the scientist's own specialty. Moreover, the same specialization and growth have made it technically difficult for actors to evaluate the merits of work being done outside their own specialties; hence, peer evaluations are often decisive. The collegial norm that scholars are best assessed by the peers in their specialty undermines a *formal* interdisciplinary regulation of professional standards.

In short, although there is a considerable amount of formal regulation in science, such regulation is concentrated on the allocation of rewards among actors who occupy similar positions in the scientific community. Hence, the reward system of science helps explain why scientists are concerned about, and influenced by, the judgments of their peers. This reward system does not explain how agreements arise and are maintained among scientists who work in different areas of science. There is no doubt that such agreements exist between certain areas of science (especially on methods), although in general there is not a massive consensus on all issues among scientists. If not by formal means, what (if any) are the mechanisms that regulate the activities of scientists who work in markedly different areas? A body of investigators treating this question does not exist, and since Polanyi's (1962) seminal article no progress has been made on the problem.

3.4.2 Polanyi on the Control of Scientific Practices

Polanyi proposes that interpersonal agreements on professional standards are formed on the basis of ongoing informal evaluations of scientists who are outside a particular specialty but who are competent to judge the research done in it:

> While scientists can admittedly exercise competent judgement only over a small part of science, they can usually judge an area adjoining their own special studies that is broad enough to include some fields on which other scientists have specialized. We thus have a considerable degree of overlapping between the areas over which a scientist can exercise a sound critical judgement. And, of course, each scientist who is a member of a group of overlapping competencies will also be a member of other groups of the same kind, so that the whole of science will be covered by chains and networks of overlapping neighborhoods. Each link in these chains and networks will establish

> agreement between the valuations made by scientists overlooking the same overlapping fields, and so, from one overlapping neighborhood to the other, agreement will be established throughout all the domains of science. Indeed, through these overlapping neighborhoods uniform standards of scientific merit will prevail over the entire range of science. (Polanyi 1962, p. 59)

Thus, the social differentiation of the scientific community is not inconsistent with structural conditions that foster agreements in particular parts of the community. Polanyi argues that the main structural basis of such agreements are overlapping competencies. It is, in other words, the structure of contiguity among the social positions of science that fosters interpersonal agreements that span the boundaries of disciplines and specialties.

3.5 Corporate Organization and the Unity of Science

The conclusion that interpersonal agreements in the scientific community are not mechanistically determined by institutionalized arrangements and authority structures underscores the importance of a line of inquiry concerned with the question of how such agreements are established and maintained, and it justifies the importance of addressing possible structural conditions and social processes that have a bearing on the formation of such agreements (Burt 1982; Powell and DiMaggio 1991; Strang and Meyer 1993). My approach to the study of the unity of science focuses on a setting – elite universities – where influence networks that include actors from different fields may readily form, and where the interpersonal agreements that are attained among the members of these networks may be especially consequential for the larger community of scientists. Agreements among scientists in elite universities contribute to a nascent form of corporate organization that Durkheim argued was crucial for the coordination of highly differentiated social structures.

Durkheim pursued a set of theoretical studies concerned with the consequences of social differentiation; however, he was not content to develop a theoretical understanding of these consequences. Durkheim also sought practical social devices (modifications of social structure) that would reduce anomy. His key idea was that a system of occupational groups – a so-called *corporate* organization – was lacking in most highly differentiated social structures, but that such a system might be developed. In essence, Durkheim sought to revitalize the medieval guild system that had disappeared in the Industrial Revolution. As Wallwork has noted,

> The medieval guilds succeeded in formulating a fairly complex set of rules covering such things as the respective rights and duties of employers and employees, the rights and privileges of workers, and occupational honesty in consumer relations. During the period stretching from the dawn of the High Middle Ages to the eve of the French Revolution, the guild system continued to grow in importance and dignity. . . . If the guilds had become national organizations paralleling large-scale industry, they would presumably have survived [the Industrial Revolution]. But this is precisely what they failed to do. (1972, pp. 101–2)

Durkheim, in *Professional Ethics and Civic Morals* (1958), called for organizations at the national level that would reestablish the regulatory activities previously found in the medieval guilds.

However, guild-like social organizations have not been entirely obliterated. In particular, universities (unlike other medieval institutions) have *proliferated* since they were first originated in corporate form. I suspect that the university not only reflects its medieval origin with its various rituals and trappings (Haskins 1923; Rashdall 1936), but it may also have the important social consequence of fostering agreements in the scientific community. I conjecture that as scientific activity has become more massive and variegated, universities have become a more crucial basis of social control in the scientific community and now perform a role in this community which Durkheim had in mind for a system of corporate organization in the industrial sector of modern societies.

I am not concerned with the effectiveness of universities in reducing anomy in the scientific community; my interest in universities rests on the idea that they may be strategic sites for learning about the mechanisms and structural conditions of consensus formation in highly differentiated social structures. Sociologists of science view the scientific specialty (or so-called invisible college) as the social group of primary interest, because it is within the specialty that scientific work is pursued and developed. However, a focus on scientific specialties does not allow a viewpoint on how agreements are formed within the broader scientific community. Following Durkheim's analysis of the importance of *corporate* organization in the development of macro-level consensus and coordination, I view universities (especially the elite research universities) as potentially important sites of agreements in the scientific community with respect to broad matters of problem definition, appropriate methods of inquiry, and standards of evaluation.

The university is not only a place where scientists tend to reside and vary in their productivity. The university is also a moral and political community that, under certain conditions, *interlocks with the peer review system of science* to constitute a powerful regulatory agency of diversity in the scientific community. If it is the specialty (or invisible college) that arrives at judgments about the scientific competence of individuals, it is the university community that is a powerful *executor* of the specialty's opinion.[2] For example, it is the members of a scientist's university department and not the members of his or her specialty who directly control access to research positions, since these positions are primarily located within universities. It is the university community that grants tenure, professorial status, and remuneration. It is within the university that resources are distributed that may be of instrumental importance to the success of a scientist's research program: space, time, and students.

University communities do not reflexively reinforce the judgments of the peer review system. Decisions about the reward or punishment of a fellow faculty member are made by persons who, in general, are not directly involved in the affairs of the specialty of the faculty member whom they are rewarding or punishing. The standards of evaluation that are applied by a university in assessing a faculty member's role-performance are, therefore, not necessarily the same standards that are applied to that person by the specialty peer group.

The contributions of a particular university's culture to standards within specialties depends on the national stature of its faculty. Research-oriented universities that support concentrations of active scientists at work in a variety of disciplines have a greater potential impact on the community of science than do universities that are primarily oriented to teaching. Certain universities are particularly important sites of potential contact between the elite members of different specialties. To be sure, other organizations exist in which multidisciplinary research-oriented populations are supported (e.g., the National Institutes of Health in the United States), but the university is currently the most prevalent formal organization in which there occurs a high density of elite representatives from different fields.

The formation of agreements within a university depends upon the extent to which influence networks occur within universities that allow flows of influence between scientists in different disciplines and specialties. There is little previous research on social networks composed of

2 Research universities foster transactions between specialties via governance responsibilities that require faculty to evaluate and vote on cases of merit and promotion. Strong traditions of faculty governance, which involve faculty in discussions of whom to hire and when, necessarily force an assessment of different fields.

scientists at work in different fields in the same university (Friedkin 1978; also see Camic and Xie 1994); the motivation for such research has been lacking, because the idea that multidisciplinary social networks within universities might have some theoretical significance has not been accepted. For instance, Blau (1973) is skeptical of the idea that multidisciplinary social networks within universities might be the basis of agreements between faculty members in different fields:

> The differentiation of academic institutions into specialized departments, far from integrating them by making them highly interdependent, weakens their integration by creating obstacles to communication among them. (p. 265)
>
> In other organizations, the differentiation of the common task into interdependent functions creates simultaneously a basis for integration, because the interdependence of parts requires them to cohere and helps integrate them. But the academic specialties in a university are not directly interdependent. The members of each can pursue their research and teaching independently of the work of others, and the high degree of specialization makes communication between different fields difficult. The fact – assuming it is a fact – that integration is more problematical in universities is ironical, since the very term "university" implies an integrated whole. (p. 215)

However, functional interdependence is not a prerequisite for an influence network that includes actors in different social positions, because such a network also can be established by the multidimensional interests and activities of scientists. Blau's later work on social integration draws on this idea (Blau 1977).

3.6 Concluding Remarks

In the scientific community, as in many other complexly differentiated communities, institutionalized social arrangements and power structures affect the pattern of actors' opinions, but do not reliably predict this pattern. A loose coupling of actors' settled opinions and social positions occurs because actors' opinions are affected informally, but importantly, by actors in different social positions. Such influence allows the emergence of dominant social positions with occupants who influence (directly and indirectly) actors in other social positions; and these influenced actors may come to hold opinions that do not so much reflect their own social positions as they do the dominant positions of other actors.

Thus, to explain the agreements of actors, we must attend to the structure of interpersonal influences that is constructed and maintained by them, and to the process of social influence by which their settled opinions are formed.

This chapter completes the introductory theoretical material. My aim is to advance the study of social structures via an analysis of the social influence processes that occur among the actors who occupy different social positions. I focus on the implications of social structural arrangements for the development of interpersonal agreements among actors in different social positions. Toward that aim, I have proposed a theory of social influence in which interpersonal agreements arise from the repeated efforts of actors to weigh and integrate the conflicting influences of significant others. I now turn to the development of a structural approach to the parameters of this theory.

Part B

Measures of the Theoretical Constructs

4

A Structural Parameterization

Abstract. I describe a structural approach to the theory of social influence in which measures of actors' social positions and interpersonal influences are based on their network of interpersonal visibilities. Subsequent chapters in this section (Chapters 5–7) will elaborate and support the structural approach that is introduced here. In the present chapter, I also describe the survey data upon which my measures are based and certain elementary network concepts that will be useful later.

In this chapter I outline an approach to the theory of social influence in which measures of actors' social positions and interpersonal influences are derived from their network of interpersonal visibilities. Interpersonal visibility exists when an actor i has some information about another actor j. The information may concern actor j's opinion on a particular issue, j's violation of a proscription, j's performance of a prescribed activity, j's expertise and interests, or j's personal affairs and circumstances. Visibility of role performance has been of interest to sociologists since preliminary statements on the subject by Simmel (1950), who used the term "surveyable" to refer to the extent to which the role-performances of actors may be scrutinized. While Simmel was concerned with the ability of aristocrats to observe the behavior of other members of the aristocracy, Merton (1968) has generalized this concern to any social system. The classical interest in interpersonal visibility derives from its relationship to social control (Coser 1961; Skolnick and Woodworth 1967; Merton 1968; Warren 1968).

Visibility of role-performance generally is considered a prerequisite condition of social control in that reactions to an actor's behavior cannot occur unless the behavior is first observed. This relationship is acknowledged in Ouchi's definition of control as a "process for monitoring and evaluating performance" (1977, p. 96) and in Skolnick and Woodworth's observation, much along the same lines, that

> Awareness of infraction is the foundation of any social control system. Whatever the system of normative standards, whether

> these are folkways or mores, crimes or rules, a transgression must somehow be observed and reported before sanctions can be applied. The potential efficiency of a social control system, therefore, varies directly with its capacity to observe or receive reports of transgressions. (1967, p. 9)

Similarly, Merton states,

> Effective social control presupposes social arrangements making for the observability of behavior . . . I mean the extent to which social norms and role-performances can readily become known to others in the social system. (1957, p. 114)

Social control mechanisms involve a feedback of reactions to the focal actor:

> The structural conditions which make for ready observability or visibility of role-performance will of course provide appropriate feed-back when the role-performance departs from the patterned expectations of the group. For under such conditions, the responses of other members of the group, tending to bring the deviant back into line with the norms, will begin to operate soon after the deviant behavior has occurred. Collaterally, when there are structural impediments to such direct and immediate observability, deviant behavior can cumulate, [and] depart even more widely from the prevailing norms before coming to the notice of others in the group. (Merton 1968, p. 374)

Whether or not appropriate feedback follows upon knowledge of a departure from group norms, it is certainly the case that without visibility there can be no such feedback.

However, interpersonal visibility is a precondition of social control processes, not only because it allows a response to actors whose behavior or opinion have been observed, but also because it allows the observed behavior and opinion to become influential – invisible behavior and opinion cannot be influential.[1] It is this latter aspect of interpersonal visibility that bears upon the network of endogenous interpersonal influences – the unmediated direct effects of actors' opinions – in the present theory of social influence. In the opinion-formation process that this

1 Among scientists interpersonal visibility is highly valued *because* it is a necessary condition of interpersonal influence. Cole and Cole (1968, p. 398) point out that, "One of the greatest rewards that a scientist can receive is the knowledge that his work has been read and used by his colleagues – that it has made a difference. The individual scientist therefore becomes deeply concerned with the visibility of his work."

theory describes, interpersonal influences upon opinions are based on such interpersonal visibility, and actors influence others *only* through the weight of their opinions.

Merton observes that reference group theory, in particular, and the process of social control, in general, presuppose avenues of communication by which persons become aware of the norms and role-performances of others (1968, p. 373–76, 390–407). He proposes that such visibility is not fortuitous, and that social structure determines its pattern. If interpersonal visibility of role-performance is an outcome of social structure, then the pattern of these visibilities can be employed to indicate features of social structure. Indeed, the key scope condition of the present approach is that the network of interpersonal visibilities, from which the structural measures are derived, must be formed by a status-organizing process (Berger, Rosenholtz, and Zelditch 1980) so that the network's structural features can serve as reliable indicators of actors' social positions and interpersonal influences.

To describe the social positions and interpersonal influences of actors, the network of direct interpersonal attachments or engagements (a subnet of the total pattern of interpersonal visibilities) is perhaps most fundamental. This network reflects the concrete activities of actors – conversing, reading, or listening to reports of each other's work and opinions – as opposed to the secondary flows of information that these concrete activities produce.[2] Let this network be

$$\mathbf{R} = [r_{ij}] \tag{4.1}$$

where $r_{ij} = 1$ if actor j's role-performance is visible to actor i on the basis of a direct engagement with actor j (conversing, reading, or listening), $r_{ij} = 0$ if no such basis of observability has occurred, and $r_{ii} = 0$. I refer to this subnet of interpersonal visibilities as the network of interpersonal attachments, and I base the measures of the theoretical constructs on it.

In three sections, I introduce structural measures of actors' interpersonal influences and social positions, i.e., measures of $\mathbf{A}$, $\mathbf{W}$, and $\mathbf{Y}^{(1)}$, that are based on the network of interpersonal attachments, $\mathbf{R}$. First, a measure of cohesion, defined as the probability of an interpersonal attachment, forms the basis of the interpersonal influences in $\mathbf{W}$. Second, a measure of the centrality of an actor, defined as the actor's indegree in the network of interpersonal attachments, forms the basis of the self-

2 The role-performance of actor j may be visible to actor i because of a direct engagement of actor i with the work of actor j, or because actor i has received information about actor j from third parties. Elsewhere, I have examined such secondary flows of visibility and have shown how they are patterned by certain features of the network of face-to-face communication (Friedkin 1982).

weights in **A**. Third, a measure of the structural equivalence of actors, defined as their profile similarity in the influence network **W**, forms the basis of actors' social positions and initial opinions, $\mathbf{Y}^{(1)}$.

4.1 Interpersonal Influence

A program of research on the measurement of interpersonal influence has not developed out of the early work March (1957) and Simon (1953), and this lack of development has inhibited the study of influence structures. The difficulty in pursuing the development of influence measures has to do with the nature of the phenomenon: Interpersonal influence is a causal effect (direct and unmediated) of one actor on another. It is difficult to isolate and measure this effect because an observed difference of opinion, or opinion change, is not always a reliable indicator of the direct and unmediated effect of one actor on another. If the opinion difference or change has occurred within a system of influences involving other actors, then these other actors may have induced the observed opinion difference or change. However, a structural approach to interpersonal influence is feasible (Friedkin 1993).

The greater the likelihood of an interpersonal attachment from actor i to actor j, the greater the likelihood that actor j will have some influence on actor i. Thus, I base a measure of the relative interpersonal influence of actor j on actor i on conditions that predict the probability of a tie in **R** from i to j:

$$w_{ij} = (1 - w_{ii})\frac{c_{ij}}{\sum_k c_{ik}} \tag{4.2}$$

where c_{ij} is an estimate of the probability of $r_{ij} = 1$. This estimate is obtained from a logistic regression

$$c_{ij} = \frac{1}{1 + e^{-z_{ij}}} \tag{4.3}$$

$$z_{ij} = b_0 + \sum_{h=1}^{H} b_h x_h + u \tag{4.4}$$

among ij-dyads with members who are two steps removed or less in the semipath structure of **R** (c_{ij} is set to zero for all other dyads), in which r_{ij} is regressed on structural features of the bundle of interpersonal ties to and from actors i and j in **R**:

x_1 is the outdegree of actor i, a count of the number of ties from i
x_2 is the indegree of actor i, a count of the number of ties to i

x_3 is r_{ji}, the occurrence of a tie from j to i
x_4 is the number of actors who send ties to i and j ($i \leftarrow k \rightarrow j$)
x_5 is the number of actors to whom i and j send ties ($i \rightarrow k \leftarrow j$)
x_6 is the number of actors to whom i sends a tie and from whom j receives a tie ($i \rightarrow k \rightarrow j$)
x_7 is the number of actors from whom i receives a tie and to whom j sends a tie ($i \leftarrow k \leftarrow j$)
x_8 is the outdegree of actor j, a count of the number of ties from j
x_9 is the indegree of actor j, a count of the number of ties to j

These nine variables describe the immediate network environment of the ij-dyad under which actor i may observe the role-performance of actor j via an interpersonal attachment.

In this approach, it is not the occurrence of an attachment from i to j that is of paramount importance; it is the *probability* of such an attachment under the structural conditions in which i and j are situated. An important attraction of this approach is that it may easily accommodate a more elaborate set of predictor variables. However, I presently rely on this basic set of nine structural variables. In Chapter 5, I lay out this approach in more detail and show how it integrates certain key traditions of structural analysis.

4.2 Self and Other

In contrast to the absence of work on networks of interpersonal influence, there is an extensive literature on a structural approach to individual-level influence. I advance this line of structural work with a formulation in which the weight an actor attaches to his or her own opinions is equated to the structural centrality of the actor in the network of interpersonal attachments. Two equations describe the approach. First, I link the self-weight of actors to their structural centrality, c_i:

$$w_{ii} = 1 - \sqrt{1 - c_i} \tag{4.5}$$

The greater an actor's structural centrality, the greater the actor's self-weight and, therefore (since $w_{ii} = 1 - a_{ii}$ from Eq. [2.3], the less subject the actor is to interpersonal influences and the more anchored the actor is on his or her initial opinions. Second, I define the centrality of an actor i in terms of a standardized measure of the indegree of the actor in the network of interpersonal attachments:

$$c_i = \frac{1}{1 + e^{-(d_i - 2\bar{d})}} \tag{4.6}$$

where d_i is the indegree of actor i

$$d_i = \sum_k r_{ki} \tag{4.7}$$

and $\bar{d}$ is the mean indegree of the actors

$$\bar{d} = \frac{\sum\sum r_{ij}}{N} \tag{4.8}$$

This measure of indegree (a) varies between zero and one and (b) dampens the centrality of actors in networks where the probability of an interpersonal tie is high. This approach to self-weight is the subject of Chapter 6.

4.3 Social Positions and Initial Opinions

For an approach to actors' initial opinions, $\mathbf{Y}^{(1)}$, I build directly on the tradition in structural analysis that has dealt with the description of social positions in multidimensional social space (Burt 1976; Laumann and Pappi 1976). The theoretical focus is on the expected opinions of actors in a social position, as opposed to the opinions of actors on particular issues. I assume a correspondence between actors' endogenous and exogenous social positions; hence, actors' location in social space can be based either on the matrix of exogenous conditions, $\mathbf{X}$, or on the influence network, $\mathbf{W} = [w_{ij}]$. In the absence of reliable data on the exogenous determinants of actors' opinions, this correspondence assumption allows an approach to the definition of social space based on the profile similarities of actors in the influence network.[3] The approach consists of two steps.

First, the distance between social positions is equated with the extent of individual differences in the bundle of interpersonal influences to and from actors. I assess the dissimilarity of two actors' profiles of interpersonal influences with a standardized measure of structural equivalence, $\mathbf{D} = [d_{ij}]$, where

$$d_{ij} = \left[\frac{\sum_k(\tilde{w}_{ik} - \tilde{w}_{jk})^2 + \sum_k(\tilde{w}_{ki} - \tilde{w}_{kj})^2 + (\tilde{w}_{ij} - \tilde{w}_{ji})^2}{\sum_k\tilde{w}_{ik}^2 + \sum_k\tilde{w}_{jk}^2 + \sum_k\tilde{w}_{ki}^2 + \sum_k\tilde{w}_{kj}^2 + \max(\tilde{w}_{ij}^2, \tilde{w}_{ji}^2)}\right]^{1/2} \tag{4.9}$$

for distinct actors i, j, and k, and where $\tilde{\mathbf{W}} = [\tilde{w}_{ij}]$ are the interpersonal influences to and from actors standardized for variations in self-weight:

3 A "backwards" approach to actors' social positions and initial opinions also is feasible given measures of the influence network and equilibrium opinions of actors. From $\mathbf{Y}^{(\infty)} = (\mathbf{I} - \mathbf{AW})^{-1}(\mathbf{I} - \mathbf{A})\mathbf{Y}^{(1)}$, we get $\mathbf{Y}^{(1)} = (\mathbf{I} - \mathbf{A})^{-1}(\mathbf{I} - \mathbf{AW})\mathbf{Y}^{(\infty)}$, where the dimensionality of $\mathbf{Y}^{(1)}$ is determined by the dimensionality of the equilibrium opinions.

$$\tilde{\mathbf{W}} = \mathbf{A}^{-1}\mathbf{W} \tag{4.10}$$

Hence, these standardized interpersonal influences are simply the relative probabilities of the interpersonal attachments and interpersonal influences:

$$\tilde{w}_{ij} = \frac{c_{ij}}{\sum_k c_{ik}} = \frac{w_{ij}}{\sum_k w_{ik}} \tag{4.11}$$

for $i \neq k$. The resulting measure of profile dissimilarity, d_{ij}, equals zero if the bundles of actors' interpersonal influences are identical, it equals one if these bundles are disjoint, and it is undefined for actors (such as isolates) whose self-weights are maximal (i.e., actors for whom $w_{ii} = 1 - a_{ii} = 1$).

Second, I define the social positions of actors by their coordinates in a multidimensional space that is consistent with the individual differences manifested in **D**. These coordinates are derived with a metric multidimensional scaling solution in as many dimensions as is required to obtain a close fit between the observed and derived interpersonal distances. The k coordinates for the N actors are equated with their initial opinions $\mathbf{Y}^{(1)}$.

The basic assumptions of this approach inform the interpretation of the locations of actors in the derived social space. The distances between social positions correspond to expected differences of initial opinion between actors: the greater the distance, the larger the expected opinion discrepancy. Actors in proximate social positions are expected to have more similar initial opinions on issues than actors in distant social positions. If jointly occupied positions exist, then the joint occupants of these positions are expected to form identical initial opinions. This approach to actors' social positions and initial opinions is the subject of Chapter 7.

4.4 Equilibrium Opinions and Total Interpersonal Influences

Given measures of actors' social positions and interpersonal influences, certain systemic implications of the social structure follow immediately from this theory of social influence. These implications include the destinations or settled opinions of actors

$$\mathbf{Y}^{(\infty)} = (\mathbf{I} - \mathbf{AW})^{-1}\,(\mathbf{I} - \mathbf{A})\mathbf{Y}^{(1)}$$

and the net interpersonal influence of each actor in determining the destination of other actors

$$\mathbf{V} = (\mathbf{I} - \mathbf{AW})^{-1}(\mathbf{I} - \mathbf{A})$$

These equilibrium opinions and total interpersonal influences are derived constructs [Eqs. (2.11, 2.12)], and the analysis of the influence system is based on them.

4.5 Summary of the Approach

The entire formal approach may be summarized in the following five steps. First, a network of interpersonal attachments is defined, $\mathbf{R} = [r_{ij}]$, where $r_{ij} = 1$ if actor i has an attachment to actor j, $r_{ij} = 0$ otherwise, and $r_{ii} = 0$. Second, from **R**, point centralities, $\mathbf{c} = [c_i]$, are defined:

$$c_i = \frac{1}{1 + e^{-(d_i - 2\bar{d})}}$$

where d_i is the indegree of actor i in **R** and $\bar{d}$ is the mean indegree of the actors. From **c**, the parameters w_{ii} and a_{ii} are determined:

$$\begin{aligned}\sqrt{1 - c_i} &= a_{ii} \\ &= 1 - w_{ii}\end{aligned}$$

Third, from **R**, the probabilities of interpersonal attachments, $\mathbf{C} = [c_{ij}]$, are estimated from a logistic regression of r_{ij} on a set of predictor variables that describe the bundle of ties to and from actors i and j. The estimation is restricted to dyads with members who are two steps removed or less in the semipath structure of **R** and c_{ij} is set to zero for all other dyads; also see section 5.3 on the treatment of nonrespondents. Given **C** and w_{ii}, the interpersonal influences are determined for each ordered pair of actors:

$$w_{ij} = (1 - w_{ii})\frac{c_{ij}}{\sum_k c_{ik}}$$

Fourth, from $\mathbf{A}^{-1}\mathbf{W}$, a matrix of profile dissimilarities $\mathbf{D} = [d_{ij}]$ is determined, as in Eq. (4.9), and $\mathbf{Y}^{(1)}$ is defined as the k-dimensional coordinates that are derived from a multidimensional scaling of **D**. Fifth, the equilibrium opinions that are formed from the social influence process are determined with

$$\mathbf{Y}^{(\infty)} = (\mathbf{I} - \mathbf{AW})^{-1}(\mathbf{I} - \mathbf{A})\mathbf{Y}^{(1)}$$

and the net interpersonal influences of each actor are determined with

$$\mathbf{V} = (\mathbf{I} - \mathbf{AW})^{-1}(\mathbf{I} - \mathbf{A})$$

Table 4.1. *Academic Departments Included in the Survey*

University of Chicago	Columbia University
Physical Sciences N = 141	*Physical Sciences* N = 105
Astronomy & Astrophysics	Astronomy
Chemistry	Chemistry
Geophysical Sciences	Geological Sciences
Mathematics	Mathematical Statistics
Physics	Mathematics
Statistics	Physics
Biological Sciences N = 142	*Biological Sciences* N = 153
Anatomy	Anatomy
Biochemistry	Biochemistry
Biology	Biological Sciences
Biophysics & Theoretical Biology	Genetics & Development
Microbiology	Microbiology
Pathology	Pathology
Pharmacology & Physiology	Pharmacology
	Physiology
Social Sciences N = 153	*Social Sciences* N = 157
Anthropology	Anthropology
Economics	Economics
Education	Political Science
Geography	Psychology
Behavioral Science	Sociology
Sociology	

From the results of the equations of this fifth step, an analysis of the systemic implications of the social structure is pursued.

4.6 The Survey

The empirical workhorse of this approach is the network of interpersonal attachments, **R.** In this section, I describe the data for this relation and other social relations that enter into the analysis. These other relations will serve to validate the constructs that are derived from the approach.

During the 1978–9 academic year, I conducted a survey of social networks among professors in the physical, biological, and social science faculties at two elite research universities – Columbia University and The University of Chicago. The data were gathered from the population of Assistant, Associate, and Full Professors who had appointments in at least one of the departments listed in Table 4.1.

These faculty were sent a questionnaire that listed the names of all other faculty in their academic division (i.e., either the physical, biological, or social sciences) and requested the recipient to indicate those persons on the list with whom he or she had certain types of interpersonal relations. The instructions to the respondents were:

> Below and on the following pages is a list of fellow faculty members. Scan the list, marking those persons for whom the statement "I know something of this person's work" is true. Where the statement is true please respond to the additional statement: "I have read or heard person present his/her work," "I have talked with person about his/her work, . . ." Check as many items as apply. Also, please note that the first four items refer to any research a person has done, whereas the last four items refer only to research a person is engaged in now.

Data on eight types of interpersonal relations were solicited:

i knows something of *j*'s work
i has read or heard *j* present his or her work
i has talked with *j* about *j*'s work
i and *j* have been co-workers
i knows something of *j*'s current work
i has read or heard *j* present his or her current work
i has talked with *j* about *j*'s current work
i and *j* are now co-workers

The instructions to the respondents indicate that "work" refers to research. Thus, for example, a "co-worker" is a research collaborator, rather than a joint participant in some other work-related activity. However, it is possible that some respondents may have interpreted "work" more broadly.

I will need to reference these networks in an unambiguous fashion. There will be little potential confusion about the institutional identification of a network (i.e., university and academic division). However, it will be useful to have a system for referencing each of the eight types of interpersonal relations. Let

$$\mathbf{R}_{tz} = [r_{(tz)ij}] \tag{4.12}$$

indicate a particular network, where

$$t = \begin{cases} 0 \text{ if the relation concerns past work} \\ 1 \text{ if the relation concerns current work} \end{cases}$$

$$z = \begin{cases} 1 \text{ if } i \text{ knows something of } j\text{'s work} \\ 2 \text{ if } i \text{ has read or heard } j \text{ present his/her work} \\ 3 \text{ if } i \text{ has talked with } j \text{ about } j\text{'s work} \\ 4 \text{ if } i \text{ has worked with } j \end{cases}$$

Table 4.2. *Survey Response Rates*

Network	N	Survey respondents	Respondent dyads
University of Chicago			
Physical Sciences Faculty	141	78 (55.3%)	3,003 (30.4%)
Biological Sciences Faculty	142	97 (68.3%)	4,656 (46.5%)
Social Sciences Faculty	153	94 (61.4%)	4,371 (37.6%)
Columbia University			
Physical Sciences Faculty	105	59 (56.2%)	1,711 (31.3%)
Biological Sciences Faculty	153	105 (68.6%)	5,460 (47.0%)
Social Sciences Faculty	157	96 (61.1%)	4,560 (37.2%)
Totals	851	529	23,761

and

$$r_{(tz)ij} = \begin{cases} 1 \text{ if } i \text{ reports that the relation exists with } j \\ 0 \text{ otherwise} \end{cases}$$

Thus, for example, $\mathbf{R}_{13}$ is the network of interpersonal communication in which $i \to j$ if i reports having talked to j about j's current work; and $\mathbf{R}_{11}$ is the network of interpersonal communication in which $i \to j$ if i reports knowing something about j's current work.

Separate surveys were conducted for each of the academic divisions. I was concerned that the respondents would balk at the task of scanning rosters containing several hundred names and answering questions about multiple relations for each person whose research they knew something about. So I limited the rosters to faculty members within broad academic divisions. The same concern led me to exclude certain academic units: for example, history departments, Columbia's Teachers College, and certain clinically oriented departments in the biological sciences. Thus, six sets of networks are involved in the analysis, each consisting of faculty members at work in one of the two universities and in one of three domains of academic work – the biological, physical, or social sciences. The size of these networks ranges from 105 to 157 members.

As it was, I had some difficulty in obtaining satisfactory response rates. Table 4.2 gives the response rate for each academic division. The highest response rate (68–69%) was achieved in the biological science divisions of the two universities and the lowest (55–56%) in the physical science divisions. Effects of nonresponse rates on measurement of social network structure are not well understood, though some useful work has been done on the problem (Holland and Leinhardt 1973). Nonresponse produces missing ties; however, the implications of such missing ties depends on which structural features of the network are involved in a particular analysis, and this fact makes it difficult to form confident conclusions about the effects of nonresponse. Are the present findings importantly distorted by the missing data? Although I cannot confidently assert that there is not a problem in this regard, it is unlikely that the findings are grossly misleading where I have found strong associations and uniformity of results across networks. The issue is more complex in the analysis of the systemic implications of an influence system, which entails a case study of a particular system; in such an analysis, missing ties may have severe consequences if they are not taken into account.

I take nonrespondents into account in two ways. First, in analyses that assess the construct validity of the derived measures, I typically focus on respondent dyads; that is, dyads consisting of two respondents. Given this practice, I report in Table 4.2 the number and proportion of such respondent dyads for each network. Second, in the estimation of the probabilities of an interpersonal attachment, Eq. (4.3), I employ a procedure that adjusts these probabilities in cases where nonrespondents are involved. Nonrespondents, so long as they are randomly distributed in the social structure, should not affect the measure of self-weight, because this measure is based on actors' relative indegrees; the potential problems are most severe with respect to the estimates for the probabilities of interpersonal attachment. I describe the procedure that is addressed to this problem in Chapter 5.

Whenever the membership of a network is delimited for the purposes of analysis, actors may be excluded whose relations with the selected network members make an important contribution to the network structure. This problem is present in all network studies; since it cannot be avoided, one must be clear on the defining characteristics of the network's membership and be attuned to the possibility of a distorted description of the network structure. The analysis of an *influence system* crucially depends on an adequate definition of the system's boundaries, and any such analysis must be conducted under the assumption of a closed system (i.e., a system that may influence actors who are located outside it, but whose members are not influenced by outside actors). There are two useful ways in which to deal with this assumption. First, the assumption of a closed system will be satisfied for the spectrum of issues in which only the members of the defined population have an interest and opinion. Hence, so long as we can postulate such a subset of issues, we can carry forward the analysis. Second, even when the assumption of a closed system is not satisfied, the systemic outcomes that are derived from the theory can be interpreted as outcomes that would arise in the system in the absence of outside influences.

4.7 Preliminary Social Network Concepts

I close this chapter with a brief delineation of certain preliminary social network concepts. These concepts, which will be useful later on, deal with types of connections between actors (sequences, paths, semipaths, geodesics), certain properties of these connections (reachability, joining, pair connectedness, distance, length), and certain types of collections of points (point basis, strong subnets, unilateral subnets). Readers who are familiar with these concepts should skip this section and proceed to Chapter 5.

A social network may be defined as a $N \times N$ matrix $\mathbf{M} = [m_{ij}]$ consisting of a subset of nonzero-valued directed lines $(i \xrightarrow{m_{ij} \neq 0} j)$ from actor i to actor j among the possible ordered pairs of actors. I refer to an ordered pair of actors as an ij-dyad. An actor i will be said to be *adjacent* to actor j, if there is a line from i to j. An adjacency or line between actors also may be referred to as a tie. It should be kept in mind that an adjacency is based on a *directed* line; hence, although actor i is tied to actor j, actor j may not be tied to actor i.

For example, consider the network

$$\mathbf{M} = \begin{bmatrix} 5 & 3 & 0 & 0 \\ 0 & 0 & 6 & 10 \\ 0 & 8 & 0 & 10 \\ 2 & 0 & 0 & 0 \end{bmatrix}$$

which consists of 4 actors and 7 lines. For each line $(i \xrightarrow{m_{ij} \neq 0} j)$, i is the actor from which the line originates, j is the terminus of the line, and m_{ij} is the value attached to the line. For instance, $m_{12} = 3$ is the directed line from actor 1 to actor 2 and it has a value of 3. A line that originates from and terminates on the same actor $(i \xrightarrow{m_{ii} \neq 0} i)$ is referred to as a *loop*. In $\mathbf{M}$ there is a loop on actor 1. Two distinct actors may be connected by one line $(i \xrightarrow{m_{ij} \neq 0} j$ or $i \xleftarrow[m_{ij} \neq 0]{} j)$ or by two lines $(i \xrightarrow{m_{ij} \neq 0} j$ and $i \xleftarrow[m_{ji} \neq 0]{} j)$. A social network is said to be *symmetrical* when $m_{ij} = m_{ji}$ for all i and j.

We can transform a network in various ways to derive another network. Two such transformations are important and elementary. First, we may define a new network, $\tilde{\mathbf{M}} = [m_{ij}]$, with lines from i to j which are in a designated range of values:

$$\tilde{m}_{ij} = \begin{cases} 1 \text{ if } m_{ij} > z \\ 0 \text{ if } m_{ij} \leq z \end{cases}$$

For example, letting $z = 0$, the transformed network for $\mathbf{M}$ is

$$\tilde{\mathbf{M}} = \begin{bmatrix} 1 & 1 & 0 & 0 \\ 0 & 0 & 1 & 1 \\ 0 & 1 & 0 & 1 \\ 1 & 0 & 0 & 0 \end{bmatrix}$$

Second, we may define a new network by transforming a nonsymmetrical network into a symmetrical network based on some rule. For example, we can symmetrize the matrix **M** by defining a new matrix $\tilde{\mathbf{M}} = [m_{ij}]$, where $\tilde{m}_{ij} = \max(m_{ij}, m_{ji})$:

$$\tilde{\mathbf{M}} = \begin{bmatrix} 5 & 3 & 0 & 2 \\ 3 & 0 & 8 & 10 \\ 0 & 8 & 0 & 10 \\ 2 & 10 & 10 & 0 \end{bmatrix}$$

According to this rule, a tie exists between two actors if either actor sends a tie to the other, and the value of the tie in the transformed network is the largest value of the two ties in the original network. Other rules of symmetrization are possible, e.g., we also might have symmetrized **M** with the rule $\tilde{m}_{ij} = \min(m_{ij}, m_{ji})$. According to this rule, a tie exists between two actors only if both actors send ties to each other, and the value of the tie in the transformed network is the lowest value of the two ties in the original network. Network transformations are governed by substantive concerns.

A *sequence* is a set of lines in which the terminus actor on a line is the emanating actor on the next line in the sequence. A sequence of lines is described by tracing along lines without violating the directionality of the lines; for example, $1 \xrightarrow{m_{12}\neq 0} 2 \xrightarrow{m_{23}\neq 0} 3 \xrightarrow{m_{32}\neq 0} 2 \xrightarrow{m_{24}\neq 0} 4$ is a sequence from actor 1 to actor 4 that involves actor 2 twice as an originating actor of a line. A *path* is a sequence in which no actor appears more than once as the originating actor of a line, and a *cycle* is a path that originates from and terminates on the same actor.

Actor i is said to *reach* actor j if at least one path exists from i to j, or one might say that j is reachable from i. Reachability implies the existence of a path. By convention, any actor can reach himself even if the network has no loops. A *point basis* is a minimal subset of n actors from which all the other $N - n$ actors of a network are reachable.

The *length* of a path or sequence is the number of lines that compose it. Thus, one may describe a path in terms of its length as either a one-step path or 1-path, a two-step path or 2-path, and so forth. Each ordered pair of actors, i and j, may have numerous paths of different lengths going from i to j; however, there can be only a single 1-path from i to j.

A *geodesic* is a path of shortest length from actor i to actor j. If i is adjacent to *j*, then only one geodesic exists and it is the line from *i* to *j*. However, if *i* and *j* are not adjacent, then there may be one or more geodesics of length greater than one; for example, there can be numerous geodesics of length two from *i* to *j*.

The *distance* from *i* to *j* is the length of the geodesics from *i* to *j*. Distance is not defined when there is no path from *i* to *j*. By convention it is assumed that the distance from actor *i* to actor *i* is zero.

Corresponding to the concepts of sequence, path, and cycle are the concepts of *semisequence, semipath,* and *semicycle.* A semisequence is a set of directed lines in which the terminus actor on a line is either the emanating or terminating actor on the next line in the sequence. For example, $1 \xrightarrow{m_{12} \neq 0} 2 \xleftarrow{m_{25} \neq 0} 5 \xleftarrow{m_{56} \neq 0} 6$ is a semisequence from actor 1 to actor 6 that is defined by tracing along lines *ignoring* the directionality of the lines. A semipath is a semisequence involving a set of distinct actors, and a semicycle is a semipath in which a line is added that joins the initial and terminal actors of the semipath. The length of a semisequence, semipath, or semicycle is the number of lines in them. A semipath establishes the existence of a network connection between two actors that is not predicated on the occurrence of a path between them. Two actors are said to be *joined* if there is a semipath that connects them.

Each *ij*-dyad may be categorized by the type of connection that exist between the two actors. Two actors are *disconnected* or 0-connected if they are not joined by a semipath; they are *weakly connected* or 1-connected if there is a semipath joining them; they are *unilaterally connected* or 2-connected if at least one is reachable from the other; and they are *strongly connected* or 3-connected if each actor is reachable from the other. The connectedness category of a pair of actors is its highest level of connectedness.

Similarly, *subsets* of actors may be classified according to the types of connections that exist in the subnet of these actors. For all $i \neq j$, a subnet is said to be *strongly connected* or *strong* if *i* and *j* are mutually reachable, *unilaterally connected* or *unilateral* if *i* can reach *j* or *j* can reach *i*, *weakly connected* or *weak* if *i* and *j* are joined by a semipath, and *disconnected* if there is at least one pair of actors that is not connected by a semipath. The *connectivity category* of a subnet is its highest level of connectivity.

5

Interpersonal Influence

Abstract. A measure of the probability of an interpersonal attachment is the first pillar of my approach to the social-influence process. An attachment from actor i to actor j is defined as a direct interpersonal engagement in which actor i is able to observe the opinions of actor j and in which actor i regards these opinions as salient. The likelihood of such an attachment is equated with the relative influence of actor j on actor i during the course of an issue-resolution process. An estimate of the probability of an attachment is obtained from a logistic regression of observed attachments on structural features of the network of attachments in which the two actors are situated.

5.1 Structural Bases of Interpersonal Influence

I emphasize *structural* bases of interpersonal influence – cohesion, similarity, and centrality – that are associated with an actor's ability to regularly monitor the opinions of another actor and with the salience of the observed opinions (Erickson 1988; Friedkin 1993). Actor j's influence on actor i depends on i's knowledge of j's opinions; invisible opinions cannot be directly influential. Once i knows j's opinion, then j's influence on i depends on the salience or value of j's opinion for i; irrelevant or valueless opinions cannot directly influence i. In this chapter, I describe how cohesion, similarity, and centrality affect the probability that an actor i is aware of, and attaches some weight to, the opinions of actor j on an issue; then I describe a measure of the probability of an interpersonal attachment that incorporates all three of these structural bases.

In the proposed approach, the probability of attachment governs the distribution of interpersonal influence:

$$w_{ij} = (1 - w_{ii})\frac{c_{ij}}{\sum_k c_{ik}} \tag{5.1}$$

[Eq. (4.2)], and hence,

$$\frac{w_{ij}}{\sum_k w_{ik}} = \frac{c_{ij}}{\sum_k c_{ik}} \tag{5.2}$$

[Eq. (4.11)] for $i \neq \{j, k\}$, where c_{ij} is the probability of an attachment of actor i to actor j and $1 - w_{ij} = a_{ii}$ is the aggregate weight of the interpersonal influences on actor i [Eq. (2.7)].[1] According to this approach, if two actors are situated in a structural environment in which an attachment from actor i to actor j is probable, then actor i is likely to monitor and consider salient the opinions of actor j. Conversely, if two actors are situated in a structural environment in which an attachment from actor i to actor j is improbable, then actor i is not likely to monitor or consider salient the opinions of actor j.

5.1.1 Social Cohesion

Since Cooley, Durkheim, and Tönnies wrote about the essential bonds of society, the concept of cohesion has been associated with strong interpersonal ties like kinship and friendship. A cohesive group has been defined as a clique in which each member is strongly tied to all other members. However, many structural theorists have discarded this classical approach in favor of a more general conceptualization that grounds cohesion in a network of heterogeneous interpersonal ties. In this broader approach, it is not an oxymoron to refer to a cohesive "secondary" group in which a substantial proportion of the possible interpersonal ties are weak or absent.

Key elements of cohesion, involving members' inclinations to remain in the group and members' capacities for social control and collective action, may be predicated on weak ties of acquaintance and collegiality (Granovetter 1973, 1982). Moreover, cohesion does not require a *complete* network in which all members are directly tied to each other. Instead, the cohesion of the group is based on the configuration of the group's network. Structural properties of a network of interpersonal attachments such as the connectivity category, diameter, and density of a network (Harary, Norman, and Cartwright 1965) indicate conditions that foster social cohesion. For dyads, the structural cohesion of actors i and j is a function of their joint location in a structurally cohesive group, *not* of their feelings about one another. For example, if a structurally cohesive group is defined as a strong component (i.e., a group in which all pairs of members are mutually reachable via paths of interpersonal

1 As I lay out the approach that was introduced in Chapter 4, equations previously defined are repeated. I number all the important equations in each chapter; however, I also supply the references in brackets [ ] to equations that were previously defined.

attachments), then actors *i* and *j* are structurally cohesive if, and only if, they are joint members of such a component.

Because information tends to diffuse rapidly in cohesive groups, members of a cohesive group are more likely to be aware of each other's views on an emergent issue than are actors who are not members of the group (Friedkin 1982, 1983). Moreover, visible opinions are likely to be salient in cohesive groups, because members are embedded in a field of interpersonal tensions and conflicts that encourages reciprocity and compromise. Hence, the greater the structural cohesion of actors *i* and *j*, the more likely they are to influence each other.

Face-to-face communication mediates the effects of structural cohesion on issue-related interpersonal influence (Friedkin 1993). The greater the structural cohesion of actors *i* and *j*, the more likely they will be in frequent communication on a particular issue; in turn, and independent of the actors' power bases, such issue-related communication may establish the salience of *j*'s opinion for *i*. Here the foundations of salience are elementary balancing mechanisms that are often elicited by a discussion of discrepant opinions (Newcomb 1953; Heider 1958). Because these balancing mechanisms are a response to interpersonal tensions and conflicts, they are more likely to emerge as a result of a face-to-face discussion of discrepant opinions than from a simple awareness of an opinion difference. Because of the reciprocity and compromise that cohesive groups encourage, the salience that is established by face-to-face communication is likely to be more pronounced if *i* and *j* are members of a cohesive group than if they are not.

Moreover, frequent issue-related communication is likely to secure salience during the resolution of an issue. Frequent communication tends to embed opinions in a supporting fabric of arguments and information and also allows adjusting these supports as circumstances change. Hence, the pressure toward uniformity of opinions that arises from a comparison of opinions (Festinger 1954), although predicated on interpersonal awareness, is likely to be more pronounced and more sustained when issue-related communication is frequent.

5.1.2 Structural Similarity

Consider an actor *i* who is aware of *j*'s opinions on an issue but who is not cohesively joined to *j* in a network of interpersonal attachments. For example, if the shortest path that connects these actors is a long path (i.e., goes through several other group members), the structural cohesion of actors *i* and *j* would be negligible. Nevertheless, the salience of actor *j*'s opinions for *i* may be founded on *i*'s recognition that they occupy similar social positions (i.e., that their normative, material, or interpersonal circumstances in the social structure are similar).

Structural similarity may induce a competitive orientation in which actor *i* is attentive to *j*'s status and interests (Burt 1987). Structural similarity may also be a basis of interpersonal solidarity (Durkheim 1933; Dahrendorf 1959; Hechter 1987) and identification:

> P's identification with O can be established or maintained if P behaves, believes, and perceives as O does. Accordingly O has the ability to influence P, even though P may be unaware of this referent power. A verbalization of such power by P might be, "I am like O, and therefore I shall behave or believe as O does," or "I want to be like O, and I will be more like O if I behave or believe as O does." (French and Raven 1959, p. 162)

Because actors' initial orientation on issues are influenced by their definitions of the situation, the more similar two actors' structural positions are, the more similar their initial positions on issues are likely to be. By the same token, actors' initial orientations on issues are more likely to be divergent the more dissimilar are their structural positions. Furthermore, Festinger's (1950, 1954) theory of social comparison processes suggests that the *salience* of actor *j*'s opinions for *i* is inversely related to the discrepancy between their opinions.

Differences of opinion on an issue take on additional social distance when they correspond to differences in actors' material and normative circumstances. The more dissimilar the structural positions of two actors are, the less the perceived salience of discrepant opinions. Hence, actors may not only attach more weight to similar opinions, but will attach even greater weight to opinions of actors who are in similar circumstances. Festinger (1954) argued that "if persons who are very divergent from one's own opinion . . . are perceived as different from oneself on attributes consistent with the divergence, the tendency to narrow the range of comparability becomes stronger" (p. 133).

The effects of structural similarity on interpersonal influence are contingent on interpersonal visibility. Structural similarity can establish salience, which encourages *i* to respond to *j*'s opinion on an issue. However, not only must *i* be aware of *j*'s opinion on the issue, *i* must *also* be aware of their structural similarity. Without information about *j*'s social position, *i* may not attach particular salience to *j*'s displayed opinions.

Interpersonal communication can mediate the effects of structural similarity on interpersonal influence in two ways. In the absence of other media that convey information to *i* about *j*'s structural position and opinions, *i* is more likely to possess such information the more frequently *i* and *j* communicate about an issue. Hence, the effects of structural similarity may be contingent on communication when communication determines the relevant interpersonal visibilities. Moreover, the effects of structural similarity may also be transmitted by communication when actors' structural similarity determines their probability of interpersonal communication on an issue.

5.1.3 Structural Centrality

An extensive literature indicates that an actor's structural centrality in a network of interpersonal attachments contributes to the actor's social power. Structural centrality provides a basis of interpersonal salience and visibility. Central actors more readily acquire information resources (Raven 1965) that allow their opinions to become influential than do peripheral actors. In comparison to peripheral actors, central actors are not only likely to have more numerous or shorter communication channels for conveying their opinions, but also on any given issue are likely to be more active in utilizing these channels (French and Snyder 1959). Thus, network centrality is a *hybrid* condition that combines an actor attribute of *j* (e.g., *j*'s information resources) with features of the network relationship between *j* and *i*. Assuming a center–periphery pattern, central actors tend to be resourceful and cohesively joined to other actors.[2]

The effects of centrality may or may not reinforce the effects of structural similarity. In the case of two central actors, because their positions are likely to be similar, the similarity and centrality effects are reinforcing. However, in the case of a central and peripheral actor, the effects are countervailing. The peripheral actor may dismiss the opinions of a central actor because of the difference in their social positions (the similarity effect), yet also be swayed by the information that the central actor marshals in support of his or her opinion.

As with structural cohesion and similarity, effects of structural centrality on interpersonal influence will be contingent on issue-related communication to the extent that such communication determines the visibility of *j*'s opinions on an issue to *i*. Moreover, frequent issue-related communication fosters salience, which encourages *i* to respond to *j*'s opinion on an issue. Without an awareness of the information underlying *j*'s opinion, *i* can respond to *j* only on the basis of *j*'s displayed opinions.

2 A center–periphery pattern has been observed in many social networks. This pattern consists of (a) a subset of relatively central prestigious actors who are connected by direct or short indirect communication channels, and (b) a subset of peripheral actors who are more directly connected to the central actors than to other peripheral actors.

5.2 Probability of an Interpersonal Attachment

A structural approach to interpersonal influence is possible if the salience and monitoring of opinions that are necessary for sustained interpersonal influence are coupled with the simple expectation of an interpersonal attachment; hence, the greater the probability of an interpersonal attachment under given structural conditions, the greater the probability of a sustained interpersonal influence during the course of an issue-resolution process. I implement this approach below with a measure of the probability of an interpersonal attachment.

I employ the following approach for defining the probability of an interpersonal attachment, c_{ij} in Eq. (5.1). Let the network of interpersonal attachments be

$$\mathbf{R} = [r_{ij}] \tag{5.3}$$

where $r_{ij} = 1$ if actor *j*'s role performance is visible to actor *i* on the basis of a direct engagement with actor *j* (conversing, reading, or listening), $r_{ij} = 0$ if no such basis of observability has occurred, and $r_{ii} = 0$ [Eq. (4.1)]. In the present application, this network of attachments is defined as

$$\mathbf{R} = \mathbf{R}_{02} \otimes \mathbf{R}_{03} \tag{5.4}$$

so that an attachment from *i* to *j* exists if actor *i* has talked with *j* about *j*'s work ($\mathbf{R}_{02}$) or has read or heard a presentation of *j*'s work ($\mathbf{R}_{03}$); see Eq. (4.12). Under the conditions of structural cohesion, similarity, and centrality in which the *ij*-dyad is situated (say $x_1, x_2, \ldots, x_H$), the probability of an interpersonal attachment is $c_{ij} = \mathrm{P}(r_{ij} = 1 | x_1, x_2, \ldots, x_H)$. An estimate of this probability is obtained from a logistic regression in which the units of analysis are the subset of *ij*-dyads with members who are two steps removed or less in the semipath structure of **R** (c_{ij} is set to zero for all other *ij*-dyads) and the criterion variable is r_{ij}:

$$c_{ij} = \frac{1}{1 + e^{-z_{ij}}} \tag{5.5}$$

$$z_{ij} = b_0 + \sum_{h=1}^{H} b_h x_h + u \tag{5.6}$$

[Eq. (4.3)].[3] The predictor variables ($x_1, x_2, \ldots, x_H$) are structural features of the bundle of ties to and from actors *i* and *j*:

3 I stipulate that the probability of an attachment is zero if there are no one-step or two-step semipaths that join two actors in **R**; hence, the influence domain of an actor is restricted to actors who are either in direct contact or for whom at least one mutual

x_1 is the outdegree of actor i, a count of the number of ties from i
x_2 is the indegree of actor i, a count of the number of ties to i
x_3 is r_{ji}, the occurrence of a tie from j to i
x_4 is the number of actors who send ties to i and j ($i \leftarrow k \rightarrow j$)
x_5 is the number of actors to whom i and j send ties ($i \rightarrow k \leftarrow j$)
x_6 is the number of actors to whom i sends a tie and from whom j receives a tie ($i \rightarrow k \rightarrow j$)
x_7 is the number of actors from whom i receives a tie and to whom j sends a tie ($i \leftarrow k \leftarrow j$)
x_8 is the outdegree of actor j, a count of the number of ties from j
x_9 is the indegree of actor j, a count of the number of ties to j

These nine predictor variables describe the immediate network environment of the *ij*-dyad.[4] An important attraction of this approach is that it may easily accommodate a more elaborate set of predictor variables, including *individual* attributes of the actors. However, I presently rely on this basic set of nine structural variables.

Figure 5.1 illustrates the nine predictor variables. The criterion variable is indicated by i --> j. Also presented in the figure is a summary of results from the logistic regressions for respondent dyads in the six faculties of science (A, B, . . . , F); the results of these regressions are in the Appendix. The qualitative effects of the variables, which are indicated with plus (+) and minus (−) signs, are the same across the networks.

This approach integrates the three main lines of work on structural effects that I introduced earlier – cohesion (reciprocity and balance), similarity (homophily), and centrality. Each of these lines of work has contributed hypotheses, which are supported by empirical studies, concerned with the likelihood that an interpersonal tie will exist between two actors under specified structural conditions. Thus, in combination, these theories provide a powerful basis for specifying the pertinent fea-

contact exists. This constraint is based on the finding (to be presented) that interpersonal visibility of role-performance is negligible where actors are more than two steps distant in the semipath structure of the network.

4 In this approach, the logistic regression provides a descriptive analysis of the contributions of the predictor variables in determining the occurrence of an interpersonal attachment. Ideally, the assumption of independence is satisfied, from which the likelihood function in the maximum likelihood estimation is derived. This assumption will be satisfied if the major sources of interdependence are represented in the model. I proceed with this approach under the assumption that the nine structural variables that are included in the model represent the sources of interdependence, and that the estimated probabilities of interpersonal ties are therefore conditionally independent. Even if this assumption is not satisfied, the logistic regression maximizes an objective function that is useful in discriminating environments under which the probabilities of attachment are more or less pronounced; see Figure 5.2.

Figure 5.1. Summary of findings on the probability of an interpersonal attachment.

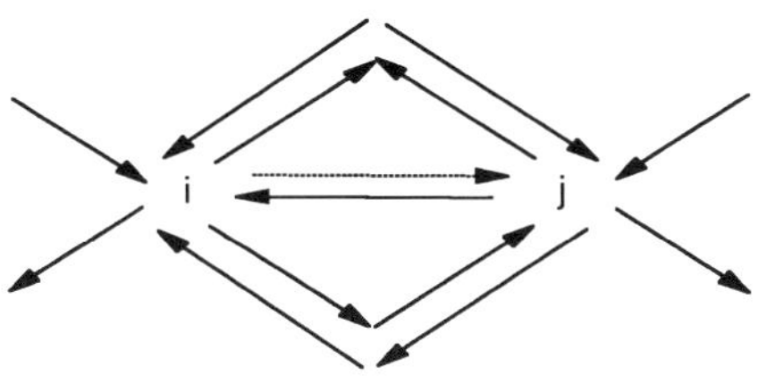

		Networks					
		A	B	C	D	E	F
$\leftarrow i$	*outdegree*	+	+	+	+	+	+
$\rightarrow i$	*indegree*	—	—	—	—	—	—
$i \leftarrow j$	*reciprocity*	+	+	+	+	+	+
$i \leftarrow k \rightarrow j$	*similarity*	+	+	+	+	+	+
$i \rightarrow k \leftarrow j$	*similarity*	+	+	+	+	+	+
$i \rightarrow k \rightarrow j$	*transitivity*	+	+	+	+	+	+
$i \leftarrow k \leftarrow j$	*circularity*	—	—	—	—	—	—
$j \leftarrow$	*indegree*	+	+	+	+	+	+
$j \rightarrow$	*outdegree*	—	—	—	—	—	—

tures of the structural environment of dyads that predict the occurrence of ties.

There is a strong tendency toward reciprocity in social relations (Gouldner 1960). If one actor has been engaged with another actor's work (talked to that actor, read that actor's work, or attended a presentation by that actor), then it is likely that *both* actors will be engaged with each other's work. Hence, the occurrence of a tie from actor j to actor i (x_3) increases the odds of a tie from i to j by a factor that ranges in these data from 5.1 to 10.3.

There is a strong tendency toward transitivity in social relations (Heider 1946; Cartwright and Harary 1956; Davis 1968; Holland and Leinhardt 1971). Hence, the occurrence of a two-step path, $i \rightarrow k \rightarrow j$, from actor i to actor j is a predictor of a tie from i to j; the greater the number of such paths (x_6), the greater the likelihood that transitivity will be satisfied. A path in the reverse direction, $i \leftarrow k \leftarrow j$, if completed by an $i \rightarrow j$ tie would form a cycle. There is no theoretical literature to support a particular tendency for such cycles; however, I find that this type of path (x_7) has a consistent negative association with the occurrence of a tie from i to j.

A third foundation of interpersonal ties is homophily or similarity (Lazarsfeld and Merton 1954; MacRae 1960; Kandel 1978).[5] The semipaths, $i \rightarrow k \leftarrow j$ and $i \leftarrow k \rightarrow j$, which indicate that i and j have matching ties, are well-established components of various measures of profile similarity (Sneath and Sokal 1973; Borgatti and Everett 1992; Wasserman and Faust 1994). Similar actors do not always have an opportunity to interact. However, because these semipaths are based on mutual contacts, they indicate not only similarity but also opportunities for interpersonal attachments for the matched actors. The greater the number of such semipaths joining i and j, the greater the likelihood of an $i \rightarrow j$ tie.

A fourth basis of interpersonal ties is the centrality of actors. Centrality has two dimensions: power (such as authority, identification, and expertise) and activity (gregariousness, expansiveness, or intensity of purpose). These two dimensions of centrality are indicated respectively by the indegree and outdegree of an actor. As with the effects of similarity, the effects of centrality on tie formation are limited to those ij-dyads where the members are no more than two steps distant in the semipath structure of the network.

As the indegree (power) of actor j increases, so does the likelihood of an $i \rightarrow j$ tie, because of a tendency to establish ties with powerful actors. As evidence mounts that other actors are oriented to actor j, the chances that actor i will be so oriented increase. However, the indegree of actor i has the opposite effect; the greater the indegree of actor i, the *lower* the likelihood of an $i \rightarrow j$ tie.[6]

As the outdegree (expansiveness) of actor i increases, so does the likelihood of an $i \rightarrow j$ tie. The most likely foundation of this effect is a simple one: As the number of actors to whom actor i is tied increases, the chances that actor i is tied to actor j increase. The outdegree of actor j has the opposite effect; the greater the expansiveness of actor j, the *lower* the likelihood of an $i \rightarrow j$ tie. A negative effect is consistent with the similarity effects noted earlier; the larger the number of j's ties to other actors, the more dissimilar are i and j, and the lower the likelihood of an $i \rightarrow j$ tie.

In this approach, the occurrence of a tie is less important than the conditions under which the tie occurs. Hence, the probability of an at-

5 Introducing his approach to the definition of cohesive subgroups, MacRae (1960, pp. 360–1) writes, "We may still consider a subgroup to be defined in terms of the linkage structure of choices, following, for example, Luce and Perry (1949), but we also hypothesize that, when there exist subgroups of this sort, members of any such group will tend to choose the same person and to be chosen by the same persons."

6 I had speculated that such an effect should occur. It is consistent with my arguments about self-weight (Chapter 6). The expected effect emerges under the full spectrum of controls, i.e., variables x_1–x_9.

tachment (c_{ij}) can differ in two pairs of actors, although both entail an interpersonal tie, if one tie has occurred under structural conditions where ties are unlikely and the other has occurred under structural conditions where ties are likely. For example, a bridging tie between two actors (a tie between two actors who have no mutual contacts) is likely to have a lower probability of attachment than a tie between two actors who have multiple mutual contacts. This implication of the approach is consistent with Granovetter's (1973) argument that bridging ties are weaker ties than ties in cliques.

Moreover, a high probability of attachment can occur in the absence of an interpersonal tie if the actors are situated in a structural environment that fosters the attachment of actors. Such high probabilities can occur given sufficient numbers of two-step semipaths (or shared contacts). This implication of the present formulation is consistent with most group-level definitions of cohesion in which two actors, who are members of a cohesive group, are cohesively attached whether or not they have a direct tie.

5.3 Nonrespondents

The implementation of this approach to the probability of an attachment (c_{ij}) is straightforward in the case of dyads involving complete data on the bundles of ties to and from the actors. Dyads involving nonrespondents must be treated somewhat differently. If an actor i or j is a nonrespondent, the value of c_{ij} predicted from Eq. (5.5) may be affected by the loss of information in the bundle of ties from the nonrespondent actor(s). If actor i is a nonrespondent, then $x_1 = x_5 = x_6 = 0$. If actor j is a nonrespondent, then $x_3 = x_5 = x_7 = x_8 = 0$. If both actors i and j are nonrespondents, then $x_1 = x_3 = x_5 = x_6 = x_7 = x_8 = 0$. However, regardless of the respondent status of actors i and j, there will be counts for x_2 (indegree of actor i), x_4 (number of actors who send ties to both i and j), and x_9 (indegree of actor j). I employ these variables as instruments to obtain an estimate of c_{ij} in cases where either actor i or actor j is a nonrespondent. Three steps are involved in generating these estimates.

First, concentrating on *respondent* dyads, a set of OLS regression equations is estimated:

$$x_k = b_0^{(k)} + b_2^{(k)}x_2 + b_4^{(k)}x_4 + b_9^{(k)}x_9 \tag{5.7}$$

for $k = 1, 5, 6, 7$, and 8. Second, the estimated coefficients in Eq. (5.7) are employed to generate predicted values ($\hat{x}_1$, $\hat{x}_5$, $\hat{x}_6$, $\hat{x}_7$, and $\hat{x}_8$) in those dyads that involve a nonrespondent. The same two steps are used to obtain a predicted value for x_3 (the occurrence of a tie from actor *j* to actor *i*) except that the estimates in the first step are based on a logistic regression, and the prediction in the second step is set to zero or one depending on whether the predicted probability of a tie is greater than 0.50. Third, these predicted values ($\hat{x}_1$, $\hat{x}_5$, $\hat{x}_6$, $\hat{x}_7$, and $\hat{x}_8$) are substituted into the model estimated for the respondent dyads, i.e., Eq. (5.5), to generate the predicted probability of an attachment in cases where a nonrespondent is involved.

5.4 Construct Validation

Figure 5.2 allows an assessment of whether the predicted probabilities of attachment actually discriminate conditions under which attachments are more or less likely. The figure plots the observed proportion of $i \rightarrow j$ ties against the predicted probability of such a tie (c_{ij}). I have collapsed the predictions into categories: 0, $0 > c_{ij} \leq 0.1$, $0.1 > c_{ij} \leq 0.2$, . . . , $0.9 > c_{ij} \leq 1$. For the respondent dyads in each of these categories, the observed proportion is the relative frequency of *ij*-dyads in which there is an $i \rightarrow j$ tie. It is evident from the plots that there is a strong association between the observed and predicted probabilities of an interpersonal tie and that the association is similar in each of the six networks. These findings support the use of the predicted probabilities as indicators of structural conditions under which actor *i* is more or less likely to be attached to actor *j*.

The structural contexts that are associated with the likelihood of an interpersonal attachment also are contexts that are associated with the likelihood of an ongoing interpersonal engagement. Figure 5.3 shows that the derived probability of attachment is associated with the likelihood of *current* visibilities of role-performance based on reading or attending a presentation of that work, conversations, or other sources; i.e., $\mathbf{R}_{11}$, $\mathbf{R}_{12}$, and $\mathbf{R}_{13}$ from Eq. (4.12). Here, as before, for the respondent dyads in each of these categories, the likelihood of an observed tie is calculated as the proportion of dyads in which actor *i* reports a tie to actor *j* among dyads with a similar probability of attachment: 0, $0 > c_{ij} \leq 0.1$, $0.1 > c_{ij} \leq 0.2$, . . . , $0.9 > c_{ij} \leq 1$. The likelihood of visibility of current work, which is slight where the probability of attachment is near zero, increases to above 0.60 in cases where the probability of attachments is high. A similar pattern of findings is obtained for interpersonal visibilities based on reading or hearing a presentation of the current work of another actor, and on conversations with that actor;

Figure 5.2. Predicted and observed likelihood of an interpersonal attachment.

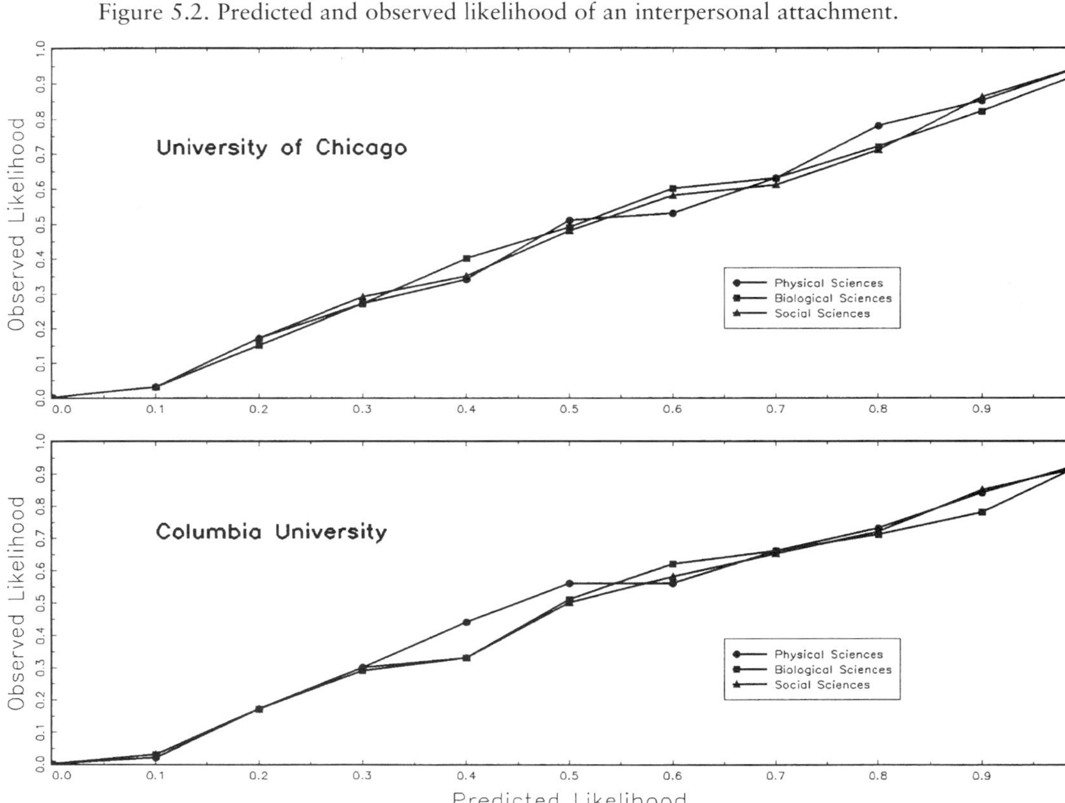

Figure 5.3. Current relations and predicted likelihood of an attachment.

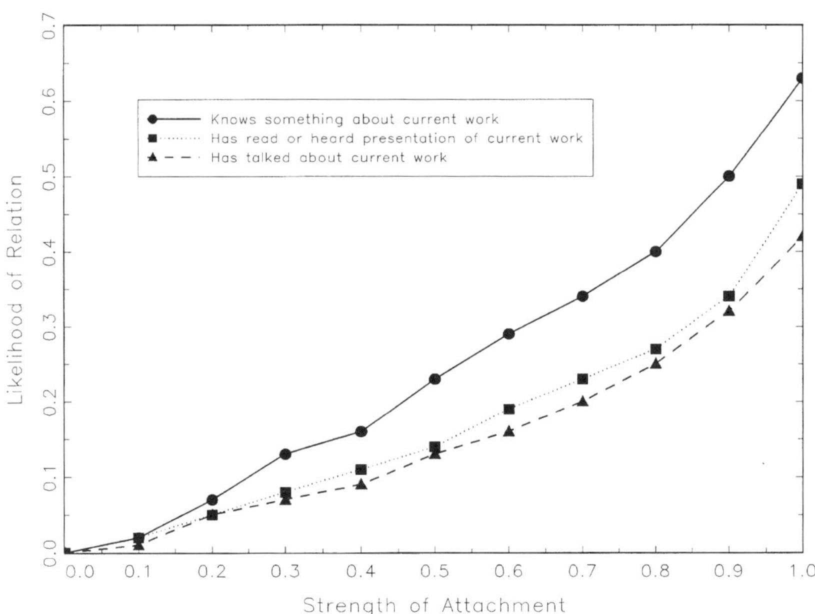

however, for these relations, the probabilities of visibility are less elevated.

I have stipulated that the probability of an attachment is zero between actors who are more than two steps removed in the semipath structure of interpersonal attachments; this constraint restricts the influence domain of actors to the members of their 2-cliques (i.e., to persons with whom the actor is in direct contact or shares at least one common contact in the semipath structure of attachments).

This constraint is imposed because of evidence that the probability of interpersonal visibility is negligible between actors who are more than two steps removed in the semipath structure of attachments. It is, of course, not surprising that the likelihood of interpersonal visibility declines as the distance between actors in the network increases, and that at some distance this likelihood approaches zero. At this point, which I have called the horizon of observability (Friedkin 1983), instances of direct (unmediated) interpersonal influence must also be absent or rare. What is not obvious is the distance to this horizon. Is it near or far? My evidence suggests that actors who are more than two steps distant in the

Table 5.1. *Network Distance and Observability*

(a) Observability of Past or Current Work ($\mathbf{R}_{01} \oplus \mathbf{R}_{11}$)

Network distance	# Dyads[a]	# *i* observes *j*	% *i* observes *j*
1	14,596	11,593	79.43
2	29,350	2,320	7.90
3	3,450	23	0.67
>3	126	0	0.00
Totals	47,522	13,936	

(b) Observability of Current Work ($\mathbf{R}_{11}$)

Network distance	# Dyads[a]	# *i* observes *j*	% *i* observes *j*
1	14,596	5,531	37.89
2	29,350	406	1.38
3	3,450	1	0.03
>3	126	0	0.00
Totals	47,522	5,938	

[a] Ordered pairs in which *i* and *j* are survey respondents

semipath structure of attachments are not likely to know anything about each other's work.

Table 5.1 shows that there is a dramatic decline in the likelihood that actor *i* will report knowing something about the work of actor *j* as the distance increases between the two actors in the semipath structure of attachments. The probability of an interpersonal visibility of role-performance is slight when two actors are three steps or more removed in the structure. There are over 3,400 *ij*-dyads with members that are three steps or more distant in the structure: In only one of these pairs does actor *i* possess any information about actor *j*'s current work and in only 23 of these pairs does actor *i* know anything at all (concerning either the past or present work) of actor *j*.

5.5 Concluding Remarks

My measure of the probability of an attachment is related to a measure that has been proposed and used extensively by Burt (1976, pp. 118–9). Burt's measure of the strength of an interpersonal attachment is:

$$c_{ij(\text{Burt})} = 1 - \frac{r_{d_{ij}}}{r_{N-1}} \tag{5.8}$$

where r_k is the number of actors that i can reach in k steps (recall that all actors reach themselves) and d_{ij} is the distance from i to j, $c_{ii} = 1$, and $c_{ij} = 0$ if i cannot reach j. If a network is strongly connected, then $r_{N-1} = N$ (i.e., the size of the network) for all i. If i is adjacent to j ($d_{ij} = 1$), then the strength of the relation declines as the degree of i increases. If i is two steps removed from j ($d_{ij} = 2$), then the strength of the relation declines as the number of actors that i can reach by paths of length one or two increases. Burt argues that this relation indicates the probability that actor i is engaged with actor j:

> The larger the group over which one has to distribute one's time and interpersonal energy, the weaker the relationship one can sustain with any one member of the group and the stronger the relations with people of relatively short path distance from you in the group. (1988, p. 7)
>
> This measure adjusts the strength of relation implied by a path distance for the structural context in which the path distance occurs. However, the measure does this in an arbitrary way. There is no systematic evidence to support the function relating relation decay to the number of persons reached at each path distance; it is simply less obviously wrong than a constant decay function. (1988, p. 10)

Although the two measures are based on somewhat different structural foundations, they are conceptually close with respect to an emphasis on structural conditions associated with the probability that an actor i will initiate and maintain interaction with actor j.

My measure of interpersonal attachment depends on features of the bundle of social ties to and from two actors. Although I have focused on these features because of long-standing lines of work, it is not my immediate aim to draw any conclusions about the relative merits or importance of the theoretical assertions of these various lines; hence, for example, I do not attempt to assess (as I have done elsewhere) the relative contributions of structural cohesion and similarity to interpersonal influence (Friedkin 1984, 1993). I simply draw on and combine these lines of work to construct a measure that discriminates structural environments under which an actor i is more or less likely to be engaged with actor j.

Hence, I have shown that the proposed measure of attachment is positively associated with the likelihood that an actor i has a direct past and current interpersonal engagement with another actor j (entailing conversation about the work of actor *j*, reading about that work, or attending a presentation of that work). Here, the important and useful conclusion is that the measure is discriminating structural environments under which an actor *i* is more or less likely to be engaged with actor *j*. I also have found that interpersonal visibility declines with the distance between actors in the semipath structure of attachments, and that it rarely occurs between actors who are more than two steps removed in the structure. Here, the important and useful conclusion is that the measure should be set to zero between actors who are more than two steps removed in the structure because visibility (which is a precondition of interpersonal influence) is largely absent in such cases.

The causal assertion that I make about interpersonal attachments is that they govern the distribution of interpersonal influence. If two actors are situated in a structural environment in which an attachment from actor *i* to actor *j* is probable, then actor *i* is likely to monitor and consider salient the opinions of actor *j*. Conversely, if two actors are situated in a structural environment in which an attachment from actor *i* to actor *j* is improbable, then actor *i* is not likely monitor or consider salient the opinions of actor *j*. This is an assumption of the model, i.e., the structural parameterization that is described by Eq. (5.1), with which any measure of attachment must be consistent.

This appendix contains results of the logistic regression analysis for each network, in which a tie from actor i to actor j ($i \rightarrow j$) is predicted by nine structural variables. In each network, the regression is based on dyads in which both i and j are respondents and joined by a semipath of length one or two.

1. University of Chicago Networks

Variables		A. Physical Sciences Logit estimate	A. Physical Sciences *t*-value	B. Biological Sciences Logit estimate	B. Biological Sciences *t*-value	C. Social Sciences Logit estimate	C. Social Sciences *t*-value
	constant	−2.56069	−13.90	−2.35385	−17.18	−2.02809	−13.23
$\leftarrow i$	*outdegree*	0.02729	5.86	0.02391	6.83	0.00504	1.45
$\rightarrow i$	*indegree*	−0.08269	−10.07	−0.08023	−13.54	−0.06479	−9.67
$i \leftarrow j$	*reciprocity*	2.33074	19.49	1.85061	22.45	2.11368	22.87
$i \leftarrow k \rightarrow j$	*similarity*	0.16303	8.80	0.13371	10.09	0.12449	7.54
$i \rightarrow k \leftarrow j$	*similarity*	0.10810	9.03	0.06539	7.43	0.09369	9.91
$i \rightarrow k \rightarrow j$	*transitivity*	0.04678	2.50	0.10007	7.81	0.11462	7.20
$i \leftarrow k \leftarrow j$	*circularity*	−0.09612	−5.02	−0.01057	−0.80	−0.05440	−3.45
$j \leftarrow$	*indegree*	0.02201	3.04	0.00497	1.05	0.01125	1.76
$j \rightarrow$	*outdegree*	−0.04597	−10.08	−0.03469	−11.00	−0.04421	−12.03

Variables		A. Physical Sciences		B. Biological Sciences		C. Social Sciences	
		Logit estimate	*t*-value	Logit estimate	*t*-value	Logit estimate	*t*-value
	constant	−2.30822	−7.69	−3.17907	−26.35	−2.96810	−19.88
$\leftarrow i$	*outdegree*	0.01587	1.28	0.01295	3.68	0.01322	2.92
$\rightarrow i$	*indegree*	−0.13655	−4.78	−0.06288	−10.81	−0.06655	−8.29
$i \leftarrow j$	*reciprocity*	1.63141	7.51	2.26171	23.58	1.93106	17.27
$i \leftarrow k \rightarrow j$	*similarity*	0.23423	4.25	0.15520	8.36	0.13293	6.12
$i \rightarrow k \leftarrow j$	*similarity*	0.25189	7.51	0.10015	8.64	0.11636	8.46
$i \rightarrow k \rightarrow j$	*transitivity*	0.20241	3.94	0.23396	12.50	0.20842	9.32
$i \leftarrow k \leftarrow j$	*circularity*	−0.23766	−4.48	−0.04453	−2.30	−0.01710	−0.75
$j \leftarrow$	*indegree*	0.08401	3.47	0.01955	3.41	0.03212	4.95
$j \rightarrow$	*outdegree*	−0.08768	−6.47	−0.04396	−10.49	−0.05105	−11.39

6

Self and Other

Abstract. A measure of structural centrality is the second pillar of my approach to the social-influence process. In this process, actors weigh the opinions of others against their own opinion, and I assume that an actor's self-weight is a function of his or her structural centrality. In the present chapter, I support the stipulated linkage between an actor's self-weight and centrality, and I carry forward the structural operationalization of the theory with the definition of a type of centrality – the indegree of an actor in the network of interpersonal attachments – in terms of which the self-weight of an actor is formulated.

> He had in him all the attitudes of others, calling for a certain response; that was the "me" of that situation, and his response is the "I."
>
> – George Herbert Mead (1956)

In classical theory, the collective other refers to the fixed consensus of opinion of other actors (a normative opinion) with respect to a particular issue. Social influence reduces to the special case of individuals who are confronted with a fixed consensus and who, therefore, are either deviants or conformists. For deviants, there is only one likely outcome – greater conformity to the normative opinion that will be more or less pronounced depending on the balance between the self and the other in the deviant actor.

The situation of a deviant in the midst of a fixed consensus is a special case of the present social influence theory. In the general case, the influence of the collective other on the individual consists of a bundle of interpersonal effects, which are of uneven strength, and which are not unified or stable: The collective other presents an array of alternative opinions and these opinions can change over time. Moreover, in the general case, each actor is faced with a different collective other (depending on their particular array of attachments), and actors can vary in the balance between self and other. Furthermore, an actor can shape the opinions of the collective other via the influence of the actor on others (in effect, forming a superego that reflects the actor's self).

In the present theory, as the self-weight of an actor increases, the weight of the collective other declines, and vice versa; these weights are two sides of the same coin. The self–other balance refers to the inverse relationship between the weight an actor places on his or her opinions, and the weight the actor accords to the opinions of others: $w_{ii} = 1 - a_{ii}$ from Eq. (2.3). In the process of forming their settled opinions on issues, actors weigh and integrate the opinions of their attachments; they also place more or less weight on their own opinion. The precise balance between self and other, which may be different for each actor, is a crucial feature of the social-influence process, because it describes the relative weight of an actor's social position and interpersonal influences in determining opinion. The coefficient of social influence ($0 \leq a_{ii} \leq 1$) describes the relative weight of the interpersonal influences for an actor and the extent to which an actor is anchored on his or her initial opinion ($1 - a_{ii}$). Because of the stipulation that $w_{ii} = 1 - a_{ii}$, the theory implies that the coefficient of social influence (a_{ii}) is equal to the *collective weight* of the interpersonal influences upon an actor ($\sum_j w_{ij}$ for $i \neq j$). Hence, a balance of forces exists, which may differ for each actor, involving the weight of a collective other (described equivalently by a_{ii} or $\sum_j w_{ij}$ for $i \neq j$) and the weight of the self (described equivalently by $1 - a_{ii}$ or w_{ii}). It is this collective weight that is distributed among an actor's significant others according to the probability of the actor's attachments to them.

6.1 Bases of Power and Measures of Centrality

In the present work, I take a structural approach to describing the self–other balance. An important agenda of research on social networks has been the development of individual-level numerical indices, so-called measures of network centrality or sociometric status, that describe the power of an actor in terms of features of his or her network environment (Wasserman and Faust 1994). An extensive literature, based on experiments and field studies, indicates that the greater the structural centrality of an actor in a communication network, the greater the influence of the actor (for example, see Laumann and Pappi 1976; Pfeffer 1981; Brass 1984).

In the previous chapter, I introduced the concept of structural centrality and showed that the probability of an attachment from actor *i* to actor *j* is positively associated with the indegree of actor *j* and negatively associated with the indegree of actor *i*. These indegrees are elementary measures of structural centrality. Hence, it can be said that actor i is more likely to be oriented toward a central actor than toward a peripheral actor and, interestingly, that actor i is less likely to be oriented toward another actor if i is central than if i is peripheral. This latter finding suggests that a central actor is more self-absorbed than a peripheral actor and is consistent with the thesis that an actor's self-confidence, self-respect, and resistance to opinion change are a function of the actor's power bases (Goldberg 1955; Cartwright 1965, pp. 33–5; Stasser, Kerr, and Davis 1980, p. 435). A central actor is less susceptible to interpersonal influence than a peripheral actor, and a manifestation of this relationship is a decline in the probability of an actor's orientation toward others with an increase in others' orientation toward the actor. Thus, structurally central actors are heavyweights and peripheral actors are lightweights with respect to the weights that they allocate to their *own* opinions.

The formal linkage between an actor's self-weight and centrality is described by the function

$$w_{ii} = 1 - \sqrt{1 - c_i} \tag{6.1}$$

[Eq. (4.5)], which is derived as follows. At each iteration of the opinion-formation process, the weight of an actor in determining his or her own revised opinion is $(1 - a_{ii}^2)$, part of which is placed on the actor's opinion at time $t(a_{ii}w_{ii})$ and part of which is placed on the actor's initial opinion $(1 - a_{ii})$. For instance, at the first iteration of the process we have

$$y_i^{(2)} = a_{ii}w_{ii}y_i^{(1)} + a_{ii} \sum_j w_{ij}y_j^{(1)} + (1 - a_{ii})y_i^{(1)} \tag{6.2}$$

which simplifies to

$$y_i^{(2)} = (1 - a_{ii}^2)y_i^{(1)} + a_{ii} \sum_j w_{ij}y_j^{(1)} \tag{6.3}$$

for $i \neq j$. At this point in the process, the self-weight of the actor is concentrated entirely on the actor's initial opinion; whereas at subsequent points in the process, this self-weight is distributed between the actor's initial and current opinions. Equating the actor's centrality and aggregate self-weight gives

$$\begin{aligned} c_i &= 1 - a_{ii}^2 \\ &= 1 - (1 - w_{ii})^2 \end{aligned} \tag{6.4}$$

and, hence, $w_{ii} = 1 - \sqrt{1 - c_i}$.

In a network of interpersonal attachments that is comprised mainly of voluntary interpersonal ties, the indegree of actors in the network is the key structural indicator of their power bases.[1] In such a network, more

1 Depending on the type of social process that is under consideration, different structural features of a network may be relevant, so it cannot be asserted that there is a single

complicated indicators of structural centrality are likely to be derivative of the centripetal tendencies of actors to form and maintain ties with actors who have noteworthy bases of power and therefore are likely to be strongly associated with indegree. This viewpoint on indegree is consistent with my earlier treatment (Chapter 5) of the structural conditions under which interpersonal ties are formed. I now develop the argument for this viewpoint and present some supporting evidence.

Degree, betweenness, and closeness are the three most widely employed measures of the centrality of actors in a network of interpersonal ties (Freeman 1979). I shall define these measures in $\mathbf{R} = [r_{ij}]$, the network of interpersonal attachments in which $r_{ij} = 1$ if actor i is tied to actor j, $r_{ij} = 0$ if actor i is not tied to actor j, and $r_{ii} = 0$. In this network, the *degree* of a point is the ordered pair [indegree(i), outdegree(i)], where indegree is the number lines to i

$$\text{indegree}(i) = \sum_j r_{ji} \tag{6.5}$$

and outdegree is the number of lines from i

$$\text{outdegree}(i) = \sum_j r_{ij} \tag{6.6}$$

If the network is symmetric, then outdegree equals indegree, and we may simply refer to these counts as the degree of an actor. Betweenness is a measure of the extent to which an actor i is involved as an intervening point on the geodesics (shortest paths) of a network:

$$\text{betweenness}(i) = \sum_j \sum_k \frac{g_{jk(i)}}{g_{jk}} \tag{6.7}$$

for distinct actors i, j, and k, where $g_{jk(i)}$ is the number of geodesics from actor j to actor k that involve actor i as an intervening point, and g_{jk} is the number of geodesics from actor j to actor k. Closeness is a measure of the distances that separate an actor from other actors in the network:

$$\text{closeness}(i) = \left(\sum_i d_{ij}\right)^{-1} \tag{6.8}$$

for $i \neq j$, where d_{ij} is the length of the shortest path (geodesic) from actor i to actor j in a network.

Structural centrality in a network of interpersonal attachments affects, and is affected by, interpersonal influence. Interpersonal attachments are a source of power when they convey informational resources and provide a medium for the flow of interpersonal influence. However, actors may have bases of power that are independent of the information they

best measure of centrality. For example, the centrality of cities in a network of trade routes is better indicated by the betweenness of the cities in the trade network than by the degree or closeness of the cities in this network (Pitts 1979).

possess (French and Raven 1959), and actors may form communication ties with influential actors to gain access to these actors' influence and resources (Berger, Rosenholtz, and Zelditch 1980). Hence, the pattern of interpersonal attachments both shapes and reflects the power of actors. This reciprocal relationship has an important implication, that is, we may rely on the *simplest* of measures of structural centrality – degree – for an approach to the self-weight of actors.

To be sure, it is possible for an actor of low degree to occupy a strategic location in a structure of interpersonal ties; for example, a liaison position between two subgroups or a position between an occupant of a powerful formal position and other subordinate positions. Actors who occupy such positions may become influential if they and others are aware of the strategic importance of their structural location, and they are used as brokers of information and agreements. Moreover, if access to a powerful actor is restricted to a small number of subordinates and peers, then the degree of the actor will not reflect that actor's power. Along these lines, experiments on communication networks have shown that different structural locations in communication networks may result in power differentials among the actors and that these power differentials do not correspond necessarily with the actors' degrees (Freeman, Roeder, and Mulholland 1980).

In natural settings, however, the structure of a network is likely to form in a manner that produces a close correspondence between the bases of interpersonal power and the degree of actors: The more noteworthy an actor's bases of power, the greater the number of actors who will seek to form, maintain, and strengthen a tie with the actor. Such centripetal forces will be centered on actors with formal authority, expertise, and information in domains of interest to other actors. Thus, in a network where new ties are being formed, powerful liaison positions will tend to be eliminated by actors who pursue direct contacts with the sources of the liaison's power, i.e., those actors with noteworthy bases of power with whom the liaison is in contact. Thus, as the perceived influence of the actor increases, so will the indegree of the actor in the network.

Interpersonal ties that are oriented toward an actor not only reflect the power bases of the actor but also *validate* the power of the actor in the minds of others and in the mind of the focal actor. First, the perception that an actor is much sought after (i.e., possesses a high indegree) reduces uncertainty about the value of the actor's resources and encourages the formation, maintenance, and strengthening of a contact with the actor. Second, and most important for the present theoretical development, this social validation (manifest positive orientation of others toward an actor) is likely to increase the focal actor's self-respect and self-confidence and lower his or her susceptibility to interpersonal influences. In short, centripetal social forces increase the weight of self and, because of this mechanism, self-weight is a *social construction* in which autonomy is accorded to particular actors by other actors who validate their bases of interpersonal power.[2]

The centripetal tendencies of other actors to form, maintain, and strengthen their ties with those actors who have noteworthy bases of power will often have secondary consequences on the actor's location in the communication network – on the betweenness and closeness centralities of the actor. If an actor has a basis of power that is broad, then ties may be formed with actors who are located in various parts of the social structure. For example, if the expertise of an actor has a general applicability or appeal, or if the actor possesses a broad basis of power to reward (such as might be the case with a high-level administrator or a charismatic personality), then ties may be formed with actors who occupy various positions in the network. An actor with such a broad basis of power not only is likely to have a high indegree but also may be "between" many pairs of actors by virtue of the heterogeneous ties with which they are involved (i.e., when actors who are pursuing ties with an influential actor are not themselves in contact, the influential actor will be "between" such actors).[3] Furthermore, such an influential actor is likely to be "close" to many actors in the communication network. Here again, the ties that are initiated by others with the influential actor (in this case by a set of heterogeneous others) are the source of the influential actor's "closeness" to numerous actors who are located in disparate parts of the social structure.

In sum, centripetal forces should serve to maintain a close correspondence between the indegrees of actors in communication networks and their interpersonal influence. Moreover, depending on the range of an

2 The centripetal forces that create large self-weights are not haphazard and have important social structural foundations, because they are based on the distribution of valued resources, status characteristics, and power bases among actors. At the same time, access to important power bases cannot be rigorously prescribed or controlled in most situations; and those interpersonal interactions that validate a power base cannot be entirely constrained or forced by circumstances. Hence, the outcome of the social construction of the self–other balance for each actor is shaped by status characteristics and unique attributes of the actor, interpersonal, historical, and institutional circumstances and arrangements, and cultural, demographic, and ecological conditions. Observed (rather than idealized) social structure is my starting point. The present approach attempts to deal with this social structure in the concrete and particularistic form that the structure assumes in a given population.

3 Of course, an actor may be between many other actors without having a high degree. However, it is unlikely that an actor of low degree will be active in transmitting a variety of information. High degree and communication activity within ties probably go hand in hand. Thus, an actor with a high degree and low betweenness is more likely to transmit information than an actor with a low degree and high betweenness.

actor's influence, such centripetal forces will move influential actors into structurally strategic positions of high betweenness and closeness with other actors. For these reasons, I rely on the indegree of an actor in a network of attachments as an indicator of socially validated bases of power.[4]

An indegree that entails interpersonal visibility is an especially appropriate indicator of the power bases and social validation that foster large self-weights in the social-influence process. Indeed, Wasserman and Faust (1994) and Knoke and Burt (1983) equate actors' visibility and centrality (prominence).[5] An actor's indegree in the network of attachments, **R**, which I have defined in Eq. (5.4), indicates the number of other actors who have oriented themselves toward that actor's work – who have conversed with the actor about his or her work, who have read his or her work, or who have attended a presentation of his or her work. Hence, this indegree is a direct measure of sources of visibility that are based on an *engagement* of actors with the work of a particular actor.

Such indegree does not necessarily include all the actors who have some awareness of a focal actor's work. Interpersonal visibility could arise via flows of information through interpersonal communication. Hence, each actor may have a degree of visibility that includes actors with whom they have not talked, and who have neither read their work nor attended a presentation of their work. I refer to such visibility as *supplemental* to distinguish it from the visibility that is based on a direct interpersonal engagement.

Table 6.1 shows that the indegree of an actor in **R** has a strong association with supplemental visibility and that indegree has a stronger effect on such visibility than does either betweenness or closeness of the actor in $\tilde{\mathbf{R}} = [\tilde{r}_{ij}]$, where $\tilde{r}_{ij} = \max(r_{ij}, r_{ji})$. In this table, I also show that the indegree of an actor in **R** has a stronger association with supplemental visibility than does the outdegree of the actor in **R**.

These findings suggest that an actor's indegree in the network of attachments can serve as a measure of the general visibility of the actor. Moreover, these findings are consistent with my argument that indegree

4 Where a distinction between indegree and outdegree is possible in a social relation, the former should be the more sensitive indicator of a power base. Actors are oriented toward those with power bases; hence, a high outdegree may reflect a pursuit of power and prestige rather than a manifestation of their possession.

5 In this literature on centrality, visibility is not only a precondition of interpersonal influence but also an indicator of interpersonal salience; hence, visibility implies influence. Visible opinions may be influential simply by virtue of their visibility; moreover, visibility may be a basis of power or a direct reflection of the power bases held by an actor. Still, it is useful not to confound visibility and salience entirely, because there are situations in which the occurrence of one does not imply the other.

Table 6.1. *Regression o Supplemental Visibility on Indegree, Betweenness, and Outdegree*

(a) Regression of Supplemental Visibility on Indegree and Betweenness (N = 851; R^2 = .574)

Variable	Estimate	Standard error	t-value	Prob >|t|	Standardized estimate	Corr with dep var
CONSTANT	0.729495	0.211065	3.456264	0.001	—	—
INDEGREE	0.236259	0.007739	30.528670	0.000	0.735723	0.755772
BETWEENNESS	0.002351	0.001037	2.267769	0.024	0.054652	0.324552

(b) Regression of Supplemental Visibility on Indegree and Closeness (N = 851; R^2 = .574)

Variable	Estimate	Standard error	t-value	Prob >|t|	Standardized estimate	Corr with dep var
CONSTANT	−0.856820	0.977808	−0.876266	0.381	—	—
INDEGREE	0.249872	0.008422	29.668056	0.000	0.778114	0.755772
CLOSENESS	0.005090	0.003089	1.647864	0.100	0.043219	−0.359018

(c) Regression of Supplemental Visibility on Indegree and Outdegree (N = 851; R^2 = .571)

Variable	Estimate	Standard error	t-value	Prob >|t|	Standardized estimate	Corr with dep var
CONSTANT	0.724994	0.213931	3.388910	0.001	—	—
INDEGREE	0.243516	0.007818	31.149155	0.000	0.758324	0.755772
OUTDEGREE	−0.001157	0.004230	−0.273448	0.785	−0.006657	0.283967

is a key indicator of structural centrality, especially in networks where the interpersonal ties are voluntary. In such networks, betweenness and closeness are derivative consequences of the centripetal tendencies for actors to pursue ties with actors who possess noteworthy power bases. Total degree (i.e., the number of distinct actors with whom an actor communicates) masks an important distinction between indegree and outdegree. Thus, a total degree that mostly reflects a high outdegree may be misleading with respect to the status of an actor.

6.2 Indegree and the Self–Other Balance

I employ a standardized measure of indegree that dampens the centrality of actors in networks where the probability of an interpersonal tie is high. The measure [Eq. (4.6)] is:

$$c_i = \frac{1}{1 + e^{-(d_i - 2\bar{d})}} \tag{6.9}$$

Table 6.2. *Centrality Values as a Function of Indegree and Mean Indegree*

Indegree	Mean indegree 2	4	6	8	10
0	0.018	0.000	0.000	0.000	0.000
1	0.047	0.001	0.000	0.000	0.000
2	0.119	0.002	0.000	0.000	0.000
3	0.269	0.007	0.000	0.000	0.000
4	0.500	0.018	0.000	0.000	0.000
5	0.731	0.047	0.001	0.000	0.000
6	0.881	0.119	0.002	0.000	0.000
7	0.953	0.269	0.007	0.000	0.000
8	0.982	0.500	0.018	0.000	0.000
9	0.993	0.731	0.047	0.001	0.000
10	0.998	0.881	0.119	0.002	0.000
11	0.999	0.953	0.269	0.007	0.000
12	1.000	0.982	0.500	0.018	0.000
13	1.000	0.993	0.731	0.047	0.001
14	1.000	0.998	0.881	0.119	0.002
15	1.000	0.999	0.953	0.269	0.007
16	1.000	1.000	0.982	0.500	0.018
17	1.000	1.000	0.993	0.731	0.047
18	1.000	1.000	0.998	0.881	0.119
19	1.000	1.000	0.999	0.953	0.269
20	1.000	1.000	1.000	0.982	0.500

where d_i is the indegree of actor i

$$d_i = \sum_j r_{ji}$$

and $\bar{d}$ is the mean indegree of the actors in the communication network

$$\bar{d} = \frac{\sum\sum r_{ij}}{N}$$

This measure takes into account the general level of indegree in two ways. First, I standardize indegree by dealing with deviation scores from the mean indegree of actors. Hence, the measure indicates the relative status of an actor in the network. Second, I devalue indegree counts to the extent that they occur in a network where indegrees are generally high. Hence, a relatively large indegree will indicate a higher level of centrality in networks where average indegree is low than in networks where average indegree is high.

Table 6.2 gives illustrative centrality scores for different combinations of indegree and mean indegree. Because the mean indegree of a network is the same for all actors in the network, actors in the same network vary in their centrality strictly as a function of their indegree. Thus, the rank-order of centrality among actors in the same network for this measure will not differ from that of the simple raw count of the indegree for the actors. In two networks with the same mean indegree, actors in different networks will have the same centrality only if their relative status (deviation from mean indegree) is the same.

Two actors with an equivalent relative status in different networks will differ in their centralities depending on the mean indegrees of the networks; the higher the mean indegree, the lower the centrality. Relative differences of indegree indicate power differentials, but these relative differences become less meaningful as the mean indegree of a network increases.

Consider a "star" network of N actors, in which one actor receives ties from $N - 1$ members, and these $N - 1$ actors each receive a tie from the focal actor and no other ties. For $N = 5$ this network is

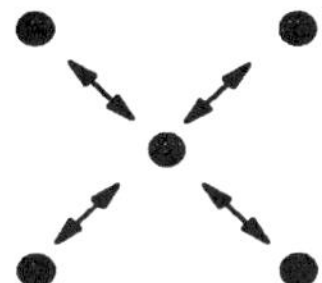

In such "star" networks, the indegree of the central actor is $N - 1$, the indegree of the other actors is 1, and the mean indegree is $2(N - 1)/N$. In such networks, the centrality scores for the central actor increase as the size of the network increases:

N	3	4	5	6
c_i	0.339	0.500	0.690	0.841

Now consider a "complete" network in which every actor sends a tie to every other actor. If the size of the network is N, then the indegree of all actors is $N - 1$ (i.e., the same count as for the central actor in the "star" network), and the mean indegree is $N - 1$. Hence, the centrality of an actor with an indegree of $N - 1$ is higher in the "star" than in the "complete" network. Moreover, unlike the situation in the "star" network, the centrality of actors in a "complete" network *declines* as the size of the network increases:

N	2	3	4	5
c_i	0.269	0.119	0.047	0.018

In a network where all actors have noteworthy bases of power and high indegrees, centralization is not as meaningful as in a network where power bases are concentrated in a subset of actors. The structural situation of the group is more consistent with that of a "company of equals" than with that of a group in which there is marked stratification of interpersonal influences.

Table 6.3 presents coefficients for self-weight as a function of the indegree and average indegree of actors. An increase in the density of interpersonal ties (mean indegree) lowers self-weight. An increase of indegree raises self-weight, especially where the density of ties is low. If the density of the network is high, then self-weights are dampened. If the density of the network is low, then only a few actors if any are likely to have noteworthy self-weights. Hence, if the density of ties in a population is either sufficiently high or sufficiently low (and stratified), then the population is likely to contain either no heavily self-weighted actors or a small number of such actors; most actors will not be anchored on their initial opinions and will be highly responsive to the opinions of others.

Table 6.4 describes the distribution of the derived coefficient of social influence (a_{ii}) in each of the faculties of science. In each of these networks, the coefficient is near its maximum for most actors, which implies that, for these actors, the collective other is dominant and exogenous conditions have little direct impact on opinions (other than forming the actors' initial opinions on an issue):

$$y_i^{(t)} = \sum_{j=1}^{n} w_{ij} y_j^{(t-1)} \tag{6.10}$$

for $t = 2, 3, \ldots, \infty$. At the same time, the ties in these populations are highly stratified, so that a few actors appear in each population who have large self-weights; unlike most of their peers, these heavyweights are subject to a trivial or modest aggregate weight of endogenous interpersonal influences. At the extreme, for an actor with a self-weight that is at the maximum, interpersonal influences are absent and the initial opinion of the actor is fixed:

$$y_i^{(\infty)} = y_i^{(1)} \tag{6.11}$$

Thus the equilibrium opinions of heavyweights tend to reflect their social positions.[6]

6 Equations (6.10) and (6.11) are special cases of Eq. (5.2) that are obtained by setting $\mathbf{A} = \mathbf{I}$ and $\mathbf{A} = \mathbf{0}$, respectively.

Table 6.3. *Self-Weight as a Function of Indegree and Mean Indegree*

Indegree	Mean indegree				
	2	4	6	8	10
0	0.009	0.000	0.000	0.000	0.000
2	0.061	0.001	0.000	0.000	0.000
4	0.293	0.009	0.000	0.000	0.000
6	0.665	0.061	0.001	0.000	0.000
8	0.866	0.293	0.009	0.000	0.000
10	0.950	0.655	0.061	0.001	0.000
12	0.982	0.866	0.293	0.009	0.000
14	0.993	0.950	0.655	0.061	0.001
16	0.998	0.982	0.866	0.293	0.009
18	0.999	0.993	0.950	0.655	0.061
20	1.000	0.998	0.982	0.866	0.293

This distribution of the coefficient of social influence, i.e., a self–other balance in which the collective other (or superego) frequently dominates, is consistent with classical theory on the prerequisites of society. Typically, actors are highly socialized and other-directed. As I have sought to emphasize repeatedly, however, in the present theory (unlike classical theory) such an imbalance does not entail a massive preexisting and fixed consensus to which actors conform or from which they deviate.

6.3 Concluding Remarks

Coombs reminds us that "a measurement or scaling model is actually a theory about behavior, admittedly on a miniature level, but nevertheless theory" (1964, p. 5). In this chapter I have developed the relationship between self and other and have proposed a model of the balance between the two. I have argued that an actor's structural centrality, as indicated by his or her indegree in a network of interpersonal attachments, is a measure of this balance.

Because self-weight and other-weight are counterbalanced, any condition that affects self-weight automatically affects other-weight and vice versa. A dominant self may be based on conditions that foster greed and rational calculation. A dominant collective other may be based on pressures toward uniformity, conformity, and deindividuation (Diener 1980; Prentice-Dunn and Rogers 1989). Self-weight may be diminished by a

Table 6.4. *Distribution of the Coefficient of Social Influence*

Coefficient	Cumulative frequency of actors					
	University of Chicago			Columbia University		
a_{ii}	Phy	Bio	Soc	Phy	Bio	Soc
.01	2	1	0	0	5	3
.05	3	4	1	0	6	4
.10	3	5	2	0	6	4
.20	4	6	3	1	8	5
.40	11	6	4	1	8	6
.80	12	7	4	4	10	8
.90	13	7	4	4	11	8
.95	14	8	4	7	11	11
.99	15	10	5	17	14	14
1	141	142	153	105	153	157

demand for consensus on issues and by societal traditions that value deference and compromise over debate and conflict. Moreover, within a common set of contextual conditions, the balance between self and other may vary for different types of issues. In short, there is plenty of scope in the proposed framework for an elaborated special theory of the self–other balance. My approach, which links the self–other balance to the centrality of an actor in the network of interpersonal attachments and to the status-organizing processes that have shaped this network, is a starting point for such a theory.

With the developments of this and the previous chapter, we can describe the network of interpersonal influences among actors. We have measures of the coefficient of social influence and self-weight for each actor i in terms of the centrality of i,

$$a_{ii} = \sqrt{1 - c_i} \tag{6.12}$$

and

$$w_{ii} = 1 - \sqrt{1 - c_i} \tag{6.13}$$

We also get a measure of the direct interpersonal effect of actor j on actor i for each ordered pair of actors

$$w_{ij} = \sqrt{1 - c_i}\frac{c_{ij}}{\sum_k c_{ik}} \tag{6.14}$$

and, since $a_{ii}^2 = 1 - c_i$,

$$a_{ii}w_{ij} = (1 - c_i)\frac{c_{ij}}{\sum_k c_{ik}} \tag{6.15}$$

Hence, the relative interpersonal effect of actor j on actor i is a positive function of the probability of i's attachment to j (c_{ij}) and a negative function of i's centrality (c_i). In turn, given the matrices $\mathbf{A} = [a_{ij}]$ and $\mathbf{W} = [w_{ij}]$, we get the interpersonal effects $\mathbf{V} = [v_{ij}]$,

$$\mathbf{V} = (\mathbf{I} - \mathbf{AW})^{-1} (\mathbf{I} - \mathbf{A})$$

which describe the total effect of actor j (which arises from all the flows of influence in the system) on the equilibrium opinion of actor i, for all i and j. Thus, the centrality and attachments of actors serve to specify their interpersonal effects.

7

Social Positions

Abstract: A measure of structural equivalence is the third pillar of my approach to the social-influence process. I equate the distance between actors in social space and their structural equivalence in the network of interpersonal influences. This correspondence permits an empirical approach to social positions, and it invests the derived positions with important theoretical properties. I discuss this approach to social positions, and I assess the construct validity of the derived positions. I introduce the concept of social manifolds, which are objects in the multidimensional space of social positions.

An actor's social position is defined by variables that determine the actor's opinions in a domain of issues. The variables may include socioeconomic characteristics (gender, ethnicity, education, income, occupation), material conditions (economy, demography, ecology), and cultural items (beliefs, norms, rules); the variables also may include opinions of significant others. The former set of variables describe exogenous effects on opinions and determine actors' initial opinions, as in Eq. (2.1). The latter set of variables describe endogenous effects on opinions, i.e., the response of actors to the opinions of others, as in Eq. (2.2). The different social positions of actors are based on individual differences in actors' profiles of exogenous status characteristics (**X**) or endogenous interpersonal influences (**W**).

Actors with identical status characteristics are not necessarily subject to identical interpersonal influences. In many social structures, however, an intimate correspondence between the two patterns emerges from status-organizing processes (Berger, Rosenholtz, and Zelditch 1980); in these processes, interpersonal influences become organized and come to reflect the status differences among actors. I assume such a correspondence in the present work: Two actors with an identical profile of interpersonal influences in **W** also have an identical status on each of the variables in **X** that determine their initial opinions, and vice versa. Hence, the joint occupants of a social position are subject to the same set of conditions (including influential opinions), and they are affected by these conditions and opinions in an identical way; the immediate implications are (a) that the joint occupants of a social position have identical initial opinions on issues and (b) that the expected differences of initial opinion among actors (which correspond to the distances between their social positions) are obtainable from an analysis of the actors' profile similarities in the influence network. In the present chapter, I implement this approach to social positions and initial opinions; however, before I describe this implementation, three broad features of the approach are discussed.

First, this approach to social positions links the classical definition of a social position as a location in social space (Laumann and Pappi 1976; Blau 1977; McPherson and Ranger-Moore 1991) to a network of interpersonal influences. In this approach, a social position is a distinctive combination of conditions that affect occupants' opinions; it also is defined by and embedded in a network of interpersonal influence that allows flows of influence among positions. Thus, although I do not employ the blockmodel approach to social structure, the simultaneous definition of social positions and interpositional bonds, which was a key theoretical attraction of the blockmodel approach, also is attained with the present approach and given a firmer theoretical foundation. This linkage of social positions and influence networks opens the door to a structural social psychology by which it is possible to address the systemic effects of social structures.

Second, this approach stipulates that the joint occupants of a social position have identical initial opinions on issues and that this equivalence of opinions is maintained throughout the social-influence process. The stipulated within-position homogeneity of opinion does not imply the absence of individuality. Individuality is manifested by the extent to which actors are differentiated into discrete social positions; indeed, it is likely that most social positions will be occupied by a single actor. If a position is jointly occupied, however, then its occupants are inextricably bound together as a coherent unit; their shared opinion on issues can be transformed by the influences of actors who occupy different positions in the social structure, but (whatever the transformation that takes place) their interpersonal agreement will be maintained. Hence, the occupants of a social position are "fellow-travelers," and their destination is an outcome of the social structure in which they are situated and the process of social influence that is played out in this structure.

Third, in this approach to social positions a *single* social relation – **W**, i.e., the network of endogenous interpersonal influences – provides sufficient information for a description of the distribution of actors in social space. A variety of variables and social relations can enter into the specification of these influences, but once the influence network is in hand, so are the social positions of actors.

7.1 Defining Social Positions

I now detail the methodology of implementing this approach to social positions. A reader who is not interested in these details should proceed directly to section 7.2, where I assess the construct validity of the social positions that have been derived by these methods in the science faculties at The University of Chicago and Columbia University.

I derive the positions of actors in social space from a multidimensional scaling of the actors' profile dissimilarities in the network of endogenous interpersonal influence – **W**. I assess the dissimilarity of two actors' profiles of interpersonal influences with a measure of structural equivalence [Eq. (4.9)]; that is, $\mathbf{D} = [d_{ij}]$,

$$d_{ij} = \left[\frac{\sum_k (\tilde{w}_{ik} - \tilde{w}_{jk})^2 + \sum_k (\tilde{w}_{ki} - \tilde{w}_{kj}) + (\tilde{w}_{ij} - \tilde{w}_{ji})^2}{\sum_k \tilde{w}_{ik}^2 + \sum_k \tilde{w}_{jk}^2 + \sum_k \tilde{w}_{ki}^2 + \sum_k \tilde{w}_{kj}^2 + \max(\tilde{w}_{ij}^2, \tilde{w}_{ji}^2)} \right]^{1/2} \tag{7.1}$$

for distinct actors i, j, and k, where $\tilde{\mathbf{W}} = [\tilde{w}_{ij}]$ are interpersonal influences that are standardized for variations in self-weight, i.e.,

$$\tilde{\mathbf{W}} = \mathbf{A}^{-1}\mathbf{w} \tag{7.2}$$

This standardized interpersonal influence is simply the relative weight of an influential actor, and it corresponds to the relative probability of the interpersonal attachment

$$\tilde{w}_{ij} = \frac{c_{ij}}{\sum_k c_{ik}} = \frac{w_{ij}}{\sum_k w_{ik}} \tag{7.3}$$

for $i \neq \{j, k\}$.

The resulting measure of profile dissimilarity, d_{ij}, equals zero if the bundles of actors' interpersonal influences are identical, it equals one if these bundles are disjoint, and it is undefined for actors (such as isolates) whose self-weights are maximal ($w_{ii} = 1 - a_{ii} = 1$). Two actors i and j occupy the same social position only if $d_{ij} = 0$. Such actors will hold identical initial opinions throughout the social-influence process (Friedkin and Johnsen 1997). This strict stipulation of the conditions under which actors i and j are joint occupants of a social position (i.e., $d_{ij} = 0$) does not preclude or discourage the definition of *clusters* of similar positions.

The social positions of actors are defined by their *coordinates* in a multidimensional space consistent with the individual differences manifested in **D**. For the present analysis, the social positions of the actors were obtained by submitting the profile dissimilarities in **D** to a metric multidimensional similarity structure analysis (Borg and Lingoes 1987). The chief purpose of this multidimensional scaling is the provision of coordinates for each actor's initial opinion, i.e., $\mathbf{Y}^{(1)}$, the $N \times K$ matrix of initial opinions. The spatial visualization and heuristic clustering of positions are secondary concerns, so there is no pressure to obtain a solution in three or fewer dimensions.

The multidimensional scaling model of **D** represents the raw profile dissimilarities as distances between actors in a K-dimensional space, such that the distances between the actors in the space closely correspond to the profile dissimilarities in **D**. Formally, the scaling procedure obtains a set of coordinates that minimize stress, where stress is

$$(\text{stress})^2 = \frac{\sum_{i<j}(d_{ij} - \tilde{d}_{ij})^2}{\sum_{i<j} d_{ij}^2} \tag{7.4}$$

and $\tilde{\mathbf{D}} = [\tilde{d}_{ij}]$ is the matrix of derived distances between actors in the K-dimensional spatial representation (Kruskal 1964). Expressing stress as a percentage, Kruskal (1964) suggests that the goodness-of-fit of a multidimensional scaling solution be evaluated as follows: 20% = poor, 10% = fair, 5% = good, 2.5% = excellent, and 0% = perfect. However, absolute evaluative criteria may be misleading, and Kruskal no longer supports their use (Borg and Lingoes 1987). The acceptability of a multidimensional scaling solution depends critically on the demonstration, via ancillary analysis, that the relationship between the derived distances and other phenomena is consistent with known facts and theoretical expectations. Nevertheless, given a stress value that is near zero, the interpretation of the derived distances is straightforward, at least in regard to the underlying raw data; hence, low stress values are desirable.

Table 7.1 reports the stress values obtained in the six faculties of science for representations of their social space in one to eight dimensions.[1] In plots of such results a distinct *elbow* may appear, after which point the marginal improvements of fit associated with increasing the number of dimensions is relatively slight. If such an elbow appears in two or three dimensions, then a solution in these dimensions can be justified. However, because a pictorial representation of social positions is not crucial, the appearance of an elbow in three or fewer dimensions is not

1 Nonrespondent dyads (where both i and j are nonrespondents) were set to missing values for this analysis.

Table 7.1. *Stress Values for* K-*Dimensional Representations of Social Space*

Faculty of Science	Dimensionality (K)							
	1	2	3	4	5	6	7	8
Chicago Physical Sciences	.165	.109	.067	.056	.040	.033	.026	.022
Chicago Biological Sciences	.148	.092	.060	.045	.035	.025	.020	.017
Chicago Social Sciences	.181	.125	.067	.054	.042	.030	.024	.021
Columbia Physical Sciences	.213	.145	.092	.061	.040	.031	.024	.020
Columbia Biological Sciences	.131	.099	.069	.059	.045	.036	.030	.025
Columbia Social Sciences	.164	.122	.093	.057	.046	.032	.025	.022

Note: Stress is computed as in Kruskal (1964).

a concern, and actors can be positioned in a space that has as many dimensions as are required to obtain a close fit between the raw and derived distances. In these data, a high degree of precision (i.e., stress $\leq$ 2.5%) for all cases is obtained with a solution in eight dimensions, and I base my analysis on that solution.

This approach to social positions assumes a correspondence between the profile dissimilarities of actors in the network of endogenous interpersonal influences (**W**) and the matrix of exogenous variables (**X**) that affect actors' opinions. If the profile dissimilarity of actors in **X** is equated with their profile dissimilarity in **W**, then either type of dissimilarity may be used to describe actors' social positions; and if the distances between actors' social positions are equated with their expected differences of initial opinion, then an approach to the initial opinions of actors ($\mathbf{Y}^{(1)}$) can be based on an analysis of actors' profile similarities in **W**. Without a correspondence between exogenous and endogenous profile similarities, a description of actors' social positions that is based on their structural equivalence in **W** might locate actors in distant social positions when they in fact occupy proximate positions in social space, and in doing so exaggerate the expected difference of their initial opinions.[2] Thus, the assumption of a correspondence of exogenous and en-

2 A more general definition of shared position in the network of interpersonal influences is possible – automorphic equivalence – which also satisfies the stipulation of within-position homogeneity of opinion (Friedkin and Johnsen 1997). Under this more general definition of equivalence, two actors can occupy the same social position only if they have an identical array of interpersonal influences upon them from the same *types* of actors, where the types of actors are defined by their initial opinions $\mathbf{Y}^{(1)}$. Two actors are the same type if they have identical initial opinions, which will occur if they have identical status characteristics in **X**. Under automorphic equivalence, two actors can be located in the same social position if they are influenced by different actors, but they must be influenced in an identical fashion by the array of initial opinions in the population. However, this approach requires prior information on actors' initial opinions or the exogenous determinants of their opinions.

dogenous profile similarities is crucial, and I will devote considerable space in this chapter to a validation of the social distances that are derived from this assumption (section 7.2).

7.2 Social Distance, Affiliations, and Relations

The present approach assumes that the distance between actors' social positions – their social distance – reflects actors' dissimilarity on conditions that affect their opinions and, hence, their expected differences of initial opinion. The approach bases social distance on the positions of actors in the network of interpersonal influences and, therefore, depends on a correspondence between actors' positions in the influence network and their positions in social space. The greater the profile dissimilarity of two actors in the influence network, the greater the distance between the positions of the actors in social space, and the greater their expected difference of initial opinion on issues that are determined by their social positions. Such a correspondence is a ubiquitous outcome of elementary status-organizing processes; however, instability of the social space (induced, for example, by compositional changes in the status characteristics of the population) can attenuate this correspondence and undermine the meaningfulness of the social structure that is revealed by the proposed approach. Hence, the merits of the approach (i.e., the meaningfulness of the derived social space) should be addressed on a case-by-case basis.

A direct assessment of the social space would examine associations between the derived social distances and observed differences of initial opinion on an array of issues. Such an assessment is impractical, because it concerns a relationship between actors' social positions and *initial* opinions (as opposed to their more readily observable equilibrium opinions).[3] Thus, the assessment must be indirect, i.e., an analysis of associations between actors' social positions and variables (upon which their social positions are based) that have a plausible bearing on opinions. If the derived social positions (or clusters of proximate social positions) can be shown to differentiate actors on important bases of social differentiation, then it is likely that the social distances among these positions correspond to expected differences of opinion among actors in a domain of issues. This method is practical because the main bases of social differentiation in a population usually are obvious. It is not feasible or

3 Actors' initial opinions can be transformed by the social influence process in a way that attenuates an association between their social positions and equilibrium opinions. For instance, when a consensus is formed, there will be no zero-order association between actors' social positions (or initial opinions) and their equilibrium opinions.

necessary to examine all of the possible exogenous determinants of actors' opinions. Evidence of strong associations between the derived social distances and key conditions that shape actors' predisposition on issues would support the approach; if such strong associations are not observed, then the derived distances must be viewed as unreliable measures of the expected differences of opinion among actors.

In the scientific community, affiliations with particular universities, disciplines (academic departments), and areas of specialization can importantly shape the work-related opinions of scientists. The exact social positions of scientists are affected by variables other than the cultural and material conditions that are entailed by these affiliations. However, these affiliations describe the important *gross* features of the social differentiation among scientists; and the derived social distance must differentiate the scientists along these lines in order to serve as a credible indicator of the expected differences of opinion among scientists on work-related issues.

Work-related issues in the scientific community concern standards, policies, personnel, and collective actions involved in the ongoing affairs of a profession. These issues also include matters that are specific to university settings and that are entailed in decisions about appointments, tenure, merit advancements, teaching, and resource allocation. Highly technical matters of practice (goals, methods, standards) that are specific to scientific research and that are involved in the production and evaluation of such work are also included. In each of these realms – profession, university, and specialty – work-related issues concern not only the matter of "What should be done?" in specific cases, but also the procedural matter of "How should we settle on what should be done when there are disagreements?" which focuses on the "social contract" that underlies social choice mechanisms. Thus, in these science faculties, the theoretical universe or issue-domain in which expected differences of opinion arise is large.

For the present theoretical development, it is not crucial to describe in concrete terms the matters that are discussed by faculty members. It is not necessary, for instance, to document that in the social sciences there are differences of opinion among faculty members on the importance of particular types and levels of mathematical and statistical course requirements for the training of graduate students. What is crucial is the plausibility of the assertion that there exists a subset of important issues on which actors' differences of initial opinion are strongly associated with the distances between their derived social positions. That there is a relationship between social position and opinion, and between social distance and opinion difference, in many social groups does not require support. What is more uncertain, and needs support on a case-by-case basis, is an approach to social positions that is based on the assumption of a correspondence between social distance and structural equivalence in an influence network.

I present three types of supporting data. First, I examine the association between the derived social distances and the shared departmental affiliations of scientists. Second, I examine the association between the derived social distances and social relations which are indicative of similar (commensurate or complementary) areas of specialization and interest – the research collaborations of scientists and their engagements with each other's work via reading, colloquia, and conversations. Third, I examine the association between the derived social distances and measures of individual difference (dis-equivalence) on a variety of social relations.

7.2.1 Departmental Affiliations

I begin with an analysis that describes the social positions of actors in terms of their departmental affiliations. Figure 7.1 shows that the probability of shared departmental affiliation declines with increasing social distance.[4] The decline is linear as social distance increases from zero to approximately 0.70, after which point the marginal decline is slight.

Table 7.2 presents the results of a hierarchical clustering analysis of social distances; clusters of actors are formed with a successively larger maximal internal distance L, such that any cluster at level L consists of actors who are no more than L distant from one another in the multidimensional space that describes the positions of the actors. The clusterings are described at selected levels roughly in increments of 0.05 up to 0.70; the intermediate clusters have been suppressed to simplify the presentation. Hence, at distance 0.0 actors are clustered who occupy identical or nearly identical social positions; and at distance 0.30 the joint occupants of a cluster are not more than 0.30 distant from each other. The alphabetic symbol that appears below each actor's identification code indicates the actor's primary departmental affiliation. Finally, beneath each cluster that appears at distance 0.70, there is a numerical identification code for the cluster that will come in handy later on. I set the threshold at the 0.70 level because it is roughly at this level that further increases in social distance have no effect on the likelihood of shared departmental affiliation (Figure 7.1).

The results are straightforward. Most of the clusters of diameter 0.70 or less are relatively homogeneous with respect to departmental affiliation. In Table 7.3, I have listed the clusters, the size of each cluster, and

4 In this figure, all dyads are included (whether or not the dyad involves a nonrespondent) and only proportions based on 50 dyads or more are reported.

Figure 7.1. Likelihood of shared departmental affiliation as a function of social distance.

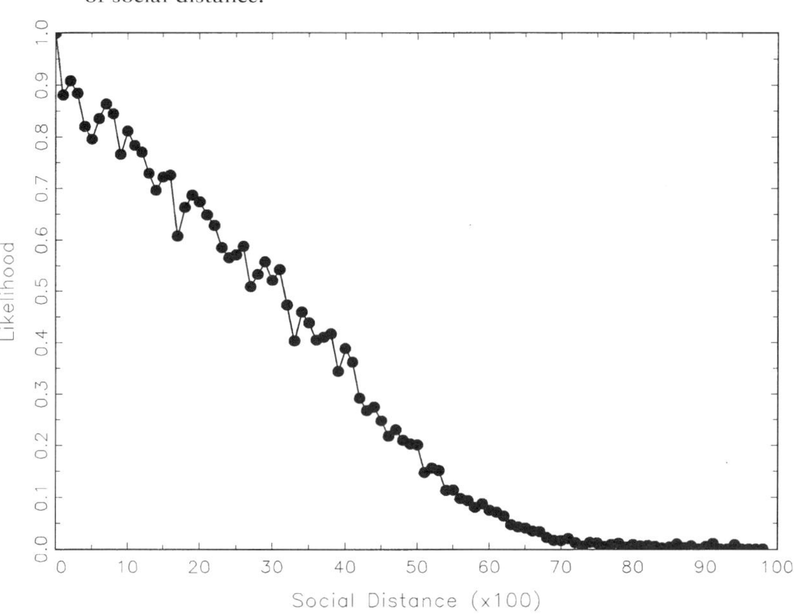

the primary departmental affiliations that are held by at least two members of a cluster.

7.2.2 Social Distance and Social Ties

While disciplinary affiliations broadly differentiate these populations, more detailed lines of differentiation are determined by areas of specialization. I draw on the occurrence of concrete social relations between scientists to indicate shared areas of specialization and interest. Figures 7.2–7.5 show that the likelihood of collaboration, reading another person's work or attending colloquia at which the work is presented, conversing about the person's work, or simply being aware of the work all decline with increasing social distance.

7.2.3 Social Distance and Dis-Equivalence

Social distance indicates the dissimilarity in actors' profiles of interpersonal influences (individual differences in the pattern of endogenous influences). I have argued that these endogenous individual differences correspond to *individual differences* on the exogenous variables that affect actors' opinions. To further buttress this argument, I now show that

Table 7.2 *Hierarchical Cluster Analysis (Diameter Method) of Social Distance*

(a) Chicago Physical Sciences

```
ALL CLUSTERS FUSED -- overall maximum distance     =  1.0948
Distance      Cluster members
-----------------------------------------------------------------
         .   4.4.1.8.1.1.1.1.1.3.4.6.1.7.6.1.2.2.1.1.9.1.1.1.9.9.7.1.8.6.1.6.1.4.1.7.7.1.6.2.1.1.1.2.1.1.9.4.1.5.1.6.9.8.9.1.3.4.1.2.3.9.7.8.5.3.5.1.2.1.2.3.5.1.1.3.1.1.1.1.
         .   3.5.0.3.3.3.3.2...0.9.7.6.8...3.5.6.7.4...0.1.1.1.4...4.5.5.2.9.0.0.2.6.9.0.1...9.2.8.2.2.3.0.2.0.4.0.3.2.7.8.1.9...3.9.2.3.3.4.1.4.7.0.3.2.1.5.5.1.2.8.0.0.1.3.
         .   ....0...4.1.8.5.......................1.....0.7.............9...3...3.....8.......6.......0.....4...6.........5.....3...................9...4.......8.2...7.1.4.5.
   0.00000   F-F.............................................................................................................................................................
   0.05248   F-F-F..........................................................................................................E-E.............E-E.................E-E.E-E...
   0.10155   F-F-F...........D-D.D-D.........D-D.....D-D.....D-D...................D-D...........................B-B.........E-E-E-E-E.E-E-E.E-E-E.E-E...E-E.....E-E.E-E-E.
   0.15062   F-F-F...........D-D-D-D.D-D.F-F.D-D.D-D.D-D-D-D-D-D...............D-D.D-D-D...B-B-B.A-E.B-B...B-B.B-E.B-B.........E-E-E-E-E-E-E-E.E-E-E.E-E-E.E-E.E-B.E-E-E-E-E.
   0.20086   F-F-F.F-D.F-F...D-D-D-D-D-D.F-F.D-D.D-D.D-D-D-D-D-D...............D-D-D-D-D...B-B-B.A-E.B-B...B-B-B-E.B-B...A-E...E-E-E-E-E-E-E-E-E-E-E.E-E-E.E-E-E-B.E-E-E-E-E-
   0.26196   F-F-F.F-D.F-F-F.D-D-D-D-D-D.F-F-D-D.D-D.D-D-D-D-D-D...............D-D-D-D-D...B-B-B-A-E.B-B-B.B-B-B-E.B-B...A-E...E-E-E-E-E-E-E-E-E-E-E-E-E-E.E-E-E-B.E-E-E-E-E-
   0.31478   F-F-F-F-D.F-F-F.D-D-D-D-D-D.F-F-D-D.D-D.D-D-D-D-D-D.......F-F.....D-D-D-D-D...B-B-B-A-E.B-B-B-B-B-B-E.B-B...A-E-D.E-E-E-E-E-E-E-E-E-E-E-E-E-E-E-E-E-B.E-E-E-E-E-
   0.36216   F-F-F-F-D.F-F-F.D-D-D-D-D-D-F-F-D-D.D-D.D-D-D-D-D-D-D.D-D.F-F.D-D.D-D-D-D-D...B-B-B-A-E.B-B-B-B-B-B-E.B-B...A-E-D.E-E-E-E-E-E-E-E-E-E-E-E-E-E-E-E-E-B.E-E-E-E-E-
   0.40404   F-F-F-F-D.F-F-F.D-D-D-D-D-D-F-F-D-D.D-D.D-D-D-D-D-D-D.D-D.F-F.D-D.D-D-D-D-D-D.B-B-B-A-E.B-B-B-B-B-B-E.B-B-C.A-E-D.E-E-E-E-E-E-E-E-E-E-E-E-E-E-E-E-E-B-E-E-E-E-E-
   0.47033   F-F-F-F-D.F-F-F.D-D-D-D-D-D-F-F-D-D-D-D.D-D-D-D-D-D-D.D-D.F-F.D-D.D-D-D-D-D-D.B-B-B-A-E-B-B-B-B-B-B-E.B-B-C.A-E-D.E-E-E-E-E-E-E-E-E-E-E-E-E-E-E-E-E-B-E-E-E-E-E-
   0.50027   F-F-F-F-D.F-F-F.D-D-D-D-D-D-F-F-D-D-D-D-D-D-D-D-D-D-D.D-D.F-F.D-D.D-D-D-D-D-D.B-B-B-A-E-B-B-B-B-B-B-E.B-B-C.A-E-D.E-E-E-E-E-E-E-E-E-E-E-E-E-E-E-E-E-B-E-E-E-E-E-
   0.55152   F-F-F-F-D.F-F-F.D-D-D-D-D-D-F-F-D-D-D-D-D-D-D-D-D-D-D.D-D-F-F.D-D.D-D-D-D-D-D.B-B-B-A-E-B-B-B-B-B-B-E-B-B-C.A-E-D.E-E-E-E-E-E-E-E-E-E-E-E-E-E-E-E-E-B-E-E-E-E-E-
   0.60145   F-F-F-F-D.F-F-F.D-D-D-D-D-D-F-F-D-D-D-D-D-D-D-D-D-D-D.D-D-F-F.D-D.D-D-D-D-D-D.B-B-B-A-E-B-B-B-B-B-B-E-B-B-C.A-E-D.E-E-E-E-E-E-E-E-E-E-E-E-E-E-E-E-E-B-E-E-E-E-E-
   0.67013   F-F-F-F-D-F-F-F.D-D-D-D-D-D-F-F-D-D-D-D-D-D-D-D-D-D-D.D-D-F-F-D-D.D-D-D-D-D-D.B-B-B-A-E-B-B-B-B-B-B-E-B-B-C.A-E-D.E-E-E-E-E-E-E-E-E-E-E-E-E-E-E-E-E-B-E-E-E-E-E-
   0.73040   F-F-F-F-D-F-F-F-D-D-D-D-D-D-F-F-D-D-D-D-D-D-D-D-D-D-D.D-D-F-F-D-D.D-D-D-D-D-D.B-B-B-A-E-B-B-B-B-B-B-E-B-B-C-A-E-D.E-E-E-E-E-E-E-E-E-E-E-E-E-E-E-E-E-B-E-E-E-E-E-
   0.78581   F-F-F-F-D-F-F-F-D-D-D-D-D-D-F-F-D-D-D-D-D-D-D-D-D-D-D.D-D-F-F-D-D.D-D-D-D-D-D.B-B-B-A-E-B-B-B-B-B-B-E-B-B-C-A-E-D-E-E-E-E-E-E-E-E-E-E-E-E-E-E-E-E-E-B-E-E-E-E-E-
   0.81759   F-F-F-F-D-F-F-F-D-D-D-D-D-D-F-F-D-D-D-D-D-D-D-D-D-D-D-D-D-F-F-D-D.D-D-D-D-D-D.B-B-B-A-E-B-B-B-B-B-B-E-B-B-C-A-E-D-E-E-E-E-E-E-E-E-E-E-E-E-E-E-E-E-E-B-E-E-E-E-E-
   0.92562   F-F-F-F-D-F-F-F-D-D-D-D-D-D-F-F-D-D-D-D-D-D-D-D-D-D-D-D-D-F-F-D-D.D-D-D-D-D-D.B-B-B-A-E-B-B-B-B-B-B-E-B-B-C-A-E-D-E-E-E-E-E-E-E-E-E-E-E-E-E-E-E-E-E-B-E-E-E-E-E-
   0.95306   F-F-F-F-D-F-F-F-D-D-D-D-D-D-F-F-D-D-D-D-D-D-D-D-D-D-D-D-D-F-F-D-D.D-D-D-D-D-D.B-B-B-A-E-B-B-B-B-B-B-E-B-B-C-A-E-D-E-E-E-E-E-E-E-E-E-E-E-E-E-E-E-E-E-B-E-E-E-E-E-
   1.03067   F-F-F-F-D-F-F-F-D-D-D-D-D-D-F-F-D-D-D-D-D-D-D-D-D-D-D-D-D-F-F-D-D.D-D-D-D-D-D.B-B-B-A-E-B-B-B-B-B-B-E-B-B-C-A-E-D-E-E-E-E-E-E-E-E-E-E-E-E-E-E-E-E-E-B-E-E-E-E-E-
   1.03662   F-F-F-F-D-F-F-F-D-D-D-D-D-D-F-F-D-D-D-D-D-D-D-D-D-D-D-D-D-F-F-D-D-D-D-D-D-D-D.B-B-B-A-E-B-B-B-B-B-B-E-B-B-C-A-E-D-E-E-E-E-E-E-E-E-E-E-E-E-E-E-E-E-E-B-E-E-E-E-E-
                   1        |              2                      |     3     |        4  |                   5               |                    6

continued-----------------------------------------------------------------
         .   1.5.1.7.1.5.5.8.7.6.7.7.8.1.9.1.5.8.4.2.8.5.9.1.6.2.4.2.5.1.6.1.4.2.3.3.7.7.1.8.1.3.1.1.1.8.1.3.6.5.1.3.4.4.1.6.9.9.1.1.8
         .   3.6.1.1.1.3.0.0.2.2.7.0.9.3.6.1...6.7.4.8.2.7.2.4.7.6.0.9.2.8.2.8.8.3.1.5.4.3.1.2...4.5.0...1.6.0.8.1.7.1.4.3.6.5.9.0.1.2
         .   2...3.....................9...1.............8...........0...7.............7...1...0...2...9.......6.......6.......5.2..
   0.00000   .........................................................................................................................
   0.05248   ............................................................B-B..........................................................
   0.10155   ........E-E.......E-E-E.E-E.......................B-B.......B-B...B-B.........................C-C..........................
   0.15062   ..A-A...E-E-E.....E-E-E.E-E-E.....................B-B-B.B-B.B-B...B-B.........................C-C.C-C.........C-C...C-C..
   0.20086   E.A-A...E-E-E.....E-E-E-E-E-E.............A-A.....B-B-B.B-B.B-B...B-B.....B-B.........C-C-C...C-C.C-C.C-C.C-C.C-C-C.C-C..
   0.26196   E.A-A-E.E-E-E-E...E-E-E-E-E-E...A-A.......A-A-A...B-B-B.B-B.B-B...B-B.B-B.B-B-B-B.C-C.C-C-C...C-C-C-C.C-C-C-C.C-C-C-C-C..
   0.31478   E.A-A-E.E-E-E-E...E-E-E-E-E-E-E.A-A...A-A.A-A-A...B-B-B-B-B.B-B-B.B-B.B-B.B-B-B-B.C-C.C-C-C...C-C-C-C.C-C-C-C.C-C-C-C-C..
   0.36216   E-A-A-E.E-E-E-E-E.E-E-E-E-E-E-E.A-A...A-A.A-A-A...B-B-B-B-B-B-B-B.B-B.B-B.B-B-B-B.C-C.C-C-C...C-C-C-C-C-C-C-C.C-C-C-C-C..
   0.40404   E-A-A-E.E-E-E-E-E.E-E-E-E-E-E-E.A-A-A.A-A.A-A-A...B-B-B-B-B-B-B-B.B-B.B-B.B-B-B-B.C-C-C-C-C...C-C-C-C-C-C-C-C.C-C-C-C-C..
   0.47033   E-A-A-E.E-E-E-E-E.E-E-E-E-E-E-E.A-A-A.A-A.A-A-A...B-B-B-B-B-B-B-B.B-B.B-B.B-B-B-B.C-C-C-C-C.C-C-C-C-C-C-C-C-C.C-C-C-C-C-C
   0.50027   E-A-A-E.E-E-E-E-E.E-E-E-E-E-E-E.A-A-A.A-A.A-A-A...B-B-B-B-B-B-B-B.B-B.B-B-B-B-B-B.C-C-C-C-C.C-C-C-C-C-C-C-C-C.C-C-C-C-C-C
   0.55152   E-A-A-E-E-E-E-E-E-E-E-E-E-E-E-E.A-A-A.A-A.A-A-A-E.B-B-B-B-B-B-B-B.B-B.B-B-B-B-B-B.C-C-C-C-C-C-C-C-C-C-C-C-C-C.C-C-C-C-C-C
   0.60145   E-A-A-E-E-E-E-E-E-E-E-E-E-E-E-E.A-A-A-A-A.A-A-A-E.B-B-B-B-B-B-B-B-B-B.B-B-B-B-B-B.C-C-C-C-C-C-C-C-C-C-C-C-C-C.C-C-C-C-C-C
   0.67013   E-A-A-E-E-E-E-E-E-E-E-E-E-E-E-E.A-A-A-A-A.A-A-A-E.B-B-B-B-B-B-B-B-B-B.B-B-B-B-B-B.C-C-C-C-C-C-C-C-C-C-C-C-C-C.C-C-C-C-C-C
   0.73040   E-A-A-E-E-E-E-E-E-E-E-E-E-E-E-E.A-A-A-A-A-A-A-A-E.B-B-B-B-B-B-B-B-B-B.B-B-B-B-B-B.C-C-C-C-C-C-C-C-C-C-C-C-C-C-C-C-C-C-C-C
   0.78581   E-A-A-E-E-E-E-E-E-E-E-E-E-E-E-E.A-A-A-A-A-A-A-A-E.B-B-B-B-B-B-B-B-B-B.B-B-B-B-B-B.C-C-C-C-C-C-C-C-C-C-C-C-C-C-C-C-C-C-C-C
   0.81759   E-A-A-E-E-E-E-E-E-E-E-E-E-E-E-E.A-A-A-A-A-A-A-A-E.B-B-B-B-B-B-B-B-B-B-B-B-B-B-B-B.C-C-C-C-C-C-C-C-C-C-C-C-C-C-C-C-C-C-C-C
   0.92562   E-A-A-E-E-E-E-E-E-E-E-E-E-E-E-E-A-A-A-A-A-A-A-A-E.B-B-B-B-B-B-B-B-B-B-B-B-B-B-B-B.C-C-C-C-C-C-C-C-C-C-C-C-C-C-C-C-C-C-C-C
   0.95306   E-A-A-E-E-E-E-E-E-E-E-E-E-E-E-E-A-A-A-A-A-A-A-A-E-B-B-B-B-B-B-B-B-B-B-B-B-B-B-B-B.C-C-C-C-C-C-C-C-C-C-C-C-C-C-C-C-C-C-C-C
   1.03067   E-A-A-E-E-E-E-E-E-E-E-E-E-E-E-E-A-A-A-A-A-A-A-A-E-B-B-B-B-B-B-B-B-B-B-B-B-B-B-B-B-C-C-C-C-C-C-C-C-C-C-C-C-C-C-C-C-C-C-C-C
   1.03662   E-A-A-E-E-E-E-E-E-E-E-E-E-E-E-E-A-A-A-A-A-A-A-A-E-B-B-B-B-B-B-B-B-B-B-B-B-B-B-B-B-C-C-C-C-C-C-C-C-C-C-C-C-C-C-C-C-C-C-C-C
                                            |         7       |       8           |       9   |                 10
```

A=Astronomy & Astrophysics   B=Chemistry   C=Geophysical Sciences   D=Mathematics   E=Physics   F=Statistics

(b) Chicago Biological Sciences

```
ALL CLUSTERS FUSED -- overall maximum distance     =    0.94832
Distance       Cluster members
----------------------------------------------------------------------
       .    2.2.3.7.1.1.1.1.1.5.1.7.7.9.1.2.7.1.1.1.3.1.5.1.7.2.1.1.1.3.1.8.9.4.9.1.5.3.6.1.5.6.1.8.5.1.6.1.1.2.4.2.5.7.6.1.2.6.1.7.9.1.9.9.1.1.8.8.4.1.7.1.6.9.1.8.1.3.6.1.
       .    1.2.1.9.1.2.4.5.2.6.0.8.2.8.0.7.3.0.1.8.2.1.2.3.5.0.3.0.4.7.1.8.5.2.1.2...0.4.1.9.1...1.5.3.7.6.2.9.3.8.3.0.5.0...2.3.6...1.0.2.4.2.7.2.1.1.4.3...4.2...4.8.0.0.
       .    ........9.2.1...6...2.............7.2.........6.....3.8.....5.........0.......6...........4.....1.............4...........4.....2.........8...7.....9...0.....1.
  0.01644   C-C...........................................................................................................................................
  0.05370   C-C...I-I...............I-D...........................B-B...............................................D-D.................................
  0.10057   C-C...I-I...............I-D...............D-B...B-B-D-B.B-B-B.....................B-B...........................D-D...D-C...........N-N.............
  0.15572   C-C-C.I-I-D-B.D-D.......I-D-D.....I-I.B-B...D-B...B-B-D-B.B-B-B-I.......C-C.............B-B.....................D-J.....B-D.D-D-D.D-C...........N-N.......N-N...
  0.20136   C-C-C.I-I-D-B.D-D.I-B...I-D-D.C-C.I-I.B-B-I.D-B...B-B-D-B.B-B-B-I-D.....C-C.B-B.N-B.....B-B-B.....B-B.B-B.......D-J.D-J.B-D-D-D-D.D-C-N.........N-N...N-N.N-N...
  0.25521   C-C-C-I-I-D-B.D-D-I-B...I-D-D-C-C.I-I.B-B-I-D-B...B-B-D-B-B-B-B-I-D.C-C.C-C.B-B.N-B.B-B.B-B-B.B-B.B-B.B-B.......D-J-D-J.B-D-D-D-D-D-C-N.........N-N...N-N.N-N-J-
  0.30178   C-C-C-I-I-D-B-D-D-I-B...I-D-D-C-C-I-I.B-B-I-D-B...B-B-D-B-B-B-B-I-D.C-C.C-C.B-B.N-B.B-B.B-B-B.B-B-B-B.B-B.......D-J-D-J.B-D-D-D-D-D-C-N.........N-N-N-N-N.N-N-J-
  0.35775   C-C-C-I-I-D-B-D-D-I-B-C.I-D-D-C-C-I-I.B-B-I-D-B-B-B-B-D-B-B-B-B-I-D.C-C.C-C-B-B.N-B.B-B.B-B-B.B-B-B-B.B-B...D-B.D-J-D-J.B-D-D-D-D-D-C-N.J-A.....N-N-N-N-N.N-N-J-
  0.40039   C-C-C-I-I-D-B-D-D-I-B-C.I-D-D-C-C-I-I.B-B-I-D-B-B-B-B-D-B-B-B-B-I-D.C-C.C-C-B-B.N-B.B-B-B-B-B.B-B-B-B.B-B-D.D-B.D-J-D-J-B-D-D-D-D-D-C-N.J-A.I-D.N-N-N-N-N.N-N-J-
  0.47650   C-C-C-I-I-D-B-D-D-I-B-C.I-D-D-C-C-I-I-B-B-I-D-B-B-B-B-D-B-B-B-B-I-D.C-C.C-C-B-B-N-B.B-B-B-B-B-B-B-B-B-B-B-D.D-B.D-J-D-J-B-D-D-D-D-D-C-N.J-A.I-D.N-N-N-N-N.N-N-J-
  0.52060   C-C-C-I-I-D-B-D-D-I-B-C.I-D-D-C-C-I-I-B-B-I-D-B-B-B-B-D-B-B-B-B-I-D.C-C.C-C-B-B-N-B.B-B-B-B-B-B-B-B-B-B-B-D.D-B.D-J-D-J-B-D-D-D-D-D-C-N.J-A-I-D.N-N-N-N-N-N-N-J-
  0.55452   C-C-C-I-I-D-B-D-D-I-B-C.I-D-D-C-C-I-I-B-B-I-D-B-B-B-B-D-B-B-B-B-I-D-C-C.C-C-B-B-N-B.B-B-B-B-B-B-B-B-B-B-B-D-D-B.D-J-D-J-B-D-D-D-D-D-C-N-J-A-I-D.N-N-N-N-N-N-N-J-
  0.60342   C-C-C-I-I-D-B-D-D-I-B-C.I-D-D-C-C-I-I-B-B-I-D-B-B-B-B-D-B-B-B-B-I-D-C-C.C-C-B-B-N-B.B-B-B-B-B-B-B-B-B-B-B-D-D-B.D-J-D-J-B-D-D-D-D-D-C-N-J-A-I-D.N-N-N-N-N-N-N-J-
  0.66969   C-C-C-I-I-D-B-D-D-I-B-C-I-D-D-C-C-I-I-B-B-I-D-B-B-B-B-D-B-B-B-B-I-D-C-C.C-C-B-B-N-B.B-B-B-B-B-B-B-B-B-B-B-D-D-B.D-J-D-J-B-D-D-D-D-D-C-N-J-A-I-D.N-N-N-N-N-N-N-J-
  0.76109   C-C-C-I-I-D-B-D-D-I-B-C-I-D-D-C-C-I-I-B-B-I-D-B-B-B-B-D-B-B-B-B-I-D-C-C-C-C-B-B-N-B.B-B-B-B-B-B-B-B-B-B-B-D-D-B.D-J-D-J-B-D-D-D-D-D-C-N-J-A-I-D.N-N-N-N-N-N-N-J-
  0.77724   C-C-C-I-I-D-B-D-D-I-B-C-I-D-D-C-C-I-I-B-B-I-D-B-B-B-B-D-B-B-B-B-I-D-C-C-C-C-B-B-N-B.B-B-B-B-B-B-B-B-B-B-B-D-D-B-D-J-D-J-B-D-D-D-D-D-C-N-J-A-I-D.N-N-N-N-N-N-N-J-
  0.81603   C-C-C-I-I-D-B-D-D-I-B-C-I-D-D-C-C-I-I-B-B-I-D-B-B-B-B-D-B-B-B-B-I-D-C-C-C-C-B-B-N-B.B-B-B-B-B-B-B-B-B-B-B-D-D-B-D-J-D-J-B-D-D-D-D-D-C-N-J-A-I-D.N-N-N-N-N-N-N-J-
  0.87964   C-C-C-I-I-D-B-D-D-I-B-C-I-D-D-C-C-I-I-B-B-I-D-B-B-B-B-D-B-B-B-B-I-D-C-C-C-C-B-B-N-B.B-B-B-B-B-B-B-B-B-B-B-D-D-B-D-J-D-J-B-D-D-D-D-D-C-N-J-A-I-D-N-N-N-N-N-N-N-J-
  0.92561   C-C-C-I-I-D-B-D-D-I-B-C-I-D-D-C-C-I-I-B-B-I-D-B-B-B-B-D-B-B-B-B-I-D-C-C-C-C-B-B-N-B-B-B-B-B-B-B-B-B-B-B-B-D-D-B-D-J-D-J-B-D-D-D-D-D-C-N-J-A-I-D-N-N-N-N-N-N-N-J-
                                     1                                                      |         2                  |         3                       |    4

continued-----------------------------------------------------------------------------
       .    1.5.1.1.7.2.9.3.1.4.6.7.5.1.1.3.2.4.1.9.9.1.2.8.4.9.4.3.1.1.4.5.4.1.2.1.6.3.8.1.1.5.1.8.1.4.8.1.1.7.1.1.3.3.4.6.8.1.8.5.6.1
       .    0.0.1.3...4.9.3.3.8.6.7.8.1.3.4.3.0.3.3.7.2.6.5.5.6.4.6.0.0.6.1...2.5.3.8...6.1.2.7.2.3.1.9.0.0.9.1.0.7.5.9.7.9.9.3.4.4.3.2
       .    6...1.1.........8.........7.5.......9.....8.............5.3.......7...0.......0.3...4...3.....0.....9.............2.......5
  0.01644   ..............................................................................................................................
  0.05370   ..............................................................................................................................
  0.10057   ..............N-N..............................J-J...J-J.......C-C.C-C.....C-D-C.............................................
  0.15572   ..N-N.....N-N.N-N-N.I-N...N-N.........N-N.......J-J-J.J-J.......C-C-C-C.....C-D-C-C-C...........A-A.........A-A.A-A...A-A..
  0.20136   ..N-N-N...N-N.N-N-N.I-N-N.N-N-N...N-N.N-N.......J-J-J.J-J-J.....C-C-C-C.....C-D-C-C-C...........A-A-C.......A-A.A-A...A-A-A
  0.25521   N.N-N-N-N.N-N-N-N-N.I-N-N.N-N-N-N.N-N-N-N...J-J.J-J-J.J-J-J.....C-C-C-C-C...C-D-C-C-C.C-C.......A-A-C...J-J.A-A.A-A-A.A-A-A
  0.30178   N.N-N-N-N.N-N-N-N-N.I-N-N.N-N-N-N-N-N-N-N...J-J.J-J-J.J-J-J.J-J.C-C-C-C-C...C-D-C-C-C.C-C...D-C.A-A-C...J-J.A-A-A-A-A.A-A-A
  0.35775   N.N-N-N-N.N-N-N-N-N-I-N-N.N-N-N-N-N-N-N-N...J-J.J-J-J.J-J-J.J-J.C-C-C-C-C-C.C-D-C-C-C.C-C-C.D-C.A-A-C-A.J-J.A-A-A-A-A.A-A-A
  0.40039   N.N-N-N-N.N-N-N-N-N-I-N-N.N-N-N-N-N-N-N-N...J-J-J-J-J.J-J-J.J-J.C-C-C-C-C-C-C-D-C-C-C.C-C-C-D-C.A-A-C-A.J-J.A-A-A-A-A.A-A-A
  0.47650   N.N-N-N-N-N-N-N-N-N-I-N-N.N-N-N-N-N-N-N-N...J-J-J-J-J.J-J-J-J-J.C-C-C-C-C-C-C-D-C-C-C.C-C-C-D-C.A-A-C-A.J-J.A-A-A-A-A.A-A-A
  0.52060   N.N-N-N-N-N-N-N-N-N-I-N-N-N-N-N-N-N-N-N-N...J-J-J-J-J.J-J-J-J-J.C-C-C-C-C-C-C-D-C-C-C.C-C-C-D-C.A-A-C-A-J-J.A-A-A-A-A.A-A-A
  0.55452   N.N-N-N-N-N-N-N-N-N-I-N-N-N-N-N-N-N-N-N-N...J-J-J-J-J.J-J-J-J-J.C-C-C-C-C-C-C-D-C-C-C.C-C-C-D-C.A-A-C-A-J-J.A-A-A-A-A-A-A-A
  0.60342   N.N-N-N-N-N-N-N-N-N-I-N-N-N-N-N-N-N-N-N-N...J-J-J-J-J-J-J-J-J-J.C-C-C-C-C-C-C-D-C-C-C-C-C-C-D-C.A-A-C-A-J-J-A-A-A-A-A-A-A-A
  0.66969   N.N-N-N-N-N-N-N-N-N-I-N-N-N-N-N-N-N-N-N-N-N.J-J-J-J-J-J-J-J-J-J.C-C-C-C-C-C-C-D-C-C-C-C-C-C-D-C.A-A-C-A-J-J-A-A-A-A-A-A-A-A
  0.76109   N-N-N-N-N-N-N-N-N-N-I-N-N-N-N-N-N-N-N-N-N.J-J-J-J-J-J-J-J-J-J.C-C-C-C-C-C-C-D-C-C-C-C-C-C-D-C-A-A-C-A-J-J-A-A-A-A-A-A-A-A
  0.77724   N-N-N-N-N-N-N-N-N-N-I-N-N-N-N-N-N-N-N-N-N.J-J-J-J-J-J-J-J-J-J.C-C-C-C-C-C-C-D-C-C-C-C-C-C-D-C-A-A-C-A-J-J-A-A-A-A-A-A-A-A
  0.81603   N-N-N-N-N-N-N-N-N-N-I-N-N-N-N-N-N-N-N-N-N-J-J-J-J-J-J-J-J-J-J.C-C-C-C-C-C-C-D-C-C-C-C-C-C-D-C-A-A-C-A-J-J-A-A-A-A-A-A-A-A
  0.87964   N-N-N-N-N-N-N-N-N-N-I-N-N-N-N-N-N-N-N-N-N-J-J-J-J-J-J-J-J-J-J.C-C-C-C-C-C-C-D-C-C-C-C-C-C-D-C-A-A-C-A-J-J-A-A-A-A-A-A-A-A
  0.92561   N-N-N-N-N-N-N-N-N-N-I-N-N-N-N-N-N-N-N-N-N-J-J-J-J-J-J-J-J-J-J.C-C-C-C-C-C-C-D-C-C-C-C-C-C-D-C-A-A-C-A-J-J-A-A-A-A-A-A-A-A
                                                                    |        5         |              6             |        7
```

A=Anatomy   C=Biology   I=Microbiology

B=Biochemistry   D=Biophysics   J=Pharmacology & Physiology   N=Pathology

(c) Chicago Social Sciences

```
ALL CLUSTERS FUSED -- overall maximum distance     =    0.89203
Distance     Cluster members
----------------------------------------------------------------------
        .    1.1.1.7.1.7.3.8.1.1.5.5.6.8.1.1.3.1.1.5.8.1.3.1.9.1.2.8.9.1.1.3.1.1.1.1.3.1.3.1.5.8.9.1.1.7.1.1.2.5.6.2.1.3.6.7.1.1.1.3.1.7.1.2.9.2.1.6.1.1.1.9.1.1.2.7.5.1.4.5.
        .    5.8.1.4.2.9.7.9.0.3.0.5.9.8.3.3.8.2.2.2.5...0.3.2.2.2.2.4.0.4.3.1.4.4.2.6.2.9.2.1.7.1.4.2.1.4.7...3...3.3.4.2.6.5.0.3...4...0.0.7.9.1.7.3.1.5.5.0.2.6.0...1.6.9.
        .    ....0...3.......4.5.........7.8...6...........4...1.......9.1...2...0.5...0...8.......2.2...3...........2.......3.7.3...8...8.......7...9.1.2...1.7.......4.....
  0.01716    C-C.............................................................................................................................................................
  0.05102    C-C...C-C...C-C...........................................................................................................................H-H...................
  0.10221    C-C-C.C-C...C-C.C-C-C.................C-C.A-A...............................A-A.B-A.............D-J.......D-J.J-H.H-J.....H-H.............H-H.H-H.......C-C.....
  0.15072    C-C-C.C-C...C-C.C-C-C...C-C.C-C.C-C...C-C.A-A-A.A-A.......A-A-A...A-A...A-A.A-A.B-A.......A-A...D-J.......D-J-J-H.H-J.....H-H-J-J.H-J.H-H.H-H.H-H-J.....C-C-J...
  0.20014    C-C-C-C-C...C-C-C-C-C-C.C-C.C-C.C-C-C.C-C.A-A-A.A-A-A.A-A.A-A-A...A-A-A.A-A-A-A.B-A.A-A...A-A...D-J...J-J.D-J-J-H-H-J.....H-H-J-J-H-J.H-H-H-H.H-H-J.J-J.C-C-J.C-
  0.25317    C-C-C-C-C-C.C-C-C-C-C-C.C-C.C-C.C-C-C.C-C.A-A-A-A-A-A.A-A.A-A-A-A.A-A-A.A-A-A-A-B-A.A-A...A-A-A.D-J-D-J-J.D-J-J-H-H-J.H-H.H-H-J-J-H-J.H-H-H-H-H-H-J.J-J.C-C-J-C-
  0.30003    C-C-C-C-C-C.C-C-C-C-C-C.C-C.C-C.C-C-C-C-C.A-A-A-A-A-A-A-A.A-A-A-A.A-A-A.A-A-A-A-B-A.A-A-A.A-A-A.D-J-D-J-J-D-J-J-H-H-J.H-H.H-H-J-J-H-J.H-H-H-H-H-H-J.J-J.C-C-J-C-
  0.35502    C-C-C-C-C-C.C-C-C-C-C-C.C-C-C-C.C-C-C-C-C.A-A-A-A-A-A-A-A-A-A-A-A.A-A-A-A-A-A-A-B-A.A-A-A.A-A-A.D-J-D-J-J-D-J-J-H-H-J.H-H-H-H-J-J-H-J-H-H-H-H-H-H-J.J-J.C-C-J-C-
  0.41493    C-C-C-C-C-C.C-C-C-C-C-C.C-C-C-C.C-C-C-C-C.A-A-A-A-A-A-A-A-A-A-A-A.A-A-A-A-A-A-A-B-A.A-A-A.A-A-A.D-J-D-J-J-D-J-J-H-H-J.H-H-H-H-J-J-H-J-H-H-H-H-H-H-J.J-J.C-C-J-C-
  0.46368    C-C-C-C-C-C-C-C-C-C-C-C-C-C-C-C.C-C-C-C-C.A-A-A-A-A-A-A-A-A-A-A-A.A-A-A-A-A-A-A-B-A-A-A-A.A-A-A.D-J-D-J-J-D-J-J-H-H-J.H-H-H-H-J-J-H-J-H-H-H-H-H-H-J-J-J.C-C-J-C-
  0.52212    C-C-C-C-C-C-C-C-C-C-C-C-C-C-C-C.C-C-C-C-C.A-A-A-A-A-A-A-A-A-A-A-A.A-A-A-A-A-A-A-B-A-A-A-A-A-A-A.D-J-D-J-J-D-J-J-H-H-J.H-H-H-H-J-J-H-J-H-H-H-H-H-H-J-J-J-C-C-J-C-
  0.55168    C-C-C-C-C-C-C-C-C-C-C-C-C-C-C-C.C-C-C-C-C.A-A-A-A-A-A-A-A-A-A-A-A.A-A-A-A-A-A-A-B-A-A-A-A-A-A-A.D-J-D-J-J-D-J-J-H-H-J-H-H-H-H-J-J-H-J-H-H-H-H-H-H-J-J-J-C-C-J-C-
  0.60588    C-C-C-C-C-C-C-C-C-C-C-C-C-C-C-C.C-C-C-C-C.A-A-A-A-A-A-A-A-A-A-A-A.A-A-A-A-A-A-A-B-A-A-A-A-A-A-A.D-J-D-J-J-D-J-J-H-H-J-H-H-H-H-J-J-H-J-H-H-H-H-H-H-J-J-J-C-C-J-C-
  0.66704    C-C-C-C-C-C-C-C-C-C-C-C-C-C-C-C-C-C-C-C-C.A-A-A-A-A-A-A-A-A-A-A-A-A-A-A-A-A-A-A-B-A-A-A-A-A-A-A.D-J-D-J-J-D-J-J-H-H-J-H-H-H-H-J-J-H-J-H-H-H-H-H-H-J-J-J-C-C-J-C-
  0.77452    C-C-C-C-C-C-C-C-C-C-C-C-C-C-C-C-C-C-C-C-C.A-A-A-A-A-A-A-A-A-A-A-A-A-A-A-A-A-A-A-B-A-A-A-A-A-A-A.D-J-D-J-J-D-J-J-H-H-J-H-H-H-H-J-J-H-J-H-H-H-H-H-H-J-J-J-C-C-J-C-
  0.81100    C-C-C-C-C-C-C-C-C-C-C-C-C-C-C-C-C-C-C-C-C.A-A-A-A-A-A-A-A-A-A-A-A-A-A-A-A-A-A-A-B-A-A-A-A-A-A-A.D-J-D-J-J-D-J-J-H-H-J-H-H-H-H-J-J-H-J-H-H-H-H-H-H-J-J-J-C-C-J-C-
  0.84530    C-C-C-C-C-C-C-C-C-C-C-C-C-C-C-C-C-C-C-C-C.A-A-A-A-A-A-A-A-A-A-A-A-A-A-A-A-A-A-A-B-A-A-A-A-A-A-A-D-J-D-J-J-D-J-J-H-H-J-H-H-H-H-J-J-H-J-H-H-H-H-H-H-J-J-J-C-C-J-C-
  0.86740    C-C-C-C-C-C-C-C-C-C-C-C-C-C-C-C-C-C-C-C-C.A-A-A-A-A-A-A-A-A-A-A-A-A-A-A-A-A-A-A-B-A-A-A-A-A-A-A-D-J-D-J-J-D-J-J-H-H-J-H-H-H-H-J-J-H-J-H-H-H-H-H-H-J-J-J-C-C-J-C-
                                1                    |                        2                             |                         3

continued-------------------------------------------------------------
        .    6.6.6.4.1.1.2.8.6.1.9.1.7.9.1.1.1.9.2.4.1.5.9.1.1.1.6.1.3.8.8.8.4.5.9.1.2.5.1.2.8.4.1.4.1.7.1.6.1.1.6.3.7.4.4.5.1.4.1.3.1.2.1.8.7.7.1.1.1.4.9.4.1
        .    3.4.5...5.9.4.1.8.0.6.4.3.9.1.0.3...7.4.1.8.8.3.4.1.0.4.5...4.6.2.4.3.3.5.6.1.1.0.8.2.3.2.8.4.1.4.6.6.2.7.0.1.7.0.5.0.1.1.8.5.3.2.5.1.0.3.7.0.9.0
        .    ........1.........2...7.....9.6.0.......6.....1.6.3...4.....................8.......4...9...9...5...............3...........0.......5.5.6.......0
  0.01716    .................................................................................................................................................
  0.05102    ..............................................J-J................................................................................................
  0.10221    ................H-H...........................J-J...............D-D.....B-B...B-B.....D-D.D-D.............................B-B-B..................
  0.15072    ......H-D-H.H-H.H-H-H...J-H...B-J.............J-J...D-B.........D-D-B-B.B-B...B-B.B-B.D-D.D-D.D-D.....B-B.B-B.B-B-B.B-B...B-B-B...........B-B....
  0.20014    C.....H-D-H.H-H.H-H-H...J-H...B-J...D-E...B-E.J-J...D-B-B.......D-D-B-B-B-B...B-B-B-B.D-D-D-D.D-D.B-B.B-B-B-B.B-B-B.B-B...B-B-B.......B-B.B-B.B-B
  0.25317    C.C-C.H-D-H-H-H.H-H-H...J-H...B-J-J.D-E-J.B-E.J-J-J.D-B-B.......D-D-B-B-B-B...B-B-B-B.D-D-D-D.D-D.B-B.B-B-B-B.B-B-B.B-B...B-B-B.B-B...B-B.B-B.B-B
  0.30003    C.C-C.H-D-H-H-H.H-H-H...J-H...B-J-J.D-E-J.B-E.J-J-J.D-B-B.......D-D-B-B-B-B-B.B-B-B-B.D-D-D-D-D-D.B-B.B-B-B-B-B-B-B.B-B-D.B-B-B-B-B...B-B.B-B-B-B
  0.35502    C-C-C.H-D-H-H-H.H-H-H-H.J-H...B-J-J.D-E-J.B-E.J-J-J.D-B-B...B-B.D-D-B-B-B-B-B.B-B-B-B-D-D-D-D-D-D.B-B.B-B-B-B-B-B-B.B-B-D.B-B-B-B-B-B.B-B.B-B-B-B
  0.41493    C-C-C.H-D-H-H-H.H-H-H-H.J-H-H.B-J-J-D-E-J.B-E.J-J-J.D-B-B-D.B-B.D-D-B-B-B-B-B-B-B-B-B-D-D-D-D-D-D.B-B-B-B-B-B-B-B-B.B-B-D.B-B-B-B-B-B.B-B.B-B-B-B
  0.46368    C-C-C.H-D-H-H-H-H-H-H-H.J-H-H.B-J-J-D-E-J.B-E-J-J-J.D-B-B-D.B-B.D-D-B-B-B-B-B-B-B-B-B-D-D-D-D-D-D.B-B-B-B-B-B-B-B-B.B-B-D.B-B-B-B-B-B.B-B.B-B-B-B
  0.52212    C-C-C.H-D-H-H-H-H-H-H-H.J-H-H.B-J-J-D-E-J.B-E-J-J-J.D-B-B-D-B-B.D-D-B-B-B-B-B-B-B-B-B-D-D-D-D-D-D-B-B-B-B-B-B-B-B-B.B-B-D.B-B-B-B-B-B.B-B.B-B-B-B
  0.55168    C-C-C.H-D-H-H-H-H-H-H-H.J-H-H.B-J-J-D-E-J.B-E-J-J-J.D-B-B-D-B-B.D-D-B-B-B-B-B-B-B-B-B-D-D-D-D-D-D-B-B-B-B-B-B-B-B-B.B-B-D.B-B-B-B-B-B-B-B.B-B-B-B
  0.60588    C-C-C.H-D-H-H-H-H-H-H-H-J-H-H.B-J-J-D-E-J.B-E-J-J-J.D-B-B-D-B-B-D-D-B-B-B-B-B-B-B-B-B-D-D-D-D-D-D-B-B-B-B-B-B-B-B-B.B-B-D.B-B-B-B-B-B-B-B-B-B-B-B
  0.66704    C-C-C-H-D-H-H-H-H-H-H-H-J-H-H.B-J-J-D-E-J-B-E-J-J-J.D-B-B-D-B-B-D-D-B-B-B-B-B-B-B-B-B-D-D-D-D-D-D-B-B-B-B-B-B-B-B-B.B-B-D.B-B-B-B-B-B-B-B-B-B-B-B
  0.77452    C-C-C-H-D-H-H-H-H-H-H-H-J-H-H.B-J-J-D-E-J-B-E-J-J-J.D-B-B-D-B-B-D-D-B-B-B-B-B-B-B-B-B-D-D-D-D-D-D-B-B-B-B-B-B-B-B-B.B-B-D.B-B-B-B-B-B-B-B-B-B-B-B
  0.81100    C-C-C-H-D-H-H-H-H-H-H-H-J-H-H-B-J-J-D-E-J-B-E-J-J-J.D-B-B-D-B-B-D-D-B-B-B-B-B-B-B-B-B-D-D-D-D-D-D-B-B-B-B-B-B-B-B-B-B-B-D-B-B-B-B-B-B-B-B-B-B-B-B
  0.84530    C-C-C-H-D-H-H-H-H-H-H-H-J-H-H-B-J-J-D-E-J-B-E-J-J-J.D-B-B-D-B-B-D-D-B-B-B-B-B-B-B-B-B-D-D-D-D-D-D-B-B-B-B-B-B-B-B-B-B-B-D-B-B-B-B-B-B-B-B-B-B-B-B
  0.86740    C-C-C-H-D-H-H-H-H-H-H-H-J-H-H-B-J-J-D-E-J-B-E-J-J-J-D-B-B-D-B-B-D-D-B-B-B-B-B-B-B-B-B-D-D-D-D-D-D-B-B-B-B-B-B-B-B-B-B-B-D-B-B-B-B-B-B-B-B-B-B-B-B

                                      |           5       |                                                        |      6
```

A=Anthropology   D=Education   J=Sociology

B=Behavioral Science   E=Geography

C= Economics   H=Political Science

(d) Columbia Physical Sciences

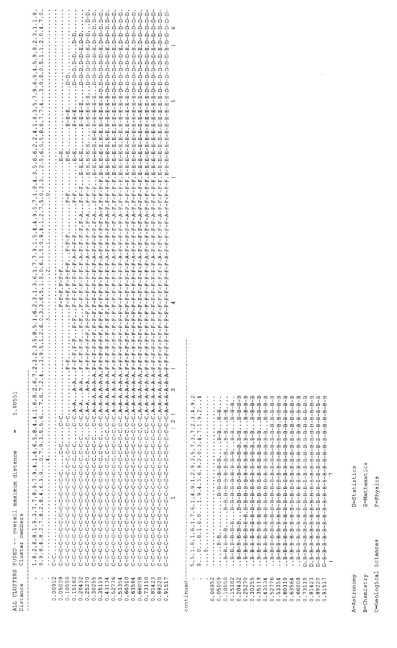

```
ALL CLUSTERS FUSED -- overall maximum distance     =     1.00551
Distance     Cluster members
---------------------------------------------------------------------
        .   1.8.2.6.8.1.9.3.7.7.8.9.7.9.4.1.4.6.5.8.4.4.1.6.8.2.6.7.2.3.2.3.5.8.5.1.6.2.3.1.3.6.1.7.7.9.1.5.4.4.9.5.7.1.8.4.3.5.6.6.2.2.4.1.8.3.5.7.9.6.9.4.5.9.8.2.3.1.1.8.
        .   9.9.8.4.8.2.7.8.2.8.4.6.9.0...0.7.9.3.5.5.6...7.6.7.2.4...3.9.5.1.2.6.0.3.3.6.5.1.8.0.6.1.5.0.8.4.1.2.7.5.0.3.3...2.5.6.0.5.8.0.7.7.4...3.0.8.0.5.1.1.2.0.4.7.0.
        .   ......................................4...............................................3...............2.......1.............0.........................................................
  0.00952   C-C.............................................................................................................................................................
  0.05009   C-C-C-C-C-C-C.C-C-C-C-C-C-C.....C-C.....C-C...................................F-F-F.F-F-F.............................E-E.........................................
  0.10550   C-C-C-C-C-C-C-C-C-C-C-C-C-C.C-C.C-C.....C-C.............F-F...............F-F-F.F-F-F-F...F-F-F.........F-F.........E-E.......E-E-E.......D-D...................
  0.15162   C-C-C-C-C-C-C-C-C-C-C-C-C-C.C-C.C-C.....C-C.A-A...A-A...F-F-F.F-F...F-F...F-F-F.F-F-F-F-A-F-F-F.........F-F.........E-E.......E-E-E.......D-D-D.D-D...D-D.......
  0.20432   C-C-C-C-C-C-C-C-C-C-C-C-C-C-C-C.C-C-C...C-C.A-A...A-A...F-F-F-F-F...F-F...F-F-F-F-F-F-F-A-F-F-F-F.F-A...F-F-F...E-E.E-E.......E-E-E-E.....D-D-D.D-D-E.D-D.......
  0.25270   C-C-C-C-C-C-C-C-C-C-C-C-C-C-C-C.C-C-C...C-C.A-A...A-A...F-F-F-F-F-F.F-F-F.F-F-F-F-F-F-F-A-F-F-F-F.F-A...F-F-F...E-E.E-E-E.....E-E-E-E-E...D-D-D-D-D-E.D-D...D-D.
  0.30255   C-C-C-C-C-C-C-C-C-C-C-C-C-C-C-C.C-C-C...C-C.A-A-A.A-A-A.F-F-F-F-F-F.F-F-F.F-F-F-F-F-F-F-A-F-F-F-F.F-A...F-F-F...E-E.E-E-E.E-E.E-E-E-E-E...D-D-D-D-D-E.D-D-D.D-D.
  0.35119   C-C-C-C-C-C-C-C-C-C-C-C-C-C-C-C.C-C-C...C-C.A-A-A.A-A-A.F-F-F-F-F-F.F-F-F.F-F-F-F-F-F-F-A-F-F-F-F-F-A-F.F-F-F-F.E-E.E-E-E.E-E.E-E-E-E-E-D.D-D-D-D-D-E.D-D-D.D-D.
  0.43134   C-C-C-C-C-C-C-C-C-C-C-C-C-C-C-C.C-C-C-C.C-C.A-A-A.A-A-A.F-F-F-F-F-F-F-F-F.F-F-F-F-F-F-F-A-F-F-F-F-F-A-F.F-F-F-F.E-E-E-E-E.E-E.E-E-E-E-E-D-D-D-D-D-D-E.D-D-D.D-D.
  0.52776   C-C-C-C-C-C-C-C-C-C-C-C-C-C-C-C.C-C-C-C.C-C.A-A-A.A-A-A.F-F-F-F-F-F-F-F-F-F-F-F-F-F-F-F-A-F-F-F-F-F-A-F.F-F-F-F.E-E-E-E-E.E-E.E-E-E-E-E-D-D-D-D-D-D-E.D-D-D-D-D.
  0.53354   C-C-C-C-C-C-C-C-C-C-C-C-C-C-C-C-C-C-C-C.C-C.A-A-A.A-A-A.F-F-F-F-F-F-F-F-F-F-F-F-F-F-F-F-A-F-F-F-F-F-A-F.F-F-F-F.E-E-E-E-E.E-E.E-E-E-E-E-D-D-D-D-D-D-E.D-D-D-D-D.
  0.60310   C-C-C-C-C-C-C-C-C-C-C-C-C-C-C-C-C-C-C-C.C-C.A-A-A-A-A-A.F-F-F-F-F-F-F-F-F-F-F-F-F-F-F-F-A-F-F-F-F-F-A-F.F-F-F-F.E-E-E-E-E-E-E.E-E-E-E-E-D-D-D-D-D-D-E.D-D-D-D-D.
  0.63564   C-C-C-C-C-C-C-C-C-C-C-C-C-C-C-C-C-C-C-C.C-C.A-A-A-A-A-A.F-F-F-F-F-F-F-F-F-F-F-F-F-F-F-F-A-F-F-F-F-F-A-F.F-F-F-F.E-E-E-E-E-E-E-E-E-E-E-E-D-D-D-D-D-D-E.D-D-D-D-D.
  0.66008   C-C-C-C-C-C-C-C-C-C-C-C-C-C-C-C-C-C-C-C.C-C.A-A-A-A-A-A.F-F-F-F-F-F-F-F-F-F-F-F-F-F-F-F-A-F-F-F-F-F-A-F-F-F-F-F.E-E-E-E-E-E-E-E-E-E-E-E-D-D-D-D-D-D-E.D-D-D-D-D.
  0.73110   C-C-C-C-C-C-C-C-C-C-C-C-C-C-C-C-C-C-C-C.C-C.A-A-A-A-A-A-F-F-F-F-F-F-F-F-F-F-F-F-F-F-F-F-A-F-F-F-F-F-A-F-F-F-F-F.E-E-E-E-E-E-E-E-E-E-E-E-D-D-D-D-D-D-E.D-D-D-D-D-
  0.81423   C-C-C-C-C-C-C-C-C-C-C-C-C-C-C-C-C-C-C-C-C-C.A-A-A-A-A-A-F-F-F-F-F-F-F-F-F-F-F-F-F-F-F-F-A-F-F-F-F-F-A-F-F-F-F-F.E-E-E-E-E-E-E-E-E-E-E-E-D-D-D-D-D-D-E-D-D-D-D-D-
  0.89220   C-C-C-C-C-C-C-C-C-C-C-C-C-C-C-C-C-C-C-C-C-C.A-A-A-A-A-A-F-F-F-F-F-F-F-F-F-F-F-F-F-F-F-F-A-F-F-F-F-F-A-F-F-F-F-F.E-E-E-E-E-E-E-E-E-E-E-E-D-D-D-D-D-D-E-D-D-D-D-D-
  0.91517   C-C-C-C-C-C-C-C-C-C-C-C-C-C-C-C-C-C-C-C-C-C-A-A-A-A-A-A-F-F-F-F-F-F-F-F-F-F-F-F-F-F-F-F-A-F-F-F-F-F-A-F-F-F-F-F.E-E-E-E-E-E-E-E-E-E-E-E-D-D-D-D-D-D-E-D-D-D-D-D-
                               1                   | 2 |      3     |                  4                                    |                     5               |    6

continued--------------------------------------------------------------------------
        .   5.5.1.8.1.6.1.7.6.1.4.9.1.2.9.3.5.7.3.7.2.3.4.9.2
        .   9...0...8.1.6.0...1.9.4.3.6.9.2.0.3.4.7.1.9.2...4
        .   ....5............................................
  0.00952   .................................................
  0.05009   ......B-B...........B-B-B-B-B-B.....B-B...B-B....
  0.10550   ..B-B.B-B-B.....B-B.B-B-B-B-B-B-B...B-B...B-B....
  0.15162   ..B-B.B-B-B-B...B-B-B-B-B-B-B-B-B...B-B...B-B-B..
  0.20432   ..B-B-B-B-B-B...B-B-B-B-B-B-B-B-B-B.B-B...B-B-B-B
  0.25270   ..B-B-B-B-B-B-B.B-B-B-B-B-B-B-B-B-B.B-B...B-B-B-B
  0.30255   ..B-B-B-B-B-B-B-B-B-B-B-B-B-B-B-B-B.B-B...B-B-B-B
  0.35119   ..B-B-B-B-B-B-B-B-B-B-B-B-B-B-B-B-B-B-B...B-B-B-B
  0.43134   ..B-B-B-B-B-B-B-B-B-B-B-B-B-B-B-B-B-B-B...B-B-B-B
  0.52776   ..B-B-B-B-B-B-B-B-B-B-B-B-B-B-B-B-B-B-B-B.B-B-B-B
  0.53354   ..B-B-B-B-B-B-B-B-B-B-B-B-B-B-B-B-B-B-B-B.B-B-B-B
  0.60310   ..B-B-B-B-B-B-B-B-B-B-B-B-B-B-B-B-B-B-B-B-B-B-B-B
  0.63564   ..B-B-B-B-B-B-B-B-B-B-B-B-B-B-B-B-B-B-B-B-B-B-B-B
  0.66008   ..B-B-B-B-B-B-B-B-B-B-B-B-B-B-B-B-B-B-B-B-B-B-B-B
  0.73110   D.B-B-B-B-B-B-B-B-B-B-B-B-B-B-B-B-B-B-B-B-B-B-B-B
  0.81423   D.B-B-B-B-B-B-B-B-B-B-B-B-B-B-B-B-B-B-B-B-B-B-B-B
  0.89220   D-B-B-B-B-B-B-B-B-B-B-B-B-B-B-B-B-B-B-B-B-B-B-B-B
  0.91517   D-B-B-B-B-B-B-B-B-B-B-B-B-B-B-B-B-B-B-B-B-B-B-B-B
             |                        7
```

A=Astronomy D=Statistics

B=Chemistry E=Mathematics

C=Geological Sciences F=Physics

(e) Columbia Biological Sciences

```
ALL CLUSTERS FUSED -- overall maximum distance     =    1.11550
Distance      Cluster members
-----------------------------------------------------------------------
         .    9.1.9.2.5.1.3.1.5.1.1.2.5.9.1.9.3.1.6.5.7.2.8.2.4.1.6.5.9.1.7.1.9.4.5.1.8.9.3.8.4.1.1.1.1.1.5.1.6.8.9.1.1.8.2.7.9.1.1.1.3.4.1.1.1.3.1.8.4.7.1.6.1.4.8.6.6.7.1.4.
         .    4.2.8.0.6.0.5.5.8.4.4.7.9.5.3.7.7.1...2.7.2.3.3.9.4.0.0.1.2.5.4.3.8.7.......0.8.7.3.3.2.5.4.3.5.4.5.0.0.3.9...3.9.0.1.2...3.0.3.7.2.1.7.0...0.3.0.4.2.7.9.2.1...
         .    ..7.......8...1.....5.......8.....2...............6.......3...2...................1...0...0...2.......1.2.........7.0.6.....5.7.....4.......6...0...........8...
   0.03265    E-E.............................................................................................................................................................
   0.05688    E-E.........E-E.................................................................................................................................................
   0.10199    E-E.........E-E.........................................................B-B.......................C-C.........................................................D-
   0.15117    E-E-D...E-E.E-E.................D-D.............F-C...............B-B...B-B.B-B.B-B...............C-C...............A-A...........A-A.........................D-
   0.20385    E-E-D...E-E.E-E-E.D-D...D-D-D...D-D.............F-C-E.F-E.........B-B...B-B.B-B.B-B.........C-C...C-C-C.....H-A.A-A.A-A.A-A-A.....A-A.................H-G.....D-
   0.25029    E-E-D-C.E-E.E-E-E.D-D-D.D-D-D...D-D.......C-C...F-C-E-F-E...F-F...B-B...B-B.B-B.B-B.....C-C.C-C...C-C-C.....H-A.A-A.A-A.A-A-A.....A-A-A...H-H.....A-A.H-G.F-F.D-
   0.30383    E-E-D-C-E-E.E-E-E.D-D-D.D-D-D...D-D-D.D-D.C-C...F-C-E-F-E...F-F...B-B-B.B-B-B-B-B-B.H-B.C-C.C-C...C-C-C.....H-A.A-A-A-A.A-A-A-A-A.A-A-A...H-H.A-A.A-A.H-G.F-F.D-
   0.35068    E-E-D-C-E-E.E-E-E.D-D-D-D-D-D...D-D-D.D-D.C-C...F-C-E-F-E-C.F-F...B-B-B.B-B-B-B-B-B.H-B.C-C.C-C...C-C-C.....H-A-A-A-A-A.A-A-A-A-A.A-A-A...H-H.A-A.A-A.H-G.F-F.D-
   0.41070    E-E-D-C-E-E.E-E-E.D-D-D-D-D-D...D-D-D.D-D.C-C...F-C-E-F-E-C.F-F-B.B-B-B.B-B-B-B-B-B.H-B.C-C-C-C-C.C-C-C-C...H-A-A-A-A-A.A-A-A-A-A.A-A-A...H-H-A-A.A-A.H-G.F-F.D-
   0.45398    E-E-D-C-E-E-E-E-E.D-D-D-D-D-D-E.D-D-D.D-D.C-C-C.F-C-E-F-E-C.F-F-B.B-B-B.B-B-B-B-B-B.H-B.C-C-C-C-C.C-C-C-C...H-A-A-A-A-A.A-A-A-A-A.A-A-A...H-H-A-A.A-A-H-G.F-F.D-
   0.50017    E-E-D-C-E-E-E-E-E.D-D-D-D-D-D-E.D-D-D-D-D.C-C-C-F-C-E-F-E-C.F-F-B.B-B-B.B-B-B-B-B-B-H-B.C-C-C-C-C.C-C-C-C-C.H-A-A-A-A-A.A-A-A-A-A.A-A-A-H.H-H-A-A.A-A-H-G.F-F.D-
   0.56092    E-E-D-C-E-E-E-E-E-D-D-D-D-D-D-E.D-D-D-D-D.C-C-C-F-C-E-F-E-C-F-F-B.B-B-B.B-B-B-B-B-B-H-B.C-C-C-C-C.C-C-C-C-C.H-A-A-A-A-A-A-A-A-A-A.A-A-A-H.H-H-A-A.A-A-H-G.F-F.D-
   0.61918    E-E-D-C-E-E-E-E-E-D-D-D-D-D-D-E.D-D-D-D-D.C-C-C-F-C-E-F-E-C-F-F-B.B-B-B.B-B-B-B-B-B-H-B.C-C-C-C-C.C-C-C-C-C.H-A-A-A-A-A-A-A-A-A-A-A-A-A-H.H-H-A-A.A-A-H-G.F-F.D-
   0.65294    E-E-D-C-E-E-E-E-E-D-D-D-D-D-D-E.D-D-D-D-D.C-C-C-F-C-E-F-E-C-F-F-B.B-B-B.B-B-B-B-B-B-H-B.C-C-C-C-C-C-C-C-C-C.H-A-A-A-A-A-A-A-A-A-A-A-A-A-H.H-H-A-A-A-A-H-G.F-F.D-
   0.70971    E-E-D-C-E-E-E-E-E-D-D-D-D-D-D-E.D-D-D-D-D-C-C-C-F-C-E-F-E-C-F-F-B.B-B-B-B-B-B-B-B-B-H-B.C-C-C-C-C-C-C-C-C-C.H-A-A-A-A-A-A-A-A-A-A-A-A-A-H.H-H-A-A-A-A-H-G.F-F.D-
   0.82196    E-E-D-C-E-E-E-E-E-D-D-D-D-D-D-E.D-D-D-D-D-C-C-C-F-C-E-F-E-C-F-F-B.B-B-B-B-B-B-B-B-B-H-B.C-C-C-C-C-C-C-C-C-C.H-A-A-A-A-A-A-A-A-A-A-A-A-A-H.H-H-A-A-A-A-H-G-F-F.D-
   0.85142    E-E-D-C-E-E-E-E-E-D-D-D-D-D-D-E-D-D-D-D-D-C-C-C-F-C-E-F-E-C-F-F-B.B-B-B-B-B-B-B-B-B-H-B.C-C-C-C-C-C-C-C-C-C.H-A-A-A-A-A-A-A-A-A-A-A-A-A-H.H-H-A-A-A-A-H-G-F-F.D-
   0.90042    E-E-D-C-E-E-E-E-E-D-D-D-D-D-D-E-D-D-D-D-D-C-C-C-F-C-E-F-E-C-F-F-B.B-B-B-B-B-B-B-B-B-H-B-C-C-C-C-C-C-C-C-C-C.H-A-A-A-A-A-A-A-A-A-A-A-A-A-H.H-H-A-A-A-A-H-G-F-F.D-
   0.91352    E-E-D-C-E-E-E-E-E-D-D-D-D-D-D-E-D-D-D-D-D-C-C-C-F-C-E-F-E-C-F-F-B.B-B-B-B-B-B-B-B-B-H-B-C-C-C-C-C-C-C-C-C-C.H-A-A-A-A-A-A-A-A-A-A-A-A-A-H.H-H-A-A-A-A-H-G-F-F.D-
   1.01395    E-E-D-C-E-E-E-E-E-D-D-D-D-D-D-E-D-D-D-D-D-C-C-C-F-C-E-F-E-C-F-F-B-B-B-B-B-B-B-B-B-B-H-B-C-C-C-C-C-C-C-C-C-C.H-A-A-A-A-A-A-A-A-A-A-A-A-A-H-H-H-A-A-A-A-H-G-F-F.D-
   1.04266    E-E-D-C-E-E-E-E-E-D-D-D-D-D-D-E-D-D-D-D-D-C-C-C-F-C-E-F-E-C-F-F-B-B-B-B-B-B-B-B-B-B-H-B-C-C-C-C-C-C-C-C-C-C-H-A-A-A-A-A-A-A-A-A-A-A-A-A-H-H-H-A-A-A-A-H-G-F-F.D-
                          1                   |     2    |    3                |         4          |       5       |          6              |            7   | 8 |

continued-------------------------------------------------------------------------
         .    7.9.1.3.4.1.1.1.1.1.5.1.3.5.9.3.6.3.7.8.2.6.4.8.1.1.7.1.1.1.1.8.1.5.4.2.2.8.1.1.1.1.1.4.7.1.1.3.1.1.1.1.6.1.1.1.1.2.6.2.6.7.2.1.1.1.1.5.3.1.1.1.7
         .    9.6.1.4.5.9.5.0.6.4.5.3.8...2.6.8.9.8.6.6.6.6.4.2.1.0.3.2.1.8.1.1.4.2.5.8.0.3.0.4.4.3.1.4.3.5.1.2.0.1.2.1.4.4.1.2.4.5.9.2.1.1.0.3.0.4.1.3.2.1.2.6
         .    ....7.......3.....1...3.......................2.3...0...6.....1...........6.9.7.8.4.....9.0...5.3...1...3.9.9.8...............2.5.4.4.....9.5.4..
   0.03265    .................................................................................................................................................
   0.05688    ..........................................................................................................G-G....................................
   0.10199    D.............................................................F-F...................................G-G...G-G....................................
   0.15117    D-D-D.....C-C.......B-B...D-D.E-D.......F-D.............F-F...F-F-F...F-F.............F-F...........G-G-G.G-G.....G-G.............G-G............
   0.20385    D-D-D.....C-C...F-F.B-B...D-D.E-D.B-B...F-D...C-H.......F-F-F.F-F-F...F-F.............F-F...........G-G-G.G-G.G-G.G-G-G.....H-H...G-G.......H-H..
   0.25029    D-D-D.E-E.C-C-C.F-F.B-B...D-D-E-D.B-B-B.F-D...C-H.......F-F-F.F-F-F...F-F-F-F...F-F...F-F.F-F.E-E...G-G-G-G-G.G-G.G-G-G.G-G.H-H...G-G...H-H.H-H..
   0.30383    D-D-D-E-E.C-C-C.F-F.B-B-B.D-D-E-D.B-B-B.F-D...C-H-B.....F-F-F-F-F-F...F-F-F-F...F-F...F-F.F-F.E-E...G-G-G-G-G.G-G.G-G-G.G-G.H-H...G-G...H-H.H-H-H
   0.35068    D-D-D-E-E.C-C-C.F-F.B-B-B.D-D-E-D.B-B-B.F-D-E.C-H-B.....F-F-F-F-F-F...F-F-F-F-F.F-F...F-F-F-F.E-E...G-G-G-G-G.G-G.G-G-G-G-G.H-H...G-G...H-H.H-H-H
   0.41070    D-D-D-E-E.C-C-C.F-F-B-B-B.D-D-E-D-B-B-B.F-D-E.C-H-B-A...F-F-F-F-F-F-F.F-F-F-F-F.F-F-F.F-F-F-F.E-E...G-G-G-G-G-G-G-G-G-G-G-G.H-H-H.G-G...H-H.H-H-H
   0.45398    D-D-D-E-E-C-C-C.F-F-B-B-B.D-D-E-D-B-B-B.F-D-E.C-H-B-A...F-F-F-F-F-F-F.F-F-F-F-F-F-F-F.F-F-F-F.E-E...G-G-G-G-G-G-G-G-G-G-G-G.H-H-H.G-G...H-H.H-H-H
   0.50017    D-D-D-E-E-C-C-C-F-F-B-B-B.D-D-E-D-B-B-B.F-D-E.C-H-B-A...F-F-F-F-F-F-F-F-F-F-F-F-F-F-F.F-F-F-F.E-E...G-G-G-G-G-G-G-G-G-G-G-G.H-H-H-G-G...H-H-H-H-H
   0.56092    D-D-D-E-E-C-C-C-F-F-B-B-B.D-D-E-D-B-B-B-F-D-E.C-H-B-A-D.F-F-F-F-F-F-F-F-F-F-F-F-F-F-F.F-F-F-F.E-E-G.G-G-G-G-G-G-G-G-G-G-G-G.H-H-H-G-G-G.H-H-H-H-H
   0.61918    D-D-D-E-E-C-C-C-F-F-B-B-B-D-D-E-D-B-B-B-F-D-E.C-H-B-A-D.F-F-F-F-F-F-F-F-F-F-F-F-F-F-F-F-F-F-F.E-E-G.G-G-G-G-G-G-G-G-G-G-G-G.H-H-H-G-G-G.H-H-H-H-H
   0.65294    D-D-D-E-E-C-C-C-F-F-B-B-B-D-D-E-D-B-B-B-F-D-E.C-H-B-A-D.F-F-F-F-F-F-F-F-F-F-F-F-F-F-F-F-F-F-F.E-E-G.G-G-G-G-G-G-G-G-G-G-G-G.H-H-H-G-G-G.H-H-H-H-H
   0.70971    D-D-D-E-E-C-C-C-F-F-B-B-B-D-D-E-D-B-B-B-F-D-E.C-H-B-A-D.F-F-F-F-F-F-F-F-F-F-F-F-F-F-F-F-F-F-F.E-E-G.G-G-G-G-G-G-G-G-G-G-G-G-H-H-H-G-G-G.H-H-H-H-H
   0.82196    D-D-D-E-E-C-C-C-F-F-B-B-B-D-D-E-D-B-B-B-F-D-E-C-H-B-A-D.F-F-F-F-F-F-F-F-F-F-F-F-F-F-F-F-F-F-F-E-E-G.G-G-G-G-G-G-G-G-G-G-G-G-H-H-H-G-G-G-H-H-H-H-H
   0.85142    D-D-D-E-E-C-C-C-F-F-B-B-B-D-D-E-D-B-B-B-F-D-E-C-H-B-A-D.F-F-F-F-F-F-F-F-F-F-F-F-F-F-F-F-F-F-F-E-E-G.G-G-G-G-G-G-G-G-G-G-G-G-H-H-H-G-G-G-H-H-H-H-H
   0.90042    D-D-D-E-E-C-C-C-F-F-B-B-B-D-D-E-D-B-B-B-F-D-E-C-H-B-A-D.F-F-F-F-F-F-F-F-F-F-F-F-F-F-F-F-F-F-F-E-E-G.G-G-G-G-G-G-G-G-G-G-G-G-H-H-H-G-G-G-H-H-H-H-H
   0.91352    D-D-D-E-E-C-C-C-F-F-B-B-B-D-D-E-D-B-B-B-F-D-E-C-H-B-A-D.F-F-F-F-F-F-F-F-F-F-F-F-F-F-F-F-F-F-F-E-E-G.G-G-G-G-G-G-G-G-G-G-G-G-H-H-H-G-G-G-H-H-H-H-H
   1.01395    D-D-D-E-E-C-C-C-F-F-B-B-B-D-D-E-D-B-B-B-F-D-E-C-H-B-A-D-F-F-F-F-F-F-F-F-F-F-F-F-F-F-F-F-F-F-F-E-E-G-G-G-G-G-G-G-G-G-G-G-G-G-H-H-H-G-G-G-H-H-H-H-H
   1.04266    D-D-D-E-E-C-C-C-F-F-B-B-B-D-D-E-D-B-B-B-F-D-E-C-H-B-A-D-F-F-F-F-F-F-F-F-F-F-F-F-F-F-F-F-F-F-F-E-E-G-G-G-G-G-G-G-G-G-G-G-G-G-H-H-H-G-G-G-H-H-H-H-H
                            9                       |     10 |             11             | 12 |             13                   |   14

A=Anatomy          C=Biological Sciences          E=Microbiology     G=Pharmacology

B=Biochemistry     D=Genetics & Development       F=Pathology        H=Physiology
```

(f) Columbia Social Sciences

```
ALL CLUSTERS FUSED -- overall maximum distance     =    0.89777
Distance     Cluster members
---------------------------------------------------------------------
         .   6.1.1.7.8.1.2.1.7.8.7.3.1.9.1.5.1.9.5.1.1.2.2.5.1.8.1.1.2.3.4.1.8.7.1.1.6.1.2.1.6.8.1.4.4.9.1.6.7.2.1.3.7.1.7.1.1.3.2.2.1.5.1.1.1.1.3.6.1.5.6.1.7.1.5.7.1.1.4.5.
         .   1.1.4.5.6.6.0.4.3.7...9.1.4.2.5.2.5.7.1.3.5...6.5.4.0.0.6.8.0.4.5.4.2.2.5.4.8.1.6.2.3.7.9.3.5...9.2.1.6.0.3.6.4.1...3.9.2.1.1.0.3.0.1.9.1.2.8.2.7.5.3.2.3.0.1.9.
         .   ..5.6.........2.............4...6.....6.3...........2.4.............0.2...4...3.....7.......2.......7.....5...0.8.......5...2.0.8.......4.....1...0.....1.1.....
   0.00628   F-F.............................................................................................................................................................
   0.05182   F-F-F-F-F-F-F-F.F-F.................................A-A.......A-A.........................................................................E-E.........E-E.......
   0.10097   F-F-F-F-F-F-F-F-F-F-F-F.......F-F.....F-F.......A-A-A-A-A.A-A.A-A-A.A-A.A-A.................................E-E.....E-E.............E-E-E.E-E...E-E...E-E...E-F.
   0.15039   F-F-F-F-F-F-F-F-F-F-F-F-F-F...F-F-F...F-F...A-A.A-A-A-A-A.A-A.A-A-A-A-A.A-A-A...........A-A.......A-A.......E-E.....E-E-E.....E-E...E-E-E-E-E-E.E-E...E-E-E.E-F-
   0.20385   F-F-F-F-F-F-F-F-F-F-F-F-F-F...F-F-F-F.F-F...A-A.A-A-A-A-A.A-A.A-A-A-A-A.A-A-A...........A-A-A.....A-A.A-A...E-E.....E-E-E.....E-E-E.E-E-E-E-E-E.E-E...E-E-E.E-F-
   0.25163   F-F-F-F-F-F-F-F-F-F-F-F-F-F-F.F-F-F-F.F-F...A-A.A-A-A-A-A-A-A.A-A-A-A-A-A-A-A.....A-A...A-A-A-A...A-A.A-A-A.E-E-E-E.E-E-E.E-E.E-E-E.E-E-E-E-E-E-E-E-E.E-E-E.E-F-
   0.30030   F-F-F-F-F-F-F-F-F-F-F-F-F-F-F-F-F-F-F.F-F...A-A-A-A-A-A-A-A-A.A-A-A-A-A-A-A-A-A...A-A-A.A-A-A-A...A-A.A-A-A.E-E-E-E.E-E-E-E-E.E-E-E.E-E-E-E-E-E-E-E-E.E-E-E.E-F-
   0.35411   F-F-F-F-F-F-F-F-F-F-F-F-F-F-F-F-F-F-F.F-F...A-A-A-A-A-A-A-A-A.A-A-A-A-A-A-A-A-A...A-A-A.A-A-A-A...A-A-A-A-A.E-E-E-E.E-E-E-E-E.E-E-E-E-E-E-E-E-E-E-E-E.E-E-E.E-F-
   0.40097   F-F-F-F-F-F-F-F-F-F-F-F-F-F-F-F-F-F-F-F-F...A-A-A-A-A-A-A-A-A-A-A-A-A-A-A-A-A-A...A-A-A.A-A-A-A-A.A-A-A-A-A.E-E-E-E.E-E-E-E-E.E-E-E-E-E-E-E-E-E-E-E-E-E-E-E.E-F-
   0.47019   F-F-F-F-F-F-F-F-F-F-F-F-F-F-F-F-F-F-F-F-F...A-A-A-A-A-A-A-A-A-A-A-A-A-A-A-A-A-A-A.A-A-A.A-A-A-A-A-A-A-A-A-A.E-E-E-E-E-E-E-E-E.E-E-E-E-E-E-E-E-E-E-E-E-E-E-E-E-F-
   0.52053   F-F-F-F-F-F-F-F-F-F-F-F-F-F-F-F-F-F-F-F-F...A-A-A-A-A-A-A-A-A-A-A-A-A-A-A-A-A-A-A-A-A-A.A-A-A-A-A-A-A-A-A-A.E-E-E-E-E-E-E-E-E.E-E-E-E-E-E-E-E-E-E-E-E-E-E-E-E-F-
   0.56585   F-F-F-F-F-F-F-F-F-F-F-F-F-F-F-F-F-F-F-F-F-F.A-A-A-A-A-A-A-A-A-A-A-A-A-A-A-A-A-A-A-A-A-A.A-A-A-A-A-A-A-A-A-A.E-E-E-E-E-E-E-E-E.E-E-E-E-E-E-E-E-E-E-E-E-E-E-E-E-F-
   0.62000   F-F-F-F-F-F-F-F-F-F-F-F-F-F-F-F-F-F-F-F-F-F.A-A-A-A-A-A-A-A-A-A-A-A-A-A-A-A-A-A-A-A-A-A.A-A-A-A-A-A-A-A-A-A.E-E-E-E-E-E-E-E-E.E-E-E-E-E-E-E-E-E-E-E-E-E-E-E-E-F-
   0.69913   F-F-F-F-F-F-F-F-F-F-F-F-F-F-F-F-F-F-F-F-F-F.A-A-A-A-A-A-A-A-A-A-A-A-A-A-A-A-A-A-A-A-A-A-A-A-A-A-A-A-A-A-A-A.E-E-E-E-E-E-E-E-E-E-E-E-E-E-E-E-E-E-E-E-E-E-E-E-E-F-
   0.73738   F-F-F-F-F-F-F-F-F-F-F-F-F-F-F-F-F-F-F-F-F-F.A-A-A-A-A-A-A-A-A-A-A-A-A-A-A-A-A-A-A-A-A-A-A-A-A-A-A-A-A-A-A-A.E-E-E-E-E-E-E-E-E-E-E-E-E-E-E-E-E-E-E-E-E-E-E-E-E-F-
   0.78230   F-F-F-F-F-F-F-F-F-F-F-F-F-F-F-F-F-F-F-F-F-F.A-A-A-A-A-A-A-A-A-A-A-A-A-A-A-A-A-A-A-A-A-A-A-A-A-A-A-A-A-A-A-A.E-E-E-E-E-E-E-E-E-E-E-E-E-E-E-E-E-E-E-E-E-E-E-E-E-F-
   0.83317   F-F-F-F-F-F-F-F-F-F-F-F-F-F-F-F-F-F-F-F-F-F-A-A-A-A-A-A-A-A-A-A-A-A-A-A-A-A-A-A-A-A-A-A-A-A-A-A-A-A-A-A-A-A.E-E-E-E-E-E-E-E-E-E-E-E-E-E-E-E-E-E-E-E-E-E-E-E-E-F-
   0.86630   F-F-F-F-F-F-F-F-F-F-F-F-F-F-F-F-F-F-F-F-F-F-A-A-A-A-A-A-A-A-A-A-A-A-A-A-A-A-A-A-A-A-A-A-A-A-A-A-A-A-A-A-A-A-E-E-E-E-E-E-E-E-E-E-E-E-E-E-E-E-E-E-E-E-E-E-E-E-E-F-
                                      1                 |                                2                              |                                      3

continued------------------------------------------------------------------
         .   4.4.6.1.1.5.1.8.9.1.1.1.9.9.5.1.2.3.4.1.5.8.6.9.1.3.1.3.1.1.1.1.9.2.6.1.7.9.1.4.1.1.1.1.1.8.3.4.1.1.8.1.1.1.1.1.1.8.1.4.1.9.1.5.7.1.3.3.6.1.1.8.1.2.6.9.4
         .   5.3.3.2.5.4.0.3.1.3.2.5.6.7...7.1.5.4.3.8...0...1.7.5.2.0.3.4.2.2.7.4.3.8.0.3.8.2.4.5.5.5.9.0.2.4...0.9.4.8.0.1.1.8.4.6.0.9.0.0.1.2.3.4.7.0.4.1.3.4.2.8..
         .   ......3.4...6.....6.7.3.........................0...7...7.2.7.........9.....4...8.9.6.1.5.......5.......1...8.9.1...8...9...3.....9.......5.3...0........
   0.00628   .........................................................................................................................................................
   0.05182   ......................................................................................................B-B...B-B-B........................................
   0.10097   ......E-E.E-E-E-E...E-E...............G-G.....................G-G...G-G.G-G...G-G.G-G.............B-B.B-B-B-B-B-B.B-B.B-B-B-B...B-B...............B-B....
   0.15039   E.B-E.E-E.E-E-E-E-E-E-E.B-G...E-F.G-G.G-G-G...G-A.G-G.........G-G-G.G-G-G-G...G-G-G-G.G-G.........B-B-B-B-B-B-B-B-B-B.B-B-B-B...B-B.B-B.B-B...B-B.B-B....
   0.20385   E.B-E-E-E.E-E-E-E-E-E-E.B-G...E-F.G-G.G-G-G-G.G-A.G-G-F.G-G...G-G-G.G-G-G-G-G.G-G-G-G.G-G...G-G...B-B-B-B-B-B-B-B-B-B.B-B-B-B-B.B-B.B-B.B-B...B-B.B-B-B..
   0.25163   E.B-E-E-E-E-E-E-E-E-E-E.B-G-A.E-F-G-G.G-G-G-G.G-A.G-G-F.G-G...G-G-G.G-G-G-G-G.G-G-G-G.G-G-G.G-G...B-B-B-B-B-B-B-B-B-B-B-B-B-B-B.B-B.B-B-B-B...B-B.B-B-B..
   0.30030   E-B-E-E-E-E-E-E-E-E-E-E.B-G-A.E-F-G-G.G-G-G-G-G-A-G-G-F.G-G...G-G-G-G-G-G-G-G-G-G-G-G.G-G-G.G-G...B-B-B-B-B-B-B-B-B-B-B-B-B-B-B.B-B.B-B-B-B...B-B.B-B-B..
   0.35411   E-B-E-E-E-E-E-E-E-E-E-E.B-G-A-E-F-G-G.G-G-G-G-G-A-G-G-F.G-G...G-G-G-G-G-G-G-G-G-G-G-G.G-G-G.G-G...B-B-B-B-B-B-B-B-B-B-B-B-B-B-B.B-B.B-B-B-B-B.B-B.B-B-B-B
   0.40097   E-B-E-E-E-E-E-E-E-E-E-E.B-G-A-E-F-G-G.G-G-G-G-G-A-G-G-F.G-G...G-G-G-G-G-G-G-G-G-G-G-G.G-G-G.G-G-E.B-B-B-B-B-B-B-B-B-B-B-B-B-B-B-B-B.B-B-B-B-B.B-B.B-B-B-B
   0.47019   E-B-E-E-E-E-E-E-E-E-E-E.B-G-A-E-F-G-G.G-G-G-G-G-A-G-G-F-G-G...G-G-G-G-G-G-G-G-G-G-G-G.G-G-G.G-G-E.B-B-B-B-B-B-B-B-B-B-B-B-B-B-B-B-B.B-B-B-B-B.B-B.B-B-B-B
   0.52053   E-B-E-E-E-E-E-E-E-E-E-E.B-G-A-E-F-G-G.G-G-G-G-G-A-G-G-F-G-G...G-G-G-G-G-G-G-G-G-G-G-G-G-G-G.G-G-E.B-B-B-B-B-B-B-B-B-B-B-B-B-B-B-B-B-B-B-B-B-B-B-B.B-B-B-B
   0.56585   E-B-E-E-E-E-E-E-E-E-E-E.B-G-A-E-F-G-G.G-G-G-G-G-A-G-G-F-G-G-B.G-G-G-G-G-G-G-G-G-G-G-G-G-G-G.G-G-E.B-B-B-B-B-B-B-B-B-B-B-B-B-B-B-B-B-B-B-B-B-B-B-B.B-B-B-B
   0.62000   E-B-E-E-E-E-E-E-E-E-E-E.B-G-A-E-F-G-G-G-G-G-G-G-A-G-G-F-G-G-B.G-G-G-G-G-G-G-G-G-G-G-G-G-G-G-G-G-E.B-B-B-B-B-B-B-B-B-B-B-B-B-B-B-B-B-B-B-B-B-B-B-B-B-B-B-B
   0.69913   E-B-E-E-E-E-E-E-E-E-E-E.B-G-A-E-F-G-G-G-G-G-G-G-A-G-G-F-G-G-B.G-G-G-G-G-G-G-G-G-G-G-G-G-G-G-G-G-E.B-B-B-B-B-B-B-B-B-B-B-B-B-B-B-B-B-B-B-B-B-B-B-B-B-B-B-B
   0.73738   E-B-E-E-E-E-E-E-E-E-E-E-B-G-A-E-F-G-G-G-G-G-G-G-A-G-G-F-G-G-B.G-G-G-G-G-G-G-G-G-G-G-G-G-G-G-G-G-E.B-B-B-B-B-B-B-B-B-B-B-B-B-B-B-B-B-B-B-B-B-B-B-B-B-B-B-B
   0.78230   E-B-E-E-E-E-E-E-E-E-E-E-B-G-A-E-F-G-G-G-G-G-G-G-A-G-G-F-G-G-B-G-G-G-G-G-G-G-G-G-G-G-G-G-G-G-G-G-E.B-B-B-B-B-B-B-B-B-B-B-B-B-B-B-B-B-B-B-B-B-B-B-B-B-B-B-B
   0.83317   E-B-E-E-E-E-E-E-E-E-E-E-B-G-A-E-F-G-G-G-G-G-G-G-A-G-G-F-G-G-B-G-G-G-G-G-G-G-G-G-G-G-G-G-G-G-G-G-E.B-B-B-B-B-B-B-B-B-B-B-B-B-B-B-B-B-B-B-B-B-B-B-B-B-B-B-B
   0.86630   E-B-E-E-E-E-E-E-E-E-E-E-B-G-A-E-F-G-G-G-G-G-G-G-A-G-G-F-G-G-B-G-G-G-G-G-G-G-G-G-G-G-G-G-G-G-G-G-E.B-B-B-B-B-B-B-B-B-B-B-B-B-B-B-B-B-B-B-B-B-B-B-B-B-B-B-B

                                    |                  4                  |                    5              |                              6
```

A=Anthropology **E=Political Science** **G=Sociology**

B=Economics **F=Psychology**

Table 7.3. *Departmental Affiliation of the Actors in Each Position-Cluster*

The University of Chicago	Columbia University
Physical Sciences:	*Physical Sciences:*
Cluster 1 Statistics (8)	Cluster 1 Geological Sciences (20)
Cluster 2 Mathematics, Statistics (19)	Cluster 2 Geological Sciences (2)
Cluster 3 Mathematics, Statistics (6)	Cluster 3 Astronomy (6)
Cluster 4 Mathematics (6)	Cluster 4 Physics (28)
Cluster 5 Chemistry, Physics (18)	Cluster 5 Mathematics, Statistics (19)
Cluster 6 Physics, Astrophysics (39)	Cluster 6 Statistics (6)
Cluster 7 Astronomy & Astrophysics (9)	Cluster 7 Chemistry (24)
Cluster 8 Chemistry (10)	
Cluster 9 Chemistry (6)	*Biological Sciences:*
Cluster 10 Geophysical Sciences (20)	Cluster 1 Genetics & Development, Microbiology (16)
Biological Sciences:	Cluster 2 Genetics & Development (5)
Cluster 1 Biology, Microbiology, Biochemistry, Biophysics (42)	Cluster 3 Biological Sciences, Microbiology, Pathology (12)
Cluster 2 Biochemistry, Biophysics (14)	Cluster 4 Biochemistry (11)
Cluster 3 Biophysics, Pharmacology & Physiology (16)	Cluster 5 Biological Sciences (10)
Cluster 4 Pathology (30)	Cluster 6 Anatomy, Physiology (15)
Cluster 5 Pharmacology & Physiology (10)	Cluster 7 Anatomy, Physiology (8)
Cluster 6 Biology, Biophysics (16)	Cluster 8 Pathology (2)
Cluster 7 Anatomy, Pharmacology & Physiology (14)	Cluster 9 Biochemistry, Biological Sciences, Genetics & Development, Microbiology, Pathology (24)
Social Sciences:	Cluster 10 (5 faculty from different disciplines)
Cluster 1 Economics (21)	Cluster 11 Pathology (11)
Cluster 2 Anthropology (27)	Cluster 12 Microbiology (3)
Cluster 3 Economics, Education, Political Science, Sociology (47)	Cluster 13 Pharmacology, Physiology (18)
Cluster 4 Behavioral Science, Geography, Sociology (11)	Cluster 14 Physiology (5)
Cluster 5 Behavioral Science, Education (35)	*Social Sciences:*
Cluster 6 Behavioral Science (12)	Cluster 1 Psychology (22)
	Cluster 2 Anthropology (32)
	Cluster 3 Political Science (38)
	Cluster 4 Anthropology, Economics, Psychology, Sociology (19)
	Cluster 5 Sociology (18)
	Cluster 6 Economics (28)

Note: The size of a cluster is reported in the parentheses; all primary departmental affiliations are reported which are held by at least two members of a cluster.

the derived social distance is related to measures of individual difference (dis-equivalence) on a variety of social relations.[5]

5 The measure of social distance is derived from several of these networks; however, the derivation involves numerous mathematical steps. Hence, it is worthwhile to directly assess the association between actors' social distance and their structural equivalence in these concrete social relations.

Figure 7.2. Likelihood of collaboration and social distance.

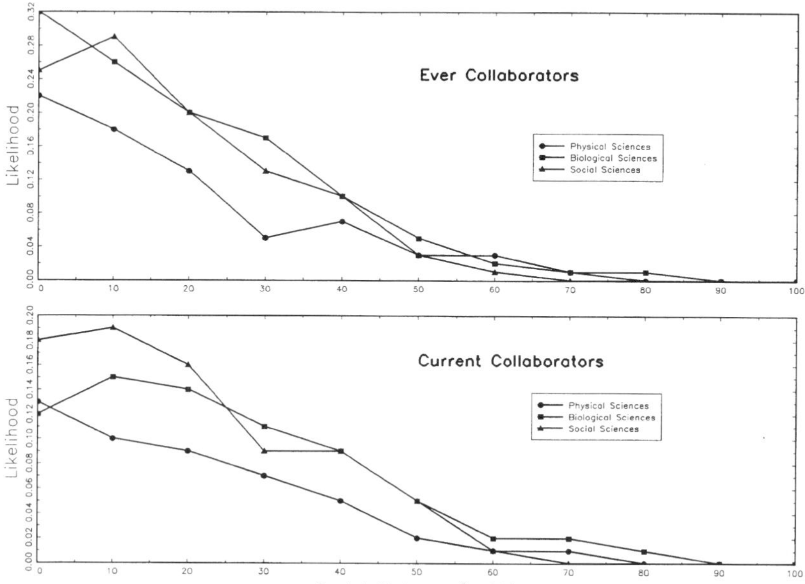

The measure of dis-equivalence is Eq. (7.1), which was used to assess the profile similarities of interpersonal influences, except that now I substitute a binary relation for the interpersonal influences. Table 7.4 shows that as the social distance between two faculty members increases, so does the extent to which they (a) have read or heard the work of different faculty members or have had their work read or heard by different faculty members, (b) have conversed with different faculty members about their work or have discussed their work with different faculty members, and (c) are aware of the work of different faculty members or have their work known by different faculty members. Hence, these data indicate that the derived social distances among these actors are associated with individual differences in their pattern of concrete social relations.

7.3 Social Manifolds and Social Differentiation

In the analysis that I have presented thus far, objects in multidimensional social space are defined that contain social positions, such that no two social positions within the boundaries of the object are more than a

Figure 7.3. Likelihood of conversation about research and social distance.

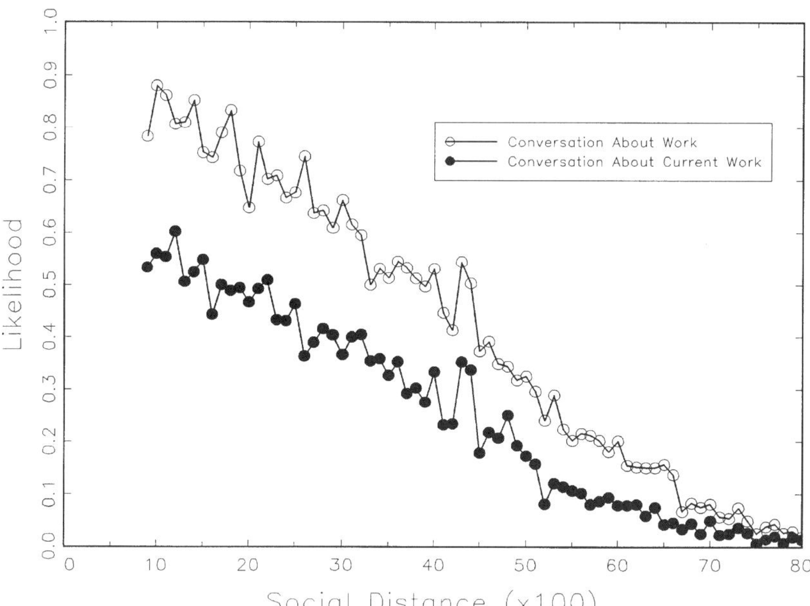

prescribed distance apart. In a two-dimensional social space, such objects would be represented by circles and the prescribed distance would be the diameter of the circle. In a three-dimensional space, such objects would be spheres. In four or more dimensions, although we cannot visualize an object, we can easily form clusters of social positions in which no distance between two members is greater than some value. When we do that, we are describing a type of *social manifold* in multidimensional space.

Social manifolds may be defined on the basis of criteria other than the "complete linkage" or "diameter" criterion that I have employed in the hierarchical cluster analysis (Table 7.2). A hierarchical cluster analysis is useful for describing clusters of proximate social positions, i.e., "occupied regions" in multidimensional space in which multiple social positions are located, and for revealing "holes" or cleavages in the space where relatively large distances separate a particular "occupied region" and the nearest other "occupied region" in the space. However, hierarchical cluster analysis does not provide a clear image of the macrostructure of social positions except in special cases. For instance, we

Figure 7.4. Likelihood of reading or attending a presentation of work and social distance.

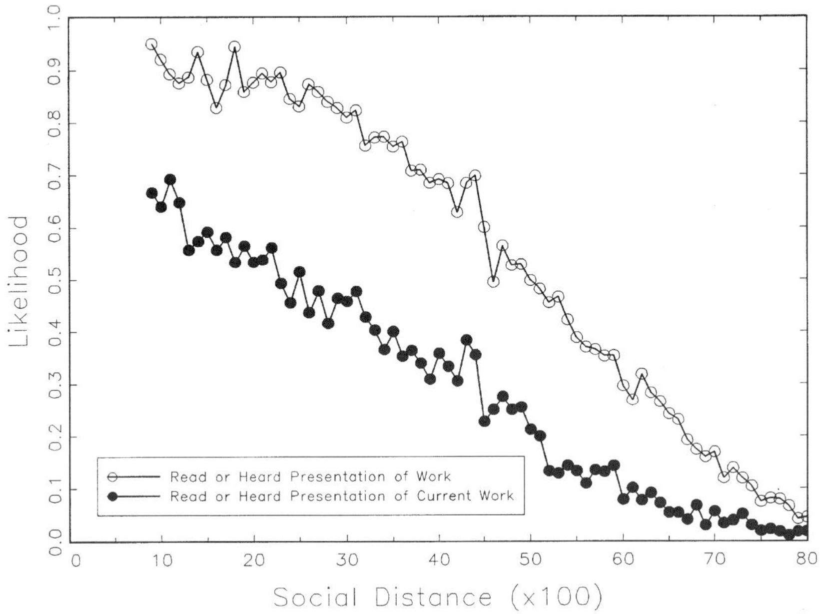

would not know directly from a hierarchical cluster analysis whether a multidimensional "Milky Way" exists that contains most of the social positions. A treatment of the organization of social space is begun in the next chapter and carried forward in Chapter 9.

7.4 Concluding Remarks

The university, academic department, discipline, and specialty are affiliations that differentiate scientists in important ways. Many other factors enter into the determination of scientists' exact social positions (and, in turn, their predisposition on issues); hence, scientists in the same university, department, and area of specialization do not necessarily occupy identical social positions and may not have identical opinions on issues. However, these several affiliations are key conditions of scientists' social environment; therefore, it should be the case that the social distance between scientists is associated with the likelihood of shared status on these conditions.

In the present chapter, I have described an approach to social positions

Figure 7.5. Likelihood of interpersonal visibility and social distance.

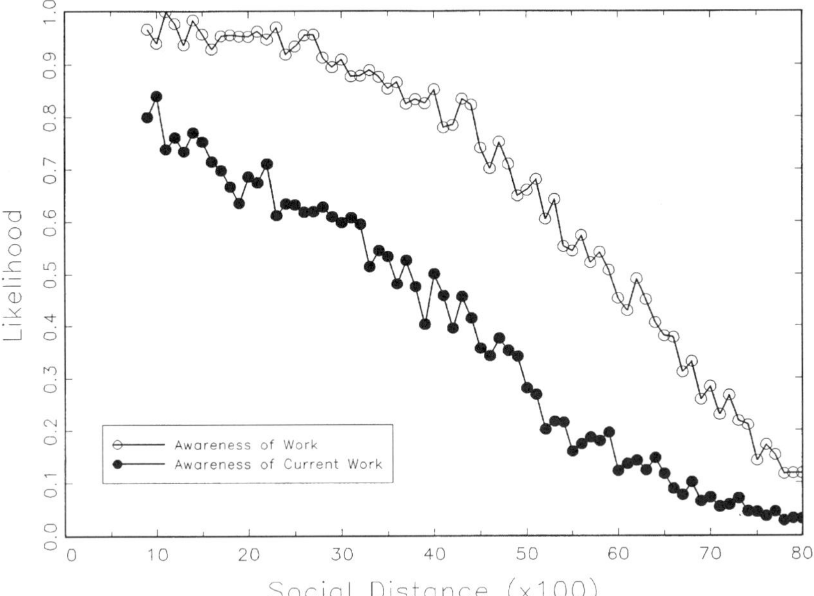

that assumes that actors' structural equivalence in the network of endogenous interpersonal influences (**W**) is associated with profile similarity on the exogenous variables that determine their initial opinions (**X**). I have supported the construct validity of the derived social positions by showing that the social distance among actors is strongly associated with the likelihood of shared affiliations and individual differences in the pattern of social ties. Taken together these associations support the viewpoint that the derived social distances indicate the expected differences of initial opinion among the actors and, assuming that this viewpoint is correct, I equate the initial opinions of actors, $\mathbf{Y}^{(1)} = [y_{ik}^{(1)}]$, with the coordinates of their positions in social space.

The third and last pillar of my approach to the social influence process is now in place. The parameterization of the theory is complete given the structural measures of actors' social positions (initial opinions) and interpersonal influences $\{\mathbf{A}, \mathbf{W}, \mathbf{Y}^{(1)}\}$. This approach to describing social positions, like the blockmodel approach described in Chapter 1, provides an image of social differentiation in which both the social distance and interrelations among social positions are represented. However, unlike the blockmodel approach, which describes interpositional bonds in terms of the density of social ties, the present approach describes these bonds

Table 7.4. *Correlation of Social Distance and Forms of Dis-Equivalence in Dyads*

	The University of Chicago			Columbia University		
Social relational basis of dis-equivalence	Physical Sciences	Biological Sciences	Social Sciences	Physical Sciences	Biological Sciences	Social Sciences
Actor *i* knows something of actor *j*'s work	0.927	0.793	0.886	0.903	0.761	0.890
Actor *i* knows something of actor *j*'s current work	0.934	0.857	0.908	0.945	0.818	0.913
Actor *i* has read or heard actor *j* present his or her work	0.852	0.777	0.865	0.906	0.770	0.860
Actor *i* has read or heard actor *j* present his or her current work	0.805	0.722	0.724	0.898	0.714	0.823
Actor *i* has talked with actor *j* about *j*'s work	0.735	0.658	0.617	0.839	0.710	0.744
Actor *i* has talked with actor *j* about *j*'s current work	0.621	0.661	0.611	0.852	0.677	0.738

Note: These findings are based on dyads in which both members are respondents.

in terms of the network of interpersonal influence that connects the actors in different positions. Depending on the influence network in which actors are situated, their social positions may or may not strongly constrain their equilibrium opinions on issues; that is, although a social position determines the *initial* opinions of the position's occupants, these actors' equilibrium opinions may have been influenced by actors who are located in positions of the social space that are distant from their own. Hence, the revealed structure of social positions and interpersonal influences is the *start point* for an analysis of the implications of the structure – it is the context in which the social influence process is played out – and we must attend to the effects of the influence process to grasp how actors' settled positions on issues have been produced and how different actors, and their social positions, have contributed to these outcomes.

The systemic implications of the social influence process can be analyzed in terms of the influence process

$$\mathbf{Y}^{(t)} = \mathbf{AWY}^{(t-1)} + (\mathbf{I} - \mathbf{A})\mathbf{Y}^{(1)}$$

for $t = 2, 3, \ldots, \infty$, which was described in Eq. (2.2.) The consequence of the opinion-formation process will be to "move" the positions of individual actors to different locations in the K-dimensional space that defines the locations of these positions. Each of the subsequent opinions held by the actors, $\mathbf{Y}^{(2)}, \mathbf{Y}^{(3)}, \ldots, \mathbf{Y}^{(\infty)}$ will be locations in the multidimensional space that is defined by $\mathbf{Y}^{(1)}$, because all these opinions must lie in the convex hull of initial opinions. Thus, it becomes possible to track and analyze the predicted movements of actors and to locate their final destinations. The final destinations of actors may be situated on or near one or more of the initial positions of the actors, or they may be compromise positions. Interpersonal agreements and effects (based on flows of influence) arise as systemic implications of this process. These matters are pursued in Chapters 9 and 10, after I describe the macro-structure of interpersonal attachments in the faculties of science.

Part C

Analysis

8

The Structure of Social Space

Abstract: The distribution of actors in social space governs the probability of interpersonal attachments which, in turn, governs the distribution of interpersonal influence. To describe the structure of social space, I develop the concept of ridge structure, which is an object in social space comprised of sequentially overlapping and densely occupied regions of social space. Because the probability of an interpersonal attachment increases with the proximity of actors in social space, a ridge structure is associated with sequentially intersecting cohesive subsets of actors. In this chapter, I support the concept of ridge structure with both theoretical and empirical results.

In this chapter I will describe the network of interpersonal attachments in each faculty of science.[1] The macro-structure of attachments allows flows of interpersonal influence to penetrate into more or less distant regions of a social space and to accumulate so that certain actors come to have a substantial effect on system outcomes. I will argue that bridges typically do not provide the most important foundations of such reachability and impact. To describe the more typical foundations of reachability and interpersonal influence in complexly differentiated social spaces, I develop the concept of *ridge structure*. A ridge structure is an object in social space (i.e., a type of social manifold) consisting of sequentially overlapping and densely occupied regions of social space. Because the probability of an interpersonal attachment increases with the proximity of actors in social space, ridge structures produce sequentially intersecting cohesive subsets of actors. In a ridge structure, each actor is embedded in a cohesive environment of interpersonal attachments which has, in turn, two consequences. First, the mean indegree of actors is high so that most self-weights are low and influence processes can lead to agreements. Second, structural connectivity is established on a robust basis so that the cessation of particular attachments and the death and

1 This network – visibilities of role-performance based on direct engagements in conversations, reading, and presentations of research – is defined in Eq. (5.4).

mobility of individuals do not substantially alter the net effects of social positions.

First, I will point to previous literature (especially balance theory) in which the idea of a ridge structure has appeared; I show that transitivity implies a ridge structure among cliques and a macro-structure of attachments in which each clique corresponds to a social position occupied by structurally equivalent actors. Second, in the faculties of science at Chicago and Columbia, I show that ridge structures exist that connect actors who are located in distant social positions. I show that, although bridging ties can be important in linking actors who are located in different ridge structures, the more robust basis of macro-level connectivity is a ridge structure that penetrates into various areas of social space and that includes a relatively large fraction of the population of actors.

8.1 Segregated Structures, Ridge Structures, and Bridges

It is an axiom of structural analysis that the probability of a social tie is negatively associated with the distance between the positions of actors in social space (Laumann and Knoke 1986; Blau 1994). I have documented such associations in the previous chapter. The association between interpersonal attachment and social distance has certain implications for the overall pattern of attachments in a population and, in turn, the structure of interpersonal influences.

8.1.1 Bridges in Segregated Structures

If the distance between each social position is sufficiently large, then nearly all of the ties will occur among those actors who occupy the same positions, and only a few ties will span the boundaries of these subgroup formations. When interpositional ties are rare, each such tie is likely to be a *local bridge* (i.e., a tie between two actors who are not joined by any semipaths of length two).[2] More generally, where social positions

2 Granovetter (1973) develops the concept of local bridge. Unlike a bridge, when a local bridge is removed from a network the members of the local bridge (and their contacts) remain joined in the network. The "degree" of a local bridge is the length of the shortest path that joins the members of a local bridge, were the local bridge removed from the network. Granovetter points out that as the degree of a local bridge increases, bridges and local bridges may tend to become equivalent in terms of their roles in networks; for example, influence will not tend to flow over very long paths, so that a local bridge of high degree or a bridge may be the only effective channel of such flow

are segregated into distant regions of the social space, and where the social positions within each of these regions are in close proximity, the expected macro-structure is a set of subgroup formations or, more precisely, position-clusters that are connected (if at all) by a small number of bridges, as shown in Figure 8.1.

Granovetter (1973) argues that the bridges between such subgroups (position-clusters) are likely to be weaker ties than those within the subgroup formations. Suppose that the *strength* of an interpersonal attachment is equated with the proximity of the attached actors in social space and, therefore, with the probability of the attachment under the conditions that have defined the social space. With this definition, an anomalous situation is generated by a strong local bridge if either actor who is involved in the bridge has at least one other strong attachment. Assume that actor i is strongly tied to actor j on a local bridge and that j also is strongly tied to some other actor k. This implies that the social distances between i, j, and k are small, and that i is likely to be tied to k. But if the likely tie from i to k occurs, then the tie from i to j is not a local bridge. Thus, ties that are not strong (i.e., ties between actors who occupy distant positions in social space), because they do not entail such an anomalous closure, are more likely to be bridges.[3]

8.1.2 Ridge Structures

Drawing on balance theory, and specifically the tendency to transitive closure, Granovetter (1973) argues that segregated macro-structures are to be expected and that, therefore, bridging ties are theoretically important phenomena – the key structural foundations of connectivity in differentiated populations. I now develop an argument that a segregated macro-structure is a special case of a broader class of macro-structures – ridge structures – and that in many of the macro-structures that belong to this broader class, bridges do not provide the key structural foundations of macro-level connectivity.

To introduce the idea of a ridge structure, consider a contour map of a mountain range on which lines are drawn that connect points on the

between two persons and their direct contacts. Local bridges have a minimum degree, which is three; thus, directly joined dyads with one or more common contacts (paths of length two) are not local bridges.

3 If the strength or weakness of a tie is based on criteria other than the probability of its occurrence, then strong bridges are not entirely precluded (Friedkin 1982, p. 285). The importance of local bridges is the connectivity they provide between different parts of the macro-structure. This is most clear in a formal hierarchy of authority composed of strong interpersonal ties; in such a macro-structure every interpersonal tie is a strong bridge.

Figure 8.1. Segregated macro-structure.

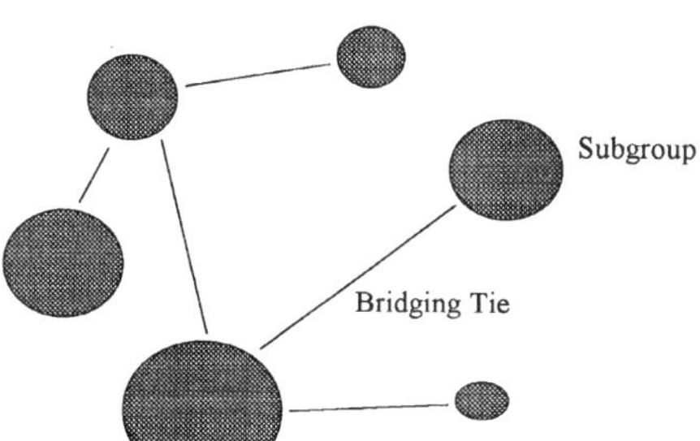

land surface that are at a certain elevation. Setting the elevation of the contour lines sufficiently high will serve to reveal the mountain peaks, but will provide a poor visualization of the overall structure of the mountain range. If we set the elevation of the contour lines somewhat lower, we may reveal a structure of elevated ridges along which we can traverse (trace a contour line) and move between distant points in the mountain range. These *ridge structures* may entail more or less steep negative gradients, and where these gradients are sufficiently steep, we can conceptualize the areas between the ridges as *gaps* or *holes*. Any phenomenon that spans such gaps (e.g., a bridge, an agreement) is a *boundary-spanning* phenomenon. A local bridge may connect different ridge structures or connect parts of the same ridge structure, but it does not constitute the structure.

Now if the *elevation* of a pair of actors is defined in terms of their proximity in social space, then a social structure may be described in terms of the high-elevation (highly proximate) subgroup formations that occur in a population. By the same token, a high-elevation *ridge structure* also may occur in which actors in different parts of the social structure are connected by one or more chains of sequentially overlapping, densely occupied, regions of social space. Such a high-elevation ridge structure is based on the same structural foundations as the "peaks" that occur in this structure – high levels of proximity in social space and probabilities of interpersonal attachment.

Social differentiation simultaneously establishes both "peaks" and "ridges," and it is the configuration of the "ridge" structure that I take to be a key (frequently occurring) foundation for the development of shared agreements between actors who are located in different parts of complexly differentiated social structures. A ridge structure is a type of social manifold (i.e., an object in social space) consisting of sequentially overlapping, densely occupied regions of social space. Because the probability of an interpersonal attachment increases with the proximity of actors in social space, ridge structures are associated with a framework of sequentially contiguous zones (overlapping neighborhoods or intersecting social circles) of structural cohesion. The framework of interpersonal attachments governs the distribution of interpersonal influence, and it is the structure of this framework that determines the relative influence of social positions. In this view, social differentiation does not simply engender cohesive subgroup formations; the concept of discrete, cohesive subgroups is an oversimplification that I discard and replace with the more general concept of *ridge structures*.[4]

8.2 Blockmodels, Link-Pin Organizations, and Social Circles

The concept of ridge structure has appeared previously in the literature in different guises. I now pull this related work together and show how different theoretical analyses have entertained the idea of a ridge structure. This related work includes White, Boorman, and Breiger's (1976) concept of a blockmodel, Likert's (1961) analysis of "linking pins," Alba and Kadushin's (1976) concept of "social circles," and generalizations of Cartwright and Harary's (1956) balance theory.

8.2.1 Ridge Structures and Blockmodels

I introduced the concept of a blockmodel in Chapter 1. A blockmodel is an image of the macro-structure of a social network in which the points are social positions (or position-clusters) and the lines are defined on the basis of the density (or average value) of the network ties among either the occupants of the same social position or two different social positions. Let $\mathbf{M} = [m_{ij}]$ be a valued network, where m_{ij} is the value of the line $(i \xrightarrow{m_{ij}} j)$ from actor i to actor j. When the actors are partitioned into position-clusters, the macro-structure of the social relation $\mathbf{M}$ can be described by a $k \times k$ blockmodel, $\mathbf{M}^* = [m^*_{ij}]$, where k is the number of distinct social positions (position-clusters), and m^*_{ij} is the mean value of the social relation $\mathbf{M}$ among actors in the same position-cluster (for $i = j$) or between actors in two different position-clusters (for $i \neq j$). From $\mathbf{M}^*$, a simplified image of the blockmodel can be developed, that is,

4 Ridge structures include as special cases the occurrence of disconnected internally cohesive subgroups and segmented structures in which such subgroups are connected by bridging ties. In these cases, the ridges are the subgroups themselves.

$\hat{\mathbf{M}}^* = [\hat{m}^*_{ij}]$, in which the adjacency of social positions is defined in terms of a threshold value of m^*_{ij}:

$$\hat{m}^*_{ij} = \begin{cases} 1 \; if \; m^*_{ij} > e \\ 0 \; if \; m^*_{ij} \leq e \end{cases} \tag{8.1}$$

For example, if **M** is an adjacency matrix (i.e., m_{ij} has the value of zero or one), then blockmodel image $\hat{\mathbf{M}}^*$ indicates which of the network densities within and between position-clusters are above the threshold value *e:* If the threshold is $e > 0$, then a line will exist in the image given at least one line in **M** from a member of position *i* to a member of position *j* (the so-called zeroblock criterion); and if the threshold is sufficiently close to 1, then a line will exist in the image only if there is a line in **M** from each of the members of position *i* to all of the members of position *j* (the so-called oneblock criterion). Typically, when **M*** is a density matrix, a framework of linkages or bonds between social positions is obtained by setting the threshold density to an intermediate value between zero and one. However, if the actors in the position-cluster are structurally equivalent in **M,** then the density of ties within and between the position-clusters must be either zero or one.

Consider a population of actors that is partitioned into social positions in which actors *i* and *j* ($i \neq j$) jointly occupy a social position only if they are structurally equivalent, where structural equivalence requires identical profiles of sent and received ties on a social relation, $\mathbf{M} = [m_{ij}]$, i.e.,

$$m_{ii} = m_{jj} \qquad m_{ij} = m_{ji} \qquad m_{ik} = m_{jk} \qquad and \qquad m_{ki} = m_{kj} \tag{8.2}$$

for all $k \neq i, j$. In such a population, a blockmodel image of the macro-structure of the social relation can be constructed on a zeroblock or oneblock criterion with the same result, because the densities of ties within and between social positions will be either zero or one. The existence of a tie between two actors *i* and *j* also implies the existence of a tie to actor *j* from all the actors who are structurally equivalent to *i;* and since actor *j* has received a tie, all actors who are structurally equivalent to *j* must also receive a tie from *i;* and so forth. Hence, to the extent that the actors within a set of empirically defined position-clusters are structurally equivalent on a social relation, the densities within and between such position-clusters should be close either to one or zero.[5]

In short, a *ridge structure* of social ties is entailed in a macro-structure

5 Similarly, with respect to a valued social relation, the variance of the values on the lines should be zero for each subset of lines within and between positions containing structurally equivalent actors.

that consists of social positions in which the joint occupants of each social position are structurally equivalent on the social relation.[6] All of the social ties might be within social positions, or there might be a framework of dense social positions and interfaces between certain positions. A social position within which the density of ties is zero is not precluded. However, zero-density positions are exceedingly unlikely; if the probability of a social tie increases as the social distance between two actors declines, then a jointly occupied social position is likely to be dense.

If there are no jointly occupied positions in social space, then a position-cluster that is defined in such a space will consist of more or less structurally equivalent actors. In this case, it cannot be assumed that a valued line from an actor in position-cluster *A* to an actor in position-cluster *B* implies lines with an identical value from all actors in *A* to all actors in *B*. However, to the extent that actors are proximal in social space, the pattern of their ties will be similar.

8.2.2 "Linking Pins" in Formal Hierarchies

The concept of a ridge structure also appears in the classic work of Likert (1961), as part of an analysis of authority hierarchies in organizations. This work is especially noteworthy because Likert argued, in effect, that ridge structures are crucial to the coordination of organizational activities (which also is my argument).

Consider a formal hierarchy of authority (a tree) in which each member has only one immediate supervisor and in which ties of interpersonal communication and influence are restricted to the lines of formal authority. Such a network is unipathic, i.e., there is only one path (or semipath) connecting each pair of actors. The pairs of actors who are in direct contact have no shared contacts. The actors who are not in direct contact have either one shared contact (an intervening supervisor) or none at all. Each tie is a *bridge* and every supervisor is a *liaison* (cut point). Severing a tie between any two actors or removing a supervisor disconnects the network.

Linking Pins. Likert (1961) argued that in effective organizations this hierarchical arrangement is modified in two ways. First, interpersonal influences are symmetric rather than anti-symmetric. Although the influ-

6 Whether the macro-structure of the population can be condensed into a *simple* image of the ridge structure depends on the number of distinct social positions in the population. To the extent that a large population is partitioned into a small number of distinct social positions, a simplified image of the macro-structure is possible. Moreover, given information on the number of occupants of each social position, the blockmodel image is a complete representation of the network of social ties.

Figure 8.2. Likert's linking pin organization.

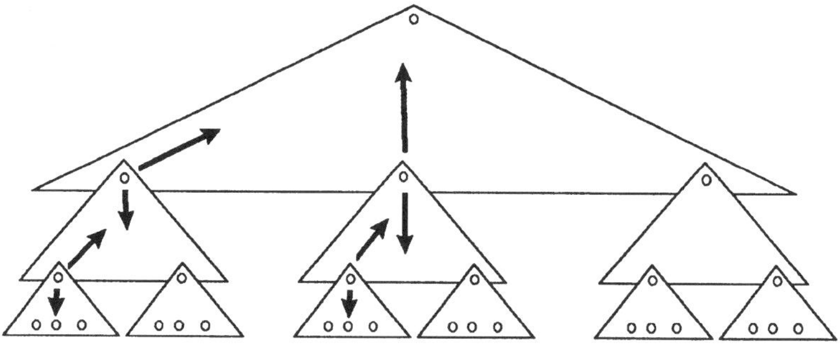

(The arrows indicate the linking pin function)

ences between a supervisor and subordinate may be markedly unbalanced in favor of the supervisor, in effective organizations subordinates usually have some influence on their immediate supervisors. Because of the hierarchical arrangement of authority, all supervisors (except for the supreme authority) are also subordinates. Likert argued that the effectiveness of supervisors depends on their ability to influence their immediate supervisors: "Subordinates expect their supervisors to be able to exercise an influence upward in dealing with problems on the job and in handling problems which affect them and their well-being" (p. 113).

Hence, effective organizations tend to be ones in which influences between subordinates and supervisors are mutual. Second, effective organizations entail additional lines of influential communication among the immediate subordinates of each supervisor. Likert states:

> Effective groups with high group loyalty are characterized by efficient and full communication and by the fact that their members respect each other, welcome attempts by the other members to influence them, and are influenced in their thinking and behavior when they believe that the evidence submitted by the other members warrants it. (1961, p. 114)

Likert (1961, p. 113) illustrates these structural arrangements as in Figure 8.2. Each triangle represents a work group of size greater than two, consisting of a supervisor and his or her immediate subordinates. The supervisor of each such work group operates as a linking pin because, being a member of two work groups, he or she serves to connect the groups. Thus, the "link-pin" organization eliminates all bridges. However, the liaison (cut point) position of the supervisors is maintained.

Figure 8.3. A linking pin organization with short circuits.

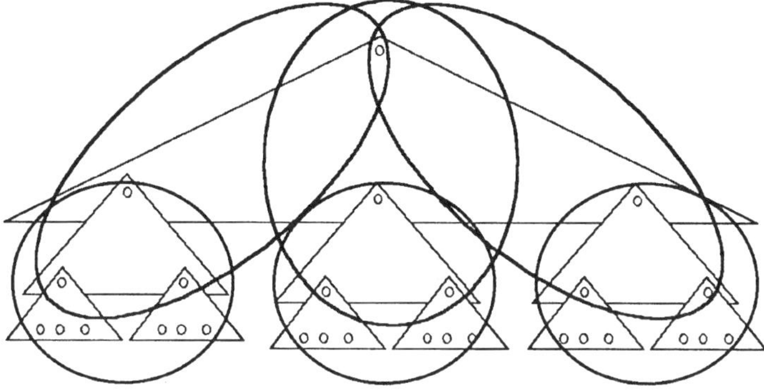

Short Circuits. Lateral extensions of influential communication raise the problem of a subordinate encountering two equivalent superiors. Vertical extensions of influential communication do not raise this problem in as severe a form. I refer to these additional vertical communications as short circuits. Likert (1961) introduces the idea of short circuits as follows: "To help maintain an effective organization, it is desirable for superiors not only to hold group meetings of their own subordinates, but also to have occasional meetings over two hierarchical levels" (p. 115).

With short circuits, a work group now entails all possible direct contacts between a supervisor, the supervisor's immediate subordinates, and these subordinates' immediate subordinates. Likert (1961) states that

> An organization takes a serious risk when it relies on a single linking pin or single linking process to tie the organization together. . . . An organization is strengthened by having staff groups and *ad hoc* committees provide multiple overlapping groups through which linking functions are performed and the organization is bound together. (p. 115)

Hence, a "tree-like" macro-structure of influential communications may arise (a) in which there are chains of sequentially overlapping zones of structural cohesion and influence and (b) in which these chains conform roughly to the shape of the authority hierarchy, as shown in Figure 8.3. This short-circuit organization not only eliminates bridges but also eliminates liaisons. Instead of "linking pins," the interfaces between the work groups have been thickened. We get a pattern of sequentially overlapping zones of structural cohesion and influence on the basis of which the social positions (organizational roles) can be coordinated.

Figure 8.4. Intersecting social circles in a two-dimensional social space.

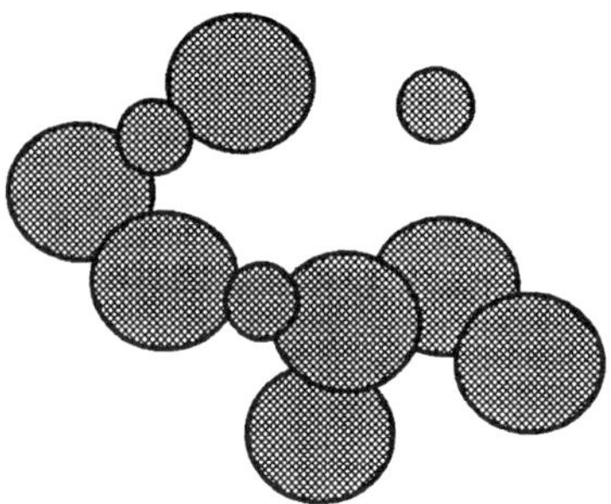

8.2.3 Social Circles

Likert's concept of linking pin organization is closely related to Alba and Kudushin's concept of a *social circle* (Kadushin 1966, 1968; Alba and Kadushin 1976):

> The social circle offers a sort of group structure appropriate for studying large-scale social organization. In contrast to the clique, with its emphasis on face-to-face interaction among all or almost all of a clique's members, the social circle's cohesion is founded on short chains of indirect interaction. . . . Circles can be thought of as knitted out of many extensively overlapping cliques. The dispersal of overlap guarantees that influences flow readily throughout a circle's extent, as individuals who participate in more than one clique act as key points of diffusion. (Alba 1982, p. 58)

Along these lines, we might represent a macro-structure as a Venn diagram consisting of a pattern of more or less overlapping subsets of structurally cohesive actors; see Figure 8.4. If a social circle is defined on the basis of subsets of actors who are not only structurally cohesive but also proximate in social space, then a ridge structure is implied. For Simmel (1955), a social circle is based on common affiliations on one or more social dimensions, and therefore a social circle is most likely to encompass actors who are proximate in social space. A sequence of overlapping social circles provides a structural foundation for a ridge structure that can encompass most of the social positions in a social space.

As Figure 8.4 suggests, it is possible that one framework of overlapping cohesive regions of the social space may include most of the actors in a population. At the other extreme, in a segregated social space

Figure 8.5. Bridging ties in a ridge structure.

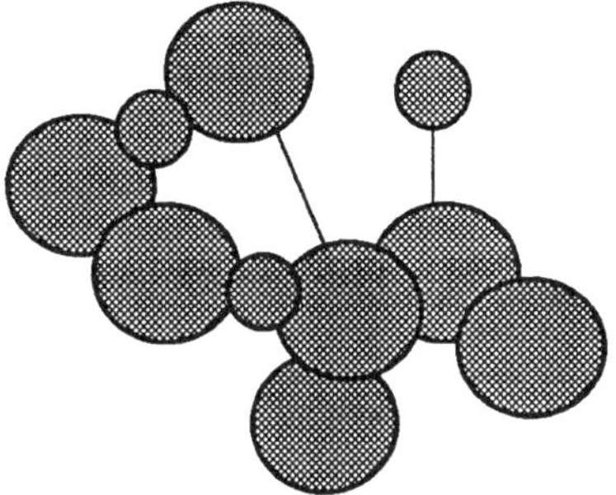

there would be multiple nonoverlapping social circles, and any bridging ties between these distinct social circles would be crucial to the occurrence of flows of influence throughout the system. However, to the extent that a single interconnected framework of social circles is present, local bridges lose theoretical status as the crucial structural components of macro-level connectivity. The more systematic foundation of such connectivity is provided by the configuration of the ridge structure.

Granovetter's (1973) argument that local bridges tend to link actors who are located in different parts of a social structure is not inconsistent with the occurrence of a ridge structure that penetrates into the various occupied regions of a social space. Bridging ties are rare events and, as I show below, are anomalous phenomena from the point of view of balance theory. However, when a bridging tie occurs, it is likely to connect actors who are situated in distinct ridge structures, or actors who are at some distance from each other in the *same* ridge structure. Hence, as Figure 8.5 illustrates, local bridges may provide either the only basis for a flow of influence between two subsets of actors, or a basis for shorter sequences of interpersonal influence that contribute (more or less) to other influence flows.

8.3 Macro-Structural Models and Transitivity

Granovetter's (1973) arguments draw on a rich vein of theoretical development concerned with the structure of sentimental or affect relations. This work, referred to as balance theory, describes certain expected patterns of affect relations in triads and the implications of these patterns for the organization of a macro-structure of affect relations. However, it is not widely recognized that the theoretical work on balance theory has been generalized so that it is no longer restricted to affect relations, and that simplified images of macro-structure can be derived from an analysis of the pattern of interpersonal ties in the $\binom{N}{3}$ triads that are entailed in a population of N actors (Johnsen 1985, 1986, 1989).

To the extent that balance theory accurately describes the structure of an observed network, a bridging tie is an anomalous or rare event, and when a bridge does occur, it is likely to join distant parts of a social structure. This assertion of balance theory is consistent with Granovetter's argument about bridges, i.e., bridges connect actors who occupy distant social positions. However, from the theoretical perspective of balance theory, there are more systematic foundations of connectivity between the parts of a social structure than bridges. These systematic foundations are dense interfaces between cliques. In balance theory these cliques are structurally equivalent positions (in a certain sense to be defined), and a ridge structure that encompasses several social positions is established by those cliques which are connected by dense interfaces.

The theoretical analysis that supports the above conclusions is presented in sections 8.3.1–8.3.7. This analysis is highly detailed, and a reader who is not interested in these details should proceed directly to section 8.3.8.

8.3.1 Elementary Concepts

Balance theory originated with the work of Heider (1946) and has been advanced by a series of papers concerned with formal models of structures of affective or sentimental relations (Newcomb 1953, 1961, 1968; Cartwright and Harary 1956; Davis 1963, 1967, 1970; Holland and Leinhardt 1970, 1971, 1973, 1976; Davis and Leinhardt 1972; Hallinan 1974; Johnsen 1985, 1986, 1989). This generalization has been carried forward to the point that the development of macro-structural models from a triad analysis may be applied to any network $\mathbf{R} = [r_{ij}]$ in which there is either a tie from actor i to actor j ($r_{ij} = 1$), or there is not ($r_{ij} = 0$), and $r_{ii} = 1$ for all ordered pairs of actors (compare with Freeman 1992). In the classical work on balance theory, the network of interpersonal ties took the form of a complete *signed* network in which the ties were equal to + (indicating positive affect) or − (indicating negative affect). The matrix **R** can be used to describe the pattern of positive and negative affect relations, but it also applies to other types of social relations in which a simple interpersonal adjacency and its absence is being represented rather than the occurrence of positive and negative sentiments.

The dyads in **R** are one of three types: mutual (M), asymmetric (A), or null (N). Actors i and j are M related if $r_{ij} = 1$ and $r_{ji} = 1$ ($i \leftrightarrow j$); they are N related if $r_{ij} = 0$ and $r_{ji} = 0$ (neither $i \rightarrow j$ nor $i \leftarrow j$ exists);

otherwise they are A related ($i \rightarrow j$ or $i \leftarrow j$). Among the triads in **R** there are sixteen different combinations of M, A, and N dyads. Each of these combinations is a *triad type* that is described conventionally with three numbers m:a:n, where m, a, and n are the numbers of M, A, and N dyads composing the triad ($m + a + n = 3$), together in some cases with a letter C, D, T, or U standing for "cyclic," "down," "transitive," and "up." The set Θ of sixteen different triad types is shown in Figure 8.6. Panel (a) describes the classical representation of the triad types and panel (b) provides a simplified representation of these types.

A *structural model* X is defined by the subset P_x of Θ of triad types that appear in the model, or by the subset $\overline{P}_x = \Theta - P_x$ of triad types that *don't* appear in the model. The triad types in P_x are said to be *permissible* and triad types $\overline{P}_x$ are said to be *forbidden*. Not all possible subsets of permissible triads are logically consistent; for example, it is not possible to construct a network based on $P_Y = \{300,003\}$ because such a network must involve the forbidden 102 triad. Johnsen (1989) reserves the term *micro-model* for those subsets P_x of Θ for which it is possible to construct a network in which all the possible permissible triad types appear, and he reserves the term *macro-model* (or macro-structural model) for the set of all the possible networks that are consistent with a particular micro-model.

In the next several sections I describe different micro-models that are constrained by transitivity and their corresponding macro-structural representations. The first two models, balance and clustering, appeared early in the development of this literature and describe a segregated macro-structure consisting of disconnected cliques. Generalizations of the balance and clustering models involve a pattern of dense interfaces between cliques. These models, described below, are the ranked clusters of M-cliques model, the transitivity model, and the hierarchical $\tilde{M}$-cliques model. I conclude with the description of a new model, weak transitivity, that extends this line of generalization to a micro-model that permits all triad types that are either nontransitive (i.e., do not violate transitivity) or that satisfy transitivity in part.

8.3.2 Balance Model

This micro-model permits only two types of triads: a triad consisting of three mutual links and a triad consisting of one mutual link only:

$$P_{BA} = \{300, 102\} \tag{8.3}$$

The 300 triad implies the occurrence of maximal subsets of actors who are completely connected by M links; such subsets are called *M-cliques*. Now suppose we have an M-clique and an actor, Ego, who is not a

Figure 8.6. The sixteen triad types.

(a) Classical representation

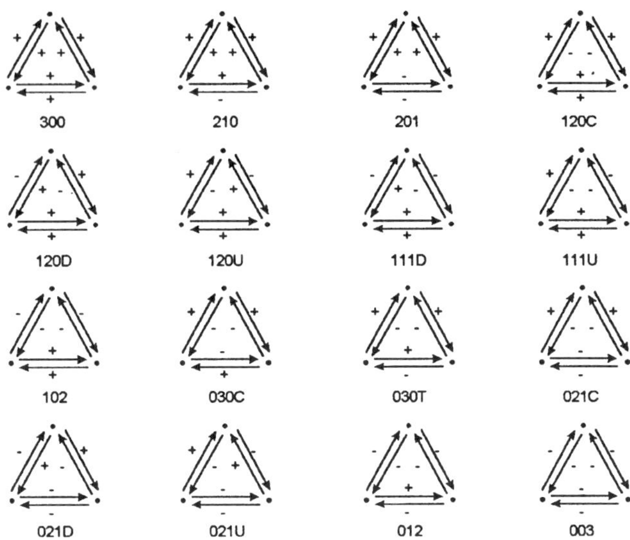

(b) Simplified representation

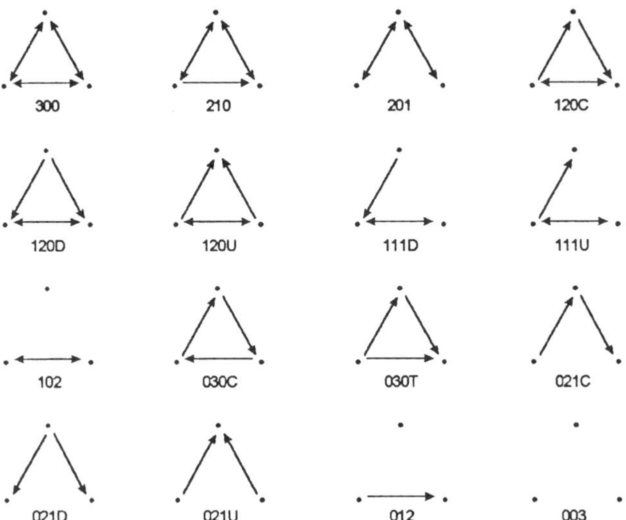

Figure 8.7. Macro-structure for balance model (Johnsen 1989).

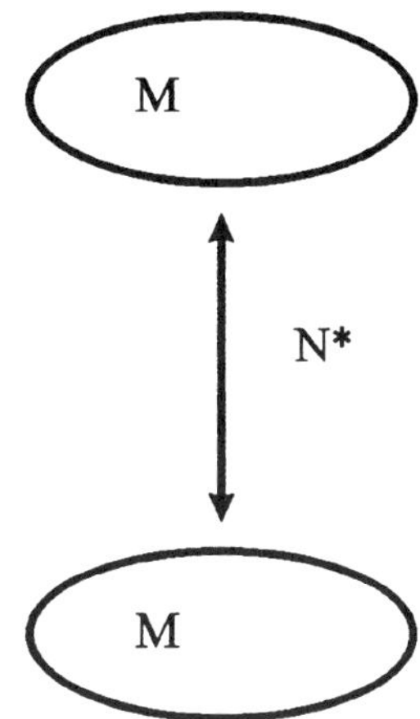

member the clique. This is a possible macro-structure because all the triads in which Ego is involved are of the 102 type. Now add to this picture an actor, Alter, who also is not a member of the original *M*-clique. Ego and Alter must be joined by an *M* link (because all other possibilities are forbidden) and, in fact, any further additions to the set of actors must be members either of the original *M*-clique or the Ego–Alter clique, and there can be no *M* or *A* links between the cliques. In short, as shown in Figure 8.7, this micro-model implies a network that consists of *at most* two *M*-cliques that are related by N^* (i.e., completely interconnected by *N* links).

8.3.3 Clustering Model

This model allows for the occurrence of three actors who have no *M* or *A* ties with each other:

$$P_{CL} = \{300, 102, 003\} \tag{8.4}$$

The resulting macro-structure, as shown in Figure 8.8, has one or more *M*-cliques that are related by N^*.

8.3.4 Ranked Clusters of *M*-Cliques Model

This model further relaxes the structural constraints and allows for *A* links in certain types of triads:

Figure 8.8. Macro-structure for clustering model (Johnsen 1989).

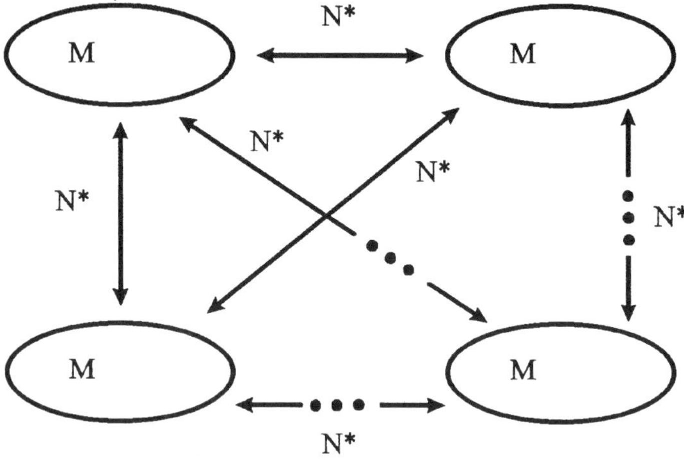

$$P_{RC} = \{300, 102, 003, 120D, 120U, 030T, 021D, 021U\} \tag{8.5}$$

Now all triad types are permitted in which there is a semipath connecting the three actors, so long as there is no violation of the principle of transitivity, i.e., if $i \to k$ and $k \to j$, then $i \to j$ for any three actors. The following triads have a semipath connecting the three actors, but entail a violation of transitivity and, therefore, are excluded: 210, 201, 120*C*, 111*D*, 111*U*, 030*C*, and 021*C*. The resulting macro-structure consists of *M*-cliques that are arranged in levels, with one or more cliques at each level, with cliques at the same level related by N^*, and with all cliques at different levels related by A^* (i.e., completely interconnected by the *A* relation with all *A* relations going in the same direction) from the lower-level to the higher-level cliques. In this structure, there are no stand-alone cliques; see Figure 8.9.

This framework of interclique relations has the following noteworthy features. Two actors *i* and *j* who are members of the same clique are structurally equivalent in the $\mathbf{R} = [r_{ij}]$ relation, i.e.,

$$r_{ii} = r_{jj} \qquad r_{ij} = r_{ji} \qquad r_{ik} = r_{jk} \qquad \text{and} \qquad r_{ki} = r_{kj} \tag{8.6}$$

for all $k \neq i, j$. Hence, each clique corresponds to a distinct social position. The interfaces between cliques are either empty or complete. All the interclique relations are *A* links: if *iAj*, then actors *i* and *j* are in different cliques and all the members of actor *i*'s clique are *A* related to

Figure 8.9. Macrostructure for ranked clusters of M-cliques model (Johnsen 1989).

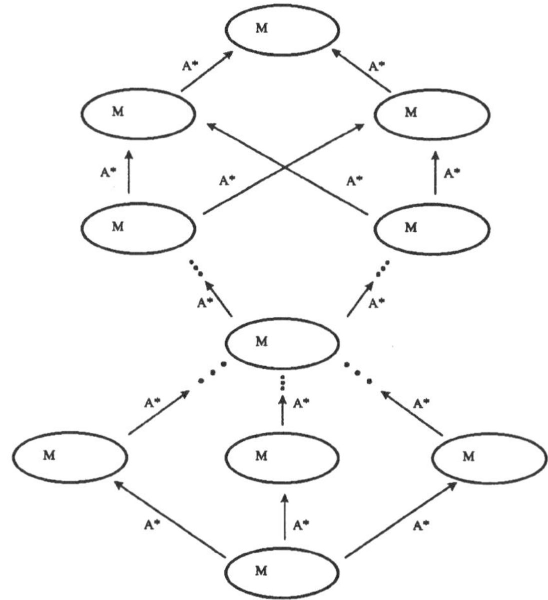

Note: All interclique A^* relations implied by transitivity are suppressed and all other missing interclique relations are N^*.

the members of actor j's clique. There are no bridges or liaisons, so long as each M-clique has two or more members. The pattern of dense interfaces is transitive; given three cliques $\{M^{(i)}, M^{(j)}, M^{(k)}\}$, if $M^{(i)} \xrightarrow{A^*} M^{(k)}$ and $M^{(k)} \xrightarrow{A^*} M^{(j)}$, then $M^{(i)} \xrightarrow{A^*} M^{(j)}$.

8.3.5 Transitivity Model

This model further relaxes the structural constraints, by permitting the 012 triad:

$$P_{TR} = \{300, 102, 003, 120D, 120U, 030T, 021D, 021U, 012\} \qquad (8.7)$$

The model is called the transitivity model because all of the forbidden triads violate transitivity and none of the permitted triads do. Triads such as 012 do not violate transitivity because a two-step path ($i \to j \to k$) does not exist. The resulting macro-structure, as shown in Figure 8.10, consists of a collection of M-cliques partially ordered by the A^* relation (by convention, every M-clique is in relation A^* to itself) where incomparable M-cliques are pairwise related by N^*.

This macro-structure is the same as the ranked clusters of M-cliques model, except that it allows for isolated subsets of M-cliques. The structural constraints do not allow for bridges or liaisons, if every M-clique consists of two or more actors. The clique interfaces are either empty or asymmetrically complete, and the A^* relation is transitive. Each M-clique is a structurally equivalent position as defined in Eq. (8.6).

8.3.6 Hierarchical $\tilde{M}$-Cliques Model

This model further relaxes the structural constraints by allowing the 210 triad:

$$P_{HC} = \{300, 102, 003, 120D, 120U, 030T, 021D, 021U, 012, 210\} \tag{8.8}$$

The set of forbidden triads is now $\overline{P}_{HC} = \{201, 120C, 111D, 111U, 030C, 021C\}$. The result is a macro-structure with the same restrictions on the framework of interclique relations that was found in the transitivity model, but in which the M-cliques are replaced by $\tilde{M}$-cliques. An $\tilde{M}$-clique is a strong component in the subnet of **R** that is obtained by eliminating the A ties; i.e., all the pairs of actors in an $\tilde{M}$-clique are connected by a path of M ties of some length. The resulting macro-structure is the same as that shown in Figure 8.10, except that the M-cliques are replaced by $\tilde{M}$-cliques.

In this macro-structure, every dyad in an $\tilde{M}$-clique is either M or A related. The subnet of M and A relations within a clique does not need to be transitive (although the subnet of A relations within such cliques is). The members of an $\tilde{M}$-clique are structurally equivalent with respect to their profiles of ties sent to and received from actors in other cliques; but they are not necessarily structurally equivalent in terms of their profiles of ties with actors in the *same* clique. Thus, two actors i and j in an $\tilde{M}$-clique are structurally equivalent in $\mathbf{R} = [r_{ij}]$ in the weaker sense of having identical profiles of interpersonal *contacts*, ignoring whether these contacts are based on an M or A relation:

$$r^*_{ii} = r^*_{jj} \qquad r^*_{ij} = r^*_{ji} \qquad r^*_{ik} = r^*_{jk} \qquad \text{and} \qquad r^*_{ki} = r^*_{kj} \tag{8.9}$$

for all $k \neq i, j$, where $r^*_{ij} = \max(r_{ij}, r_{ji})$.

The hierarchical $\tilde{M}$-cliques model is the most general of the models thus far considered. However, in an analysis of the networks in the Davis – Leinhardt data set (Davis 1970; Davis and Leinhardt 1972),

Figure 8.10. Macro-structure for transitivity model (Johnsen 1989).

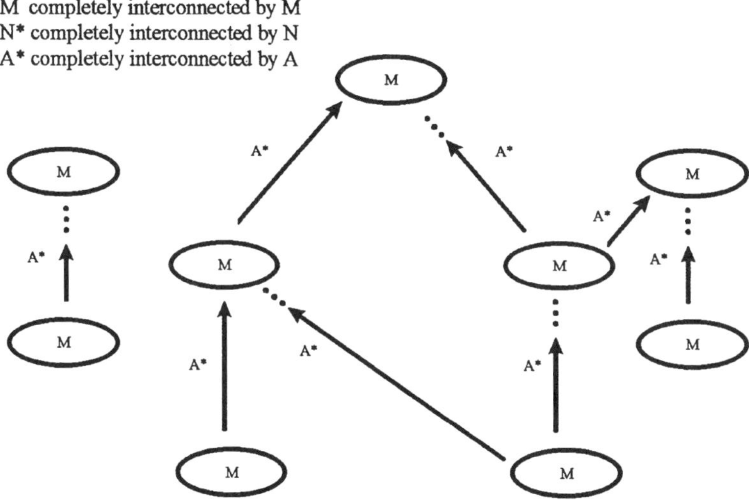

Note: All interclique A^* relations implied by transitivity are suppressed and all other missing interclique relations are N^*.

Johnsen (1989) shows that this model does not adequately deal with large groups (sizes 39–79 in the Davis–Leinhardt data), and he develops a model that appears to handle these large groups. Unlike the hierarchical $\tilde{M}$-cliques model, in Johnsen's large-group model the 120*C* triad is permitted and the 003 is prohibited:

$$P_{39+} = \{300, 102, 120D, 120U, 030T, 021D, 021U, 012, 210, 120C\}$$

Permitting the 120*C* triad entails a further relaxation of structural constraints along the same lines of the successive relaxation of constraints that we have been pursuing. However, Johnsen's large-group model also *reintroduces* the prohibition of the 003 triad, which had been permitted earlier (with the clustering model) in the sequence of generalizations. Reintroducing the 003 triad entails an unsatisfying break in the theoretical line of generalization; moreover, *especially* in large groups, the possibility of three *N* linked actors should not be forbidden. Therefore, I present a modified version of Johnsen's large-group model in which the 003 is *not* forbidden.

8.3.7 Weak Transitivity Model

This model relaxes the constraint of the hierarchical $\tilde{M}$-cliques model by allowing the 120*C* triad:

$$P_{WT} = \{300, 102, 003, 120D, 120U, 030T, 021D, 021U, 012, 210, 120C\} \tag{8.10}$$

The set of forbidden triads is now $\overline{P}_{WT} = \{201, 111D, 111U, 030C, 021C\}$. For convenience, I display these forbidden triads below:

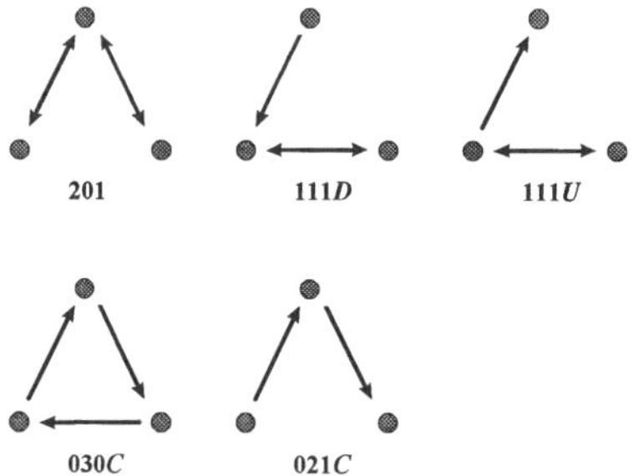

The common feature of these forbidden triads is that each possesses the conditions of transitivity (one or more two-step paths) and does not satisfy transitivity at all; i.e., the intransitivity is maximal. In the previous models, a triad was forbidden if it contained any evidence of intransitivity; hence, the 120C triad (where $i \to k \to j$ and $i \leftrightarrow j$) is intransitive. The weak transitivity model permits all triads that either are nontransitive (do not entail the conditions of transitivity and therefore cannot be intransitive) or that contain *any evidence* of a satisfaction of the conditions of transitivity. Hence, this is the *most general* of the models of macro-structure in which transitivity constrains, to some extent, the pattern of social ties.

In this weak transitivity group model, the macro-structure consists of $\tilde{M}$-cliques, and each $\tilde{M}$-clique has only M and A ties. Because 120C is now permitted, transitivity may be violated within $\tilde{M}$-cliques. The interfaces between the cliques are either empty or complete. Unlike the previous models, a clique interface is not necessarily anti-symmetric; i.e., there may be A links in both directions on a single interface. The clique interfaces in this model are either N^*, A^*, or $A^\#$, where $A^\#$ is an interface in which, for all actors i and j who are in different cliques, either iAj or jAi. Thus, A^* is a special case of $A^\#$; for two cliques, $\tilde{M}^{(i)}$ and $\tilde{M}^{(j)}$, if $\tilde{M}^{(i)} \xrightarrow{A^*} \tilde{M}^{(j)}$, then $\tilde{M}^{(i)} \xrightarrow{A\#} \tilde{M}^{(j)}$.

In this weak, transitivity model, for every three distinct $\tilde{M}$-cliques $\{\tilde{M}^{(i)}, \tilde{M}^{(j)}, \tilde{M}^{(k)}\}$, if $\tilde{M}^{(i)} \xrightarrow{A^*} \tilde{M}^{(k)}$ and $\tilde{M}^{(k)} \xrightarrow{A^*} \tilde{M}^{(j)}$, then $\tilde{M}^{(i)} \xrightarrow{A^*} \tilde{M}^{(j)}$; that is, A^* is transitive on the $\tilde{M}$-cliques. However, unlike the hierarchical $\tilde{M}$-cliques model in which the interfaces between cliques were either N^* or A^*, in this model an interface may be $A^\#$ or N^*, where it is not forced by transitivity to be A^*.

Figure 8.11. Macro-structure for weak transitivity model.

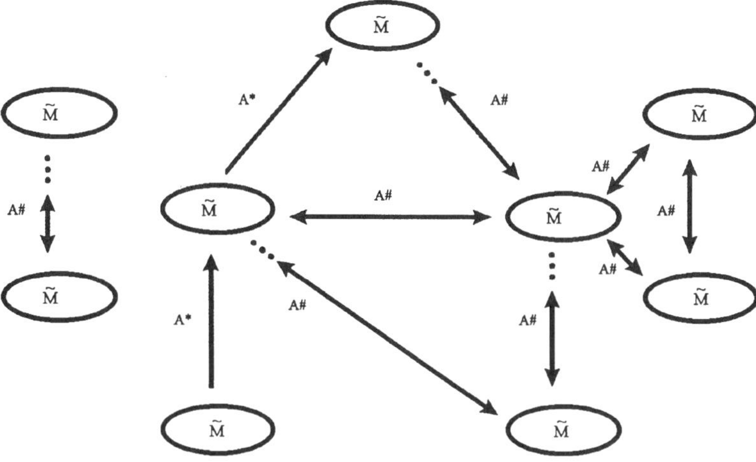

Note: All interclique A^* relations implied by transitivity are suppressed and all other missing interclique relations are N^*.

In short, as Figure 8.11 shows, we have a macro-structure consisting of subsets of $\tilde{M}$-cliques. Each of these $\tilde{M}$-cliques corresponds to a structurally equivalent position in the weak sense described by Eq. (8.9). Besides the $\tilde{M}$-cliques, there also may be a framework of dense interfaces between cliques; these interfaces may or may not join all the cliques. There are no bridges or liaisons, so long as each $\tilde{M}$-clique has two or more members. What is remarkable about this development is that we have now reduced the set of prohibited triad types to five types, on which basis we must conclude that the systematic basis of interclique connections must be the $A^{\#}$ relation, and that bridges and liaisons can exist only if they involve an actor who is a clique unto him -or herself, i.e., who has no mutual ties with any other actor.

8.3.8 Ridge Structure in Transitive Macro-Models

I have shown that the idea of a ridge structure (sequentially overlapping, densely occupied regions of social space in each of which the probability of attachments among actors is high) has appeared in various forms in the literature. Among these realizations of the concept of ridge structure, the macro-structural models related to balance theory are the most suggestive. We have seen that a ridge structure is consistent with the tendency toward transitive closure. The models of balance theory do not *require* ridge structures that encompass all the actors of a population; for example, segregated structures composed of disconnected cliques are permitted. However, balance theory suggests that interactions between cliques are *not idiosyncratic* in that the interfaces between cliques are either filled with ties or they are empty.

Hence, bridges and liaisons are structural *anomalies* or rare events to the extent that maximally intransitive triadic structures do not occur in a population. To be sure, we may find a bridge or liaison involving actors who are members of one-actor cliques; however, if there is a systematic basis of structural connectivity among cliques, then it is likely to take the form of a framework of dense interfaces between cliques.

Moreover, in the macro-models that are consistent with transitive closure, a clique is also a social position. If two actors are said to be in contact when they are joined by a semipath of length one, then all pairs of members of a clique will be in such contact with each other and they will have an identical profile of contacts with members of other cliques. Hence, cliques will consist of structurally equivalent actors in the weak sense described by Eq. (8.9). In turn, it follows that these macro-structural models can alternatively be represented as blockmodels, with the understanding that the structural equivalence of the members of a social position (clique) is based on the semipath structure of the network.

An additional implication of this perspective is that vacuous social positions (in which there are no interpersonal ties) are a theoretical anomaly. To be sure, the measure of structural equivalence permits as a *logical possibility* the occurrence of a subset of actors who are structurally equivalent and who do not have any direct ties among themselves; however, the theoretical expectation is that social positions will be filled with ties.[7] Dense social positions are implied by the prohibition of maximally intransitive triad structures. Moreover, if shared social positions (clique memberships) reflect shared positions in social space, then dense social positions are to be expected.[8]

7 Hence, peripheral actors in a center–periphery pattern, because they are one-actor cliques, occupy different social positions.

8 In my approach to influence networks and social spaces, if the actors within $\tilde{M}$-cliques are structurally equivalent as in Eq. (8.6), then they also will be structurally equivalent in the influence network and they will have identical positions in social space. The macro-structure of cohesion is a direct description of the pattern of interpersonal ties; the influence network and social positions are derived from this structure. If the actors within $\tilde{M}$-cliques are structurally equivalent as in Eq. (8.9), then the actors who belong to a common clique may not occupy an identical location in social space; however, it is likely that they will occupy proximate positions.

8.4 Analysis of the Faculties of Science

If social space is organized into ridge structures, then the organization of interpersonal attachments should be consistent with one of the macro-structural models of balance theory. In an analysis of the interpersonal attachments in the faculties of science at Chicago and Columbia presented below, I show that the networks are organized in a way that is consistent with balance theory. Then I describe the exact structure of these networks. I show that frameworks of attachments exist that connect actors who are located in distant social positions in these science faculties. I show that, although bridging ties can be important in linking actors who are in distant social positions, the more robust basis of macro-level connectivity is a framework of attachments that penetrates into various areas of social space and that includes a relatively large fraction of the population of actors.

8.4.1 Triad Analysis

In the faculties of science, I now ascertain whether the networks of interpersonal attachments, i.e., **R** as defined in Eq. (4.12), are consistent with one of the macro-structures of balance theory. The procedure is to obtain a triad census that gives the frequency of each of the sixteen types of triads and to calculate the extent to which each of the observed frequencies is above or below expectation (Holland and Leinhardt 1976). Table 8.1(a) reports the observed and expected frequencies for the triads in the respondent subnets, and Table 8.1(b) reports the standardized difference, which is the percentage difference between the observed and expected frequencies. A convention is to categorize a triad as "forbidden" if it occurs with a frequency that is 10% or more below expectation.

The important result of this analysis is that (with the exception of $111U$ in Chicago Social Science) the five forbidden triads of the weak transitivity model (P_{WT}) appear as "forbidden" in the triad analysis in each of the science faculties. In certain of the science faculties, additional "forbidden" triads appear that place restrictions on the pattern of attachments. These additional restrictions are not inconsistent with the models of balance theory. For instance, $021U$, which is not among the forbidden triads in the weak transitivity model, but which appears as forbidden in Columbia Physical Science, places a restriction on the pattern of A^* interfaces among the cliques; it precludes a situation in which two N^* related cliques are both A^* related to a third clique, but otherwise does not importantly modify the macro-structural image for the weak transitivity model.

Table 8.1(a). *Triad Analysis of the Interpersonal Attachments in the Faculties of Science*

	Observed frequency					
	Chicago			Columbia		
Triad type	Phy. $n = 78$	Bio. $n = 97$	Soc. $n = 94$	Phy. $n = 59$	Bio. $n = 105$	Soc. $n = 96$
300	2046	2008	2819	256	671	686
201	2563	4502	4916	137	2374	1507
102	16091	24718	28037	6457	27270	24718
003	20953	37076	36955	15701	85490	65684
210	2678	3913	4186	290	1689	1249
012	14881	38073	29465	7754	46676	34709
111D	3269	6205	5666	308	4871	2982
111U	3339	8839	8354	417	5171	3185
120C	558	1261	1000	58	575	404
120D	879	1306	1077	46	865	411
120U	1424	2932	2069	269	1064	868
021C	1196	4233	2788	227	3042	1764
021D	1561	5063	3304	226	3587	1758
021U	1543	4528	2195	224	2910	2180
030C	32	136	58	4	40	36
030T	988	2647	1155	135	1165	739

	Expected Frequency					
	Chicago			Columbia		
Triad type	Phy. $n = 78$	Bio. $n = 97$	Soc. $n = 94$	Phy. $n = 59$	Bio. $n = 105$	Soc. $n = 96$
300	478.13	536.53	794.94	26.63	130.65	116.57
201	4860.82	6402.35	8304.56	679.30	3358.71	2882.45
102	16433.77	25421.62	28871.73	5735.81	28715.62	23695.62
003	1876.890	33588.21	33404.20	16031.76	81647.101	64760.639
210	1488.85	2465.04	2499.52	99.48	678.40	518.40
012	16996.37	38823.81	30184.08	7053.97	49497.45	34960.75
111D	5036.30	9791.30	8693.02	840.63	5801.42	4262.78
111U	5036.30	9791.30	8693.02	840.63	5801.42	4262.78
120C	769.96	1883.21	1306.64	61.24	585.19	382.71
120D	384.98	941.60	653.32	30.62	292.59	191.36
120U	384.98	941.60	653.32	30.62	292.59	191.36
021C	2599.82	7469.79	4538.59	514.30	4994.00	3139.68
021D	1299.91	3734.90	2269.29	257.15	2497.00	1569.84
021U	1299.91	3734.90	2269.29	257.15	2497.00	1569.84
030C	132.26	478.46	227.12	12.43	167.71	93.81
030T	396.77	1435.39	681.37	37.28	503.14	281.43

Note: Based on respondent subnet in **R**.

Table 8.1(b). *Triad Analysis (cont.)*

	Standardized differences					
	Chicago			Columbia		
Triad type	Phy. $n = 78$	Bio. $n = 97$	Soc. $n = 94$	Phy. $n = 59$	Bio. $n = 105$	Soc. $n = 96$
300	3.28	2.74	2.55	8.61	4.14	4.88
201	**−0.47**	**−0.30**	**−0.41**	**−0.80**	**−0.29**	**−0.48**
102	−0.02	−0.03	−0.03	0.13	−0.05	0.04
003	0.13	0.10	0.11	−0.02	0.05	0.01
210	0.80	0.59	0.67	1.92	1.49	1.41
012	−0.00	−0.02	−0.02	0.10	−0.06	−0.01
111 D	**−0.35**	**−0.37**	**−0.35**	**−0.63**	**−0.16**	**−0.30**
111 U	**−0.34**	**−0.10**	−0.04	**−0.50**	**−0.11**	**−0.25**
120 C	**−0.28**	**−0.33**	**−0.23**	−0.05	−0.02	0.06
120 D	1.28	0.39	0.65	0.50	1.96	1.15
120 U	2.70	2.11	2.17	7.78	2.64	3.54
021 C	**−0.54**	**−0.43**	**−0.39**	**−0.56**	**−0.39**	**−0.44**
021 D	0.20	0.36	0.46	**−0.12**	0.44	0.12
021 U	0.19	0.21	−0.03	**−0.13**	0.17	0.39
030 C	**−0.76**	**−0.72**	**−0.74**	**−0.68**	**−0.76**	**−0.62**
030 T	1.49	0.84	0.70	2.62	1.32	1.63

The single anomalous result is the permitted 111*U* triad in Chicago Social Science. The 111*U* triad permits incomplete cliques and interfaces between cliques; hence, the structural equivalence of clique members becomes uncertain. However, local bridges are still precluded between nontrivial $\tilde{M}$-cliques (i.e., cliques with at least two members) even when the 111*U* triad is permitted; this is because the forbidden 111*D* triad induces a density that serves to preclude local bridges. Consider, for example, the following situation in which a bridge between two cliques appears:

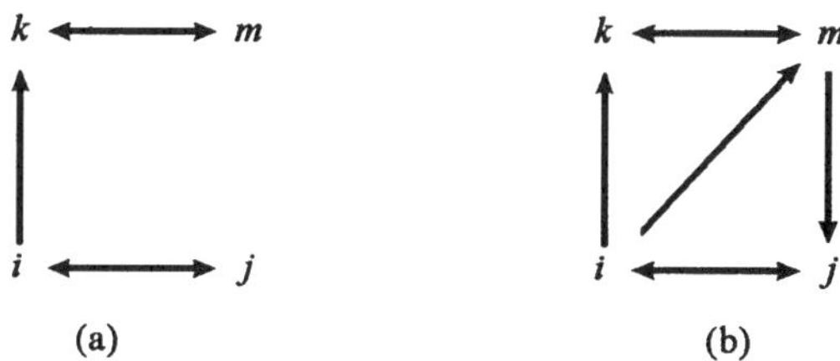

The $\{i,j,k\}$ triad in (a) is 111*U* and the tie from actor *i* to actor *j* is a bridge; but this situation entails the forbidden 111*D* triad for $\{k,m,i\}$. Therefore, a tie must exist between actors *i* and *m*, which eliminates the bridge. Situation (b) above is permissible. Given the absent tie between actors k and j, the interface between the cliques is not $A^{\#}$ as required by the weak transitivity model; nonetheless, the interface remains dense and there certainly is no local bridge.

8.4.2 Blockmodel Images of Attachments

Balance theory describes certain principles of the organization of social ties, but it is neutral on the exact configuration of attachments in a particular population of actors. The macro-models of balance theory do not specify the number and size of cliques, or the exact configuration of dense interfaces between the cliques. I now describe blockmodel images of the macro-structure of attachments in the faculties of science.

The blockmodel images are based on the position-clusters, which were defined in Chapter 7, rather than directly on a balance-theoretic (e.g., M-clique) approach. It is useful to view the tendency toward transitivity (which underlies all of the balance-theoretic macro-models) as reflecting, or as being played out in the context of, a predetermined social space, and as being constrained by the distribution of actors in that space. The social positions of actors and their social distances account for the number of distinct cliques and the configuration of dense interfaces among them. Declining social distance increases the probability of interpersonal attachment and, where attachments do occur, the configuration of these ties will be affected by status-organizing processes and balancing mechanisms. The attachments of two actors will be structurally equivalent to the extent that the actors occupy similar locations in social space. Actors in sufficiently proximate positions should be involved in a dense subnet of reciprocated ties and have either dense or empty interfaces with other such clusters. Hence, there are not separate theoretical foundations for defining social positions but instead a single consistent foundation that encompasses balance theory.

Figures 8.12–8.17 are graphical images of the mean probabilities of attachment within and among the position-clusters in the faculties of science. These probabilities are based on Eq. (4.13). In these figures, each circle represents a position-cluster. Small clusters (1–3 actors) are represented by the smallest circles; larger clusters (4–10 actors) by somewhat larger circles; and the largest clusters (greater than 10 actors) by the largest circles. For each cluster, the departmental affiliations of the members of a cluster are described (from the results reported in Chapter 7) and the mean probability of attachments within the cluster is reported. The mean probability of attachment between clusters is indicated by the width of the arrows connecting clusters. In addition, the location of bridges in the semipath structure of **R** (the network of attachments) is indicated by the dotted lines.

Figure 8.12. Chicago Physical Science blockmodel image of attachments (mean probability of interpersonal attachment within and among position-clusters).

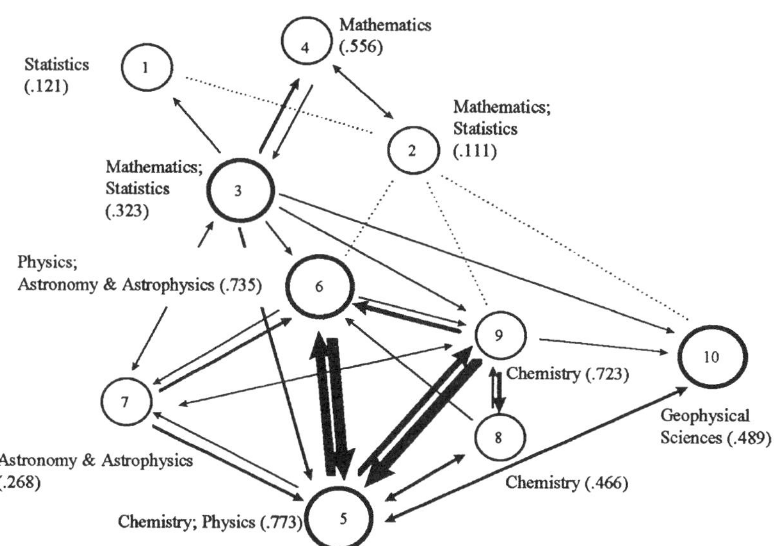

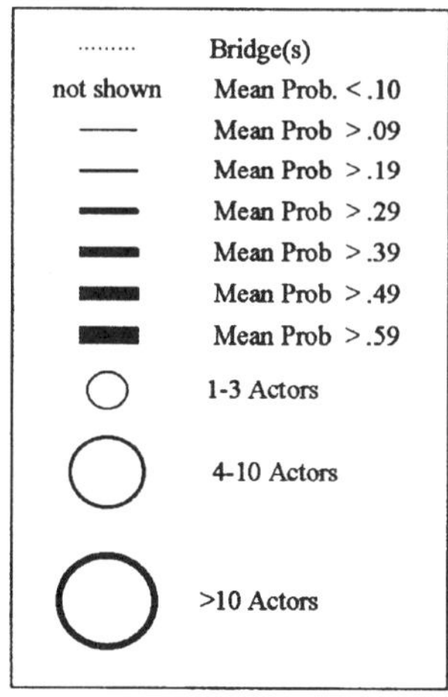

Figure 8.13. Chicago Biological Science blockmodel image of attachments (mean probability of interpersonal attachment within and among position-clusters).

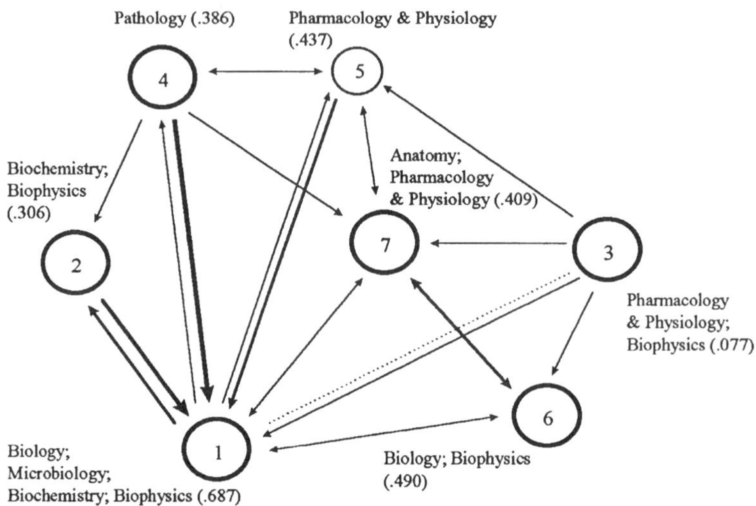

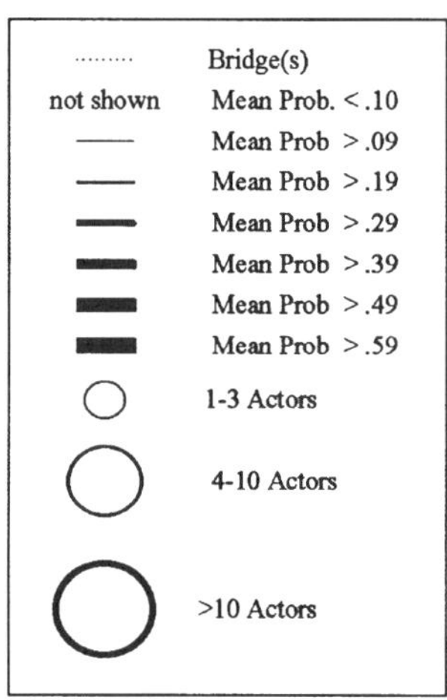

Figure 8.14. Chicago Social Science blockmodel image of attachments (mean probability of interpersonal attachment within and among position-clusters).

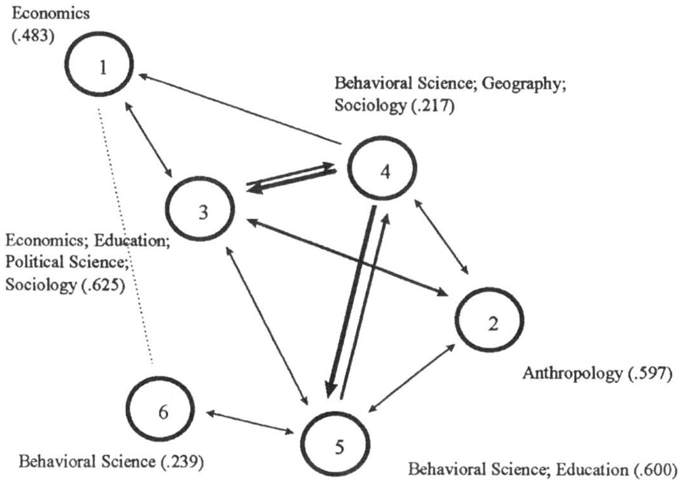

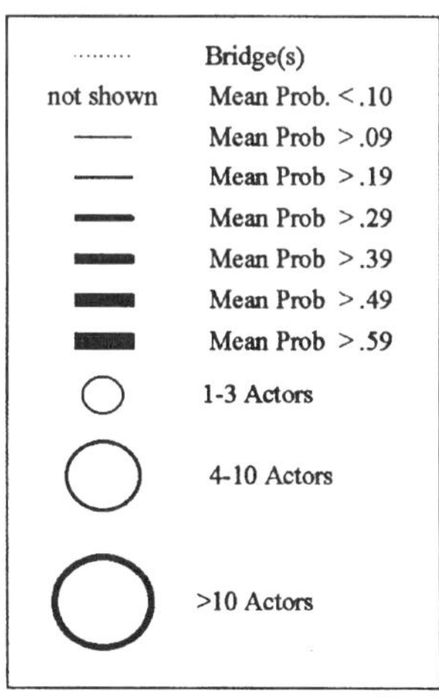

Figure 8.15. Columbia Physical Science blockmodel image of attachments (mean probability of interpersonal attachment within and among position-clusters).

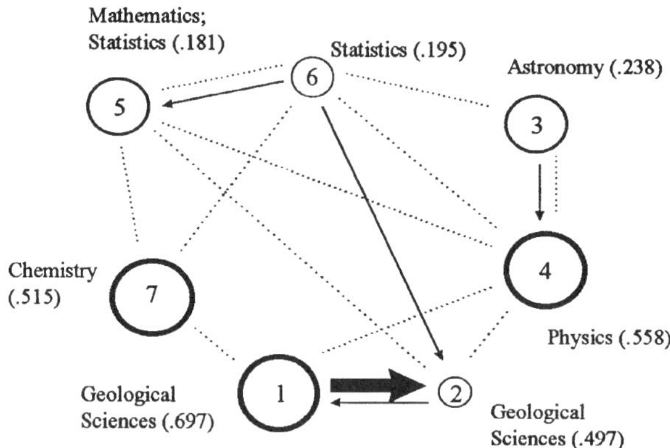

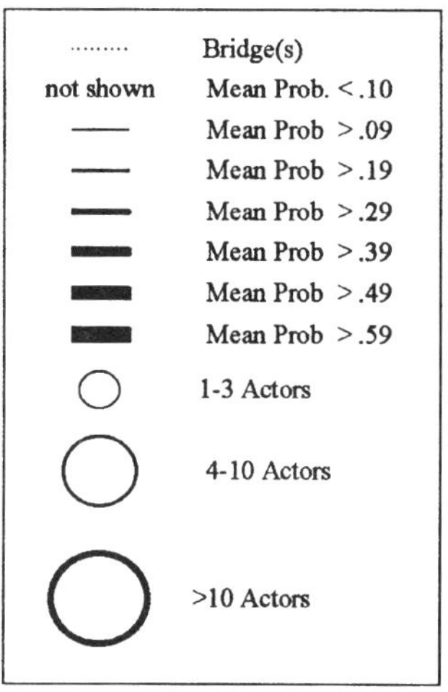

Figure 8.16. Columbia Biological Science blockmodel image of attachments (mean probability of interpersonal attachment within and among position-clusters).

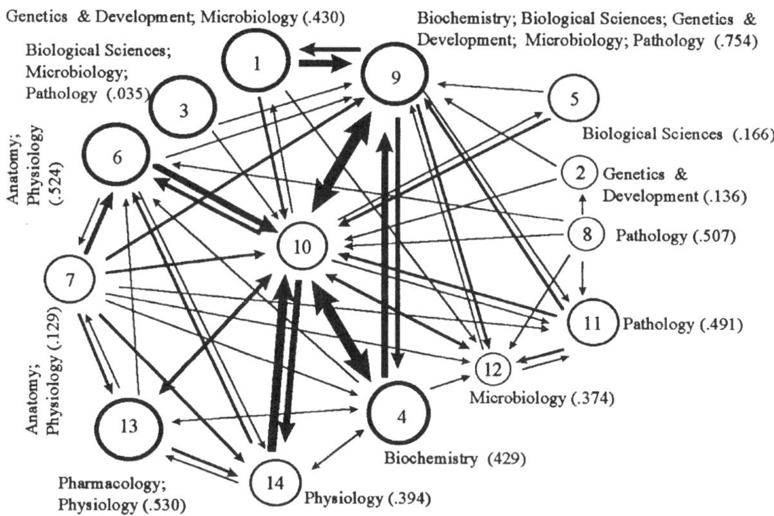

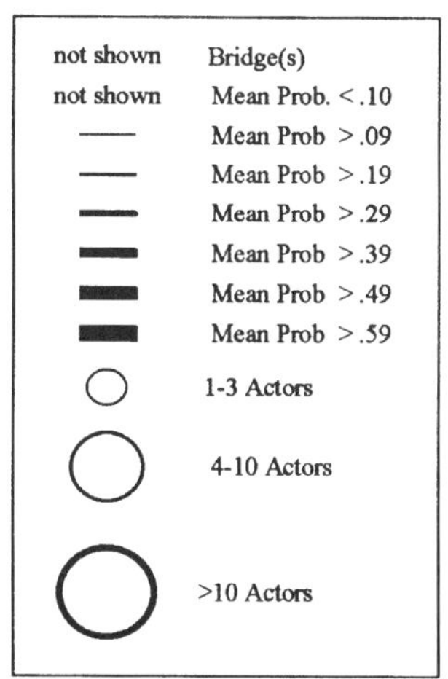

Note: Cluster 10 consists of five actors from different disciplines (.980)

Figure 8.17. Columbia Social Science blockmodel image of attachments (mean probability of interpersonal attachment within and among position-clusters).

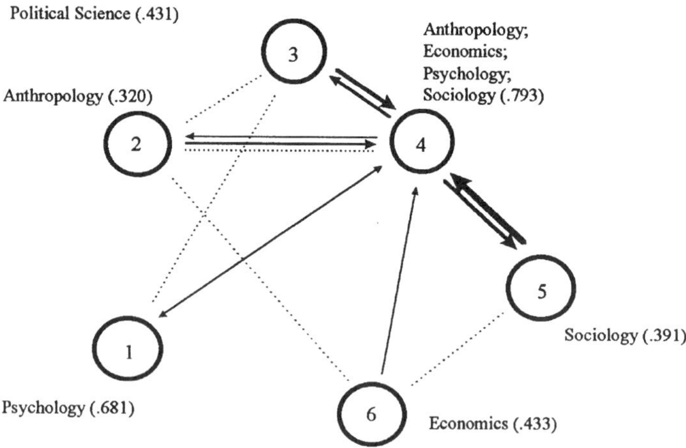

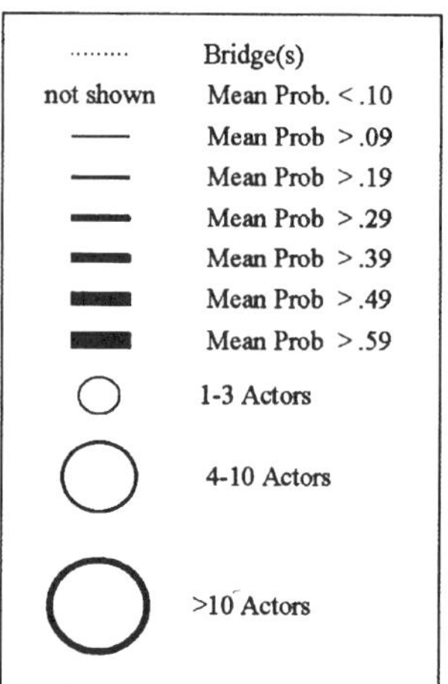

These figures have been constructed with a single purpose in mind, that is, to convey information in a relatively efficient manner about the presence and scope of a ridge structure in each faculty of science. We already know, from the results of the previous chapter, that the probability of attachments is negatively associated with social distance; hence, if the mean probability of an attachment is high on an interface between two position clusters, then this is a likely manifestation of the proximity of the clusters in social space. Distant position-clusters are most likely to have interfaces on which the probabilities of attachment are low; yet such clusters may be connected indirectly in a framework of dense interfaces between clusters.

First, it is clear from these figures that local bridges are sometimes a crucial structural foundation of the macro-level connectivity of social positions. Bridging ties are especially critical components of the connectivity of social positions in the Physical Sciences at Columbia; indeed, Columbia Physical Science closely approximates the classical model of a segregated social structure where the connectivity among position-clusters is mainly based on weak (low probability) attachments. The Astronomy and Physics clusters form a modest ridge; Mathematics, Statistics, and Geological Sciences form another modest ridge; and the Chemistry cluster forms a third ridge. The interfaces between these three ridges are ones in which the probabilities of an interpersonal attachment are low.

Second, it also is clear from these figures that cohesive interfaces between positions can form an interlocking structure that encompasses a number of distinctive positions. In the three faculties of science at The University of Chicago, and in the Biological and Social Sciences at Columbia University, there are more or less strongly interlocking ridge structures. To be sure, there are "holes" in these structures (i.e., regions where the probability of attachments is low) and across some of these "holes" there are bridges. However, there clearly exists a more robust basis of connectivity than bridging ties in these populations. If bridging ties are important structural components of the integration of a segregated population, then more cohesive interfaces between position-clusters (on which bridges are absent) must also be important to such integration.

An historical analysis of these science faculties is required to elucidate the structure of their social spaces. My interest is focused, not on the particularities of these social structures, but on the gross forms of connectivity that emerge from the activities of a differentiated population of actors. Hence, I have focused on the development of one idea: Although differentiation creates cleavages that are sometimes spanned by bridging ties, differentiation is not incompatible with a structural connectivity that is based on a ridge structure (sequentially overlapping zones of cohesion in social space) that encompasses numerous social positions. Interpersonal agreements are enabled by the high mean indegree of attachments that occur when each actor is embedded in a densely settled region of social space, and these interpersonal agreements have a robust structural basis when there are numerous channels for the flow of interpersonal influence.

8.5 Concluding Remarks

Ridge structures arise because of strong associations among the dimensions that define the social space of a population of actors and that affect the occurrence of interpersonal attachments. Hence, ridge structures entail a nonrandom distribution of interpersonal attachments, and these attachments, in turn, govern the distribution of social influence and the integration (via interpersonal agreements) of a complexly differentiated population. In this closing section of the chapter, I discuss the relationship of this argument about ridge structures with Blau's work on the structure of social space (Blau 1977, 1994; Blau and Schwartz 1984).

Blau's (1977, 1994) analysis of social space revolves on two assumptions – (a) the probability of social ties depends on opportunities for contact, and (b) proximity in social space increases the probability of social ties – and an attribute – consolidation – of the set of dimensions that define a social space. Consolidated dimensions are perfectly associated, whereas unconsolidated (intersecting) dimensions are orthogonal. Blau's argument is that unconsolidated dimensions foster social ties between actors who differ on some of the dimensions that define the social space, and that such ties are the foundation of the integration of a complexly differentiated population; much the same argument has been made by Laumann and Knoke (1986, p. 86). I will not draw on Blau's first assumption; it is not necessary for the developments that I will pursue, because the structural conditions that affect opportunities for contact are taken into account in the definition of social space.[9] It is the second assumption that is crucial.

For his argument, Blau relies on the principle of homophily. For example, under homophily, persons of similar age and wealth are more likely to interact than persons of dissimilar age and wealth. In a consol-

9 If an opportunity for contact is simply a nonzero probability of a social tie and if the association of social distance and social ties is not contingent on other variables, then the analysis of the distribution of social ties can focus strictly on the social distance between actors.

idated structure, persons who are similar in age also are likely to be similar in wealth. Consequently, the propensity toward age-peer interaction reinforces the propensity toward wealth-peer interaction. In this situation, interpersonal ties should occur disproportionately among homogeneous categories of actors (e.g., among young poor persons and among old wealthy persons) and between the most proximate age–wealth categories. In an unconsolidated situation, because wealth and age are not associated, interaction with wealth-peers will weaken the tendency to interact with age-peers. Similarly, interaction with age-peers will weaken the tendency to interact with wealth-peers.

In an unconsolidated situation, actors will be randomly dispersed in social space, and so will their interpersonal ties (Blau 1994; p. 125). Blau suggests that a decrease in the consolidation of two determinants of interpersonal relations diminishes their *salience*. For example, the weaker the association between age and wealth, the less salient either factor will be in determining the occurrence of interpersonal relations. It follows that in an unconsolidated situation, homophily is attenuated and interpersonal ties are randomly distributed among social positions that are themselves randomly distributed in social space (because the dimensions are orthogonal).

If dimensions are perfectly consolidated, then an actor's location on any one dimension predicts his or her location on each of the other dimensions, and two actors who have an identical status on one dimension will have an identical status across all dimensions. Such consolidation is consistent with the formation of a ridge structure that entails sequentially overlapping regions of structural cohesion in social space. In consolidated social spaces, where the probability of social ties declines precipitously with social distance, interpersonal ties will be nonrandomly distributed in the social space and will tend to be confined to relatively tight social manifolds.

For instance, consider a social space that is defined only by income and education and in which these two dimensions have a strong linear association. In this simple two-dimensional social space, the actors are distributed approximately in a straight line: Each actor occupies a location that might be shared with other actors, and he or she has neighboring positions on one or both sides that may be far or near and that may also be occupied by one or more actors. We might observe a segregated clustering of the actors in which there are few social ties between the clusters; i.e., all the social ties will be among actors of similar status on education and income. However, it is important to see that this formulation also allows for a situation in which all actors (apart from those in the most extreme social positions) are sequentially arrayed such that each has *proximate* nearest neighbors on either side. Because of the strong association between education and income, such a distribution of actors implies the presence of a tight social manifold that is composed of a sequence of social positions in which the probability of social ties between contiguous positions is high. This is the elemental social structural foundation of a ridge structure. If a sufficient number of actors are distributed in a sequential pattern (so that there is a continuum of overlapping and densely occupied regions of social space), then the tendency to form ties with actors who are proximate in social space will produce a framework of structural cohesion that includes the entire population.[10]

Blau recognizes the possibility of ridge structures; for example, he writes, "Whereas status diversity does not make interpersonal relations between the highest and lowest strata likely, it links them indirectly by fostering personal relations between strata that are not far apart" (1974, p. 624). However, he argues that such connectivity is less important than the intergroup ties that are fostered by homophily on single social dimensions: "Status diversity contributes to macro social integration, as heterogeneity does, though not as much, because it furnishes only indirect links between social strata that are widely separated" (1974, p. 625).

I argue that the indirect connectivity that is entailed in a ramifying ridge structure is a crucial structural foundation of macro-integration. Blau's analysis of heterogeneity gets into theoretical trouble because he ignores the social distance between actors in the multivariate social space when describing the mechanism by which social ties are formed between actors who differ on one or more of the dimensions. If actors are located in social space, then they are separated by a certain distance in that space and it is that distance which governs the probability of a social tie between them. If two actors who are distant from each other in social space happen to share an affiliation with some group, then such affiliation (when it has been taken into account in the locations of the actors) should not alter the probability of a social tie; this probability will be low regardless of any shared affiliations if the actors are sufficiently distant in social space. If two actors have proximate, nonidentical positions in social space, then they are likely to be similar on many but not all of the dimensions that define the space; their proximity in social space entails a high probability of a social tie, and this social tie, because it occurs between actors in nonidentical positions, may involve a cross-cutting of

10 The situation is complex, but not fundamentally different in a social space that is defined by many dimensions that vary in the associations among them. Depending on the character of these associations and the size of population, actors will be distributed in social space. Whether the social space is organized in a fashion that permits the emergence of a ridge structure depends on the existence of relatively tight social manifolds, each containing a contiguous zone of densely occupied regions of social space. It is the multivariate distribution of actors that determines the existence and configuration of such manifolds.

group boundaries (i.e., the two actors may be in different conditions of a nominal classification). In short, a preference to associate with persons of like characteristics is constrained by social distance.

Blau's analysis does not address the overall configuration of social ties in the social space. The occurrence of cross-cutting social ties, constrained by social distance, implies a foundation of macro-level social integration, but does so in only a limited way. Ties between actors in proximate (nonidentical) social positions are a necessary constituent of the social process that forms agreements between actors in distant locations in the social space. However, these ties may not produce a connectivity that includes the entire population of the social space. If social ties are not likely between actors who are distant from each other in social space, then macro-level integration *must* rest on the pattern of indirect connectivity among social positions.

Finally, Blau does not address the causal connection between the macro-structure of social ties and outcomes that integrate (in some concrete sense) the actors and positions. He suggests, as do Laumann and Knoke (1986), that a population will be integrated to the extent that its dimensions are unconsolidated. Unconsolidated dimensions imply a random distribution of actors in social space.[11] Because the actors are randomly distributed in the social space, both social stratification and ridge structures are unlikely events.[12] Hence, Blau's argument associates integration with the *absence* of social differentiation, and he does not address the social processes by which concrete integrative outcomes (such as interpersonal agreements and coordinated action) may be achieved within the context of a highly differentiated social structure.

I forward a hypothesis that is different from Blau's. Highly consolidated social dimensions, in a population of sufficient size, provide densely settled regions of social space, and (depending on the distribution of actors in the space) they also provide the basis of a ridge structure by which actors in distant locations are joined by sequential interlocking

11 In an unconsolidated situation, where the forces determining the occurrence of interpersonal relations are attenuated, interpersonal relations should be equally likely among all the pairs of members of the group. This implies that for any partition of the group into subgroups (obtained through a simultaneous rearrangement of the rows and columns of the adjacency matrix), the network densities within and between particular subgroups are expected to be uniform. In effect, in an unconsolidated structure there are no subgroups, if we define the occurrence of a subgroup in terms of a differential in the density of relations within and between subsets of group members. The pattern should be random.

12 A random distribution does not necessary imply a low level of structural cohesion, given a sufficiently high density of social ties. However, if weak associations also imply weak pressures to initiate a social tie, then the average number of social ties will decrease as consolidation decreases. Moreover, as the dimensions of social space become less salient, stratification of social ties will become less pronounced.

zones of structural cohesion. Such a ramifying ridge structure (which penetrates into distant regions of social space and includes most of the positions in the space) is a basis for the production of interpersonal agreements between actors who occupy distant social positions; ridge structures not only establish a robust basis of connectivity, but also (because most self-weights are diminished by a high mean indegree) enable the production of agreements via a social influence process. Hence, social differentiation segregates persons by putting social distance between actors; but while segregating actors, social differentiation also may provide a structural basis for boundary-spanning interpersonal agreements.

I do not assert that ridge structures, which allow the formation of consensus in a population, are ubiquitous or even that they are frequent. What I assert is that consensus is based on ridge structures and that the characteristics of a ridge structure determine the pattern of interpersonal agreements that get formed. The characteristics of a ridge structure depend on the distribution of actors in social space: The greater the proximity of the actors in a particular region, the greater the density of ties; and the greater the inclusiveness of the social manifold (its penetration into all the occupied regions of the social space), the greater the likelihood of a ridge structure that encompasses the entire population. Thus, a ridge structure can take the form of segregated subgroups between which few, if any, social ties exist, and it can take the form of a coherent framework of social cohesion that penetrates into all the occupied regions of the social space and that encompasses the entire population. In the former case, agreements must be predicated on social choice mechanisms, because the structural foundations of social influence processes are absent. In the latter case, the ridge structure allows a production of interpersonal agreements between the distant social positions that it includes.

I develop this argument in the next two chapters. First, in Chapter 9, I show that social influence processes, when played out in a ridge structure, can produce agreements among actors in complexly differentiated social structures. Second, in Chapter 10, I show that in large-scale complexly differentiated populations the production of consensus, via social influences, is associated with the occurrence of a dominant position-cluster, and I describe the structural foundations of such dominance.

9

The Production of Consensus

Abstract: I show how social influence network theory elucidates the development of agreements among actors in the six faculties of science. First, I present a formal analysis of the structural conditions of consensus. Second, I develop an image of the pattern of interpersonal influences among the social positions in the science faculties. Third, I assess the extent to which individual differences among the actors in the social positions are reduced, maintained, or increased by flows of interpersonal influence. Fourth, I locate the equilibrium destinations of actors that have emerged as a complex product of the social influence system.

> The essence of a group is not the similarity or dissimilarity of its members, but their interdependence. A group can be characterized as a "dynamical whole."
>
> – K. Lewin (1948, p. 84)

Were it not for the differences among actors, there would be scant interest in their interdependency. Social differentiation sets the stage for a drama (a) in which actors more or less radically modify the opinions that reflect their social positions, (b) in which the actors form, or fail to attain, interpersonal agreements, and (c) in which particular actors can emerge as dominating characters whose social positions define the content of the agreements that are formed. Each such drama has an idiosyncratic period and setting, but the thematic content is timeless and ubiquitous – a display and clash of different viewpoints that become reconciled or fixed in irreconcilable opposition. Each such drama presents a story concerned with the events that have reduced, maintained, or even increased differences of opinion between certain individuals and their social positions, but the basic process entailed in this stream of events is also timeless and ubiquitous – the repetitive balancing of Self and Other in the formation and maintenance of an opinion.

In this chapter, I describe certain characteristics of the social influence process that is played out in the physical, biological, and social science faculties at The University of Chicago and Columbia University. My analysis focuses on structural characteristics of the influence systems in these universities. First, I present a formal analysis of the connectivity of influence networks and the structural conditions for the production of consensus. Second, I describe the structure of the direct interpersonal influences among the social positions in the six faculties of science. Third, I assess the extent to which differences of opinion among actors are reduced, maintained, or increased by the flows of interpersonal influence in these communities. Fourth, I locate the expected equilibrium destinations of actors.

9.1 Structural Conditions of Consensus

I begin with the work of Harary, Norman, and Cartwright (1965, pp. 50–84) on connectedness. Recall (from section 4.7) that two actors can be classified, according to the type of network connections that exist between them, as either *disconnected* if they are not joined by a semipath, *weakly connected* if they are joined by a semipath, *unilaterally connected* if at least one actor is reachable from the other, or *strongly connected* if each actor is reachable from the other.[1] In terms of these dyadic-level connectivity categories, larger subsets of actors or subnets (including the entire network) can be classified. For all pairs of actors i and j ($i \neq j$) in a subnet, the subnet is *strongly connected* or *strong* if i and j are mutually reachable, *unilaterally connected* or *unilateral* if i can reach j or j can reach i, *weakly connected* or *weak* if i and j are joined by a semipath, and *disconnected* if there is at least one pair of actors that is not connected by a semipath.

A weak, unilateral, or strong subnet is said to be a *component* of a network if it contains all the lines in the network that occur among the members of the subnet and if it is maximal; the subnet is maximal if it contains the largest possible number of members of the network while preserving the defining characteristic of the component (i.e., its weak, unilateral, or strong connectivity). Thus, a *strong component* is a maximal strongly connected subnet; i.e., each point in such a component is mutually reachable via lines among the members of the subnet, and no other point from the network can be added to the component without destroying the strong connectivity of the component. Similarly, a *unilat-*

1 Recall that a semipath is a chain of lines that connects two points, in which the direction of the lines is ignored, and in which no line appears more than once.

eral component is a maximal unilaterally connected subnet, and a *weak component* is a maximal weakly connected subnet.

Given a partitioning of the network into components, a *condensation* of the network may be obtained that provides a simplified image of the overall structure of the network. In the condensed image of the network, the points are components and the lines between components are determined by some rule. Of particular interest are condensations with respect to strong components. Following Harary, Norman, and Cartwright (1965), let $\mathring{Z}$ denote the strong condensation of Z in which the points are the strong components of Z and a line exists from a strong component i to a strong component j in $\mathring{Z}$ if and only if there is *at least one* line in Z from a member of component i to a member of component j.

A condensation of Z in terms of its strong components, $\mathring{Z}$, provides a simplified and readily interpretable image of the pattern of influence flows. Because actors within a strong component are mutually reachable, actors within the same strong component influence each other. Any influence incoming to a strong component must influence all the members of the component. Any influence outgoing from a strong component must affect all the members of those components who are reachable in the condensed image. If there is a component that reaches all other components and that is not reachable from the other components, then that component is a potential center of power.

No cyclic paths may exist in $\mathring{Z}$, i.e., paths that originate and terminate on the same component.[2] Because $\mathring{Z}$ is acyclic, it has the following properties as has been shown by Harary, Norman, and Cartwright (1965, pp. 64–5):

> $\mathring{Z}$ has at least one component with an outdegree of zero and at least one component with an indegree of zero.
>
> If $\mathring{Z}$ contains multiple strong components that are unilaterally connected, then it has a unique receiver (a component with an outdegree of zero and an indegree greater than zero) and a unique transmitter (a component with an indegree of zero and an outdegree of greater than zero).

Hence, if $\mathring{Z}$ is a single strong component, then every actor influences directly or indirectly every other actor in Z; and if $\mathring{Z}$ has multiple strong components and is unilateral, then there is exactly one component that is not influenced by any other component and that influences all other

2 If there is path from component i to component j, there cannot also be a path from component j to component i because in that case i and j would form a single strong component. Hence, for instance, influences among pairs of strong components either must be absent or anti-symmetric.

components. These are powerful theorems, and in certain special cases they can be useful in describing and elucidating the implications of a macro-structure of interpersonal influence.

A formal analysis of the macro-level connectivity of influence networks was pursued by French (1956) and Harary (1959). They consider the implications of the pattern of all nonzero interpersonal influences, i.e., the structure of the adjacency matrix, $\mathbf{Z}^{(0)} = [z_{ij}^{(0)}]$

$$z_{ij}^{(0)} = \begin{cases} 1 \text{ if } a_{ii}w_{ij} > 0 \\ 0 \text{ if } a_{ii}w_{ij} = 0 \end{cases} \tag{9.1}$$

Their work concentrates on a special case of the present theory in which the weight of the endogenous interpersonal influences is at the maximum theoretical value, $a_{ii} = 1$, for *all* actors: that is, $\mathbf{A} = \mathbf{I}$, and hence $\mathbf{Y}^{(t)} = \mathbf{W}\mathbf{Y}^{(t-1)}$ for $t = 2, 3, \ldots$ from Eq. (2.2).[3]

French viewed the connectivity category of the influence network $\mathbf{Z}^{(0)}$ as a measure of group cohesion, and he showed that unilateral connectivity is a sufficient condition of consensus. If $\mathbf{Z}^{(0)}$ is unilateral, then it must contain one, and only one, strong component with members that influence directly or indirectly all the actors; French (1956) showed that if such a strong component contained one actor, then a consensus would emerge on the initial opinion of the actor. Harary (1959) subsequently showed that strong connectivity also is a sufficient condition of consensus:

> For $\mathbf{A} = \mathbf{I}$, if the adjacency network $\mathbf{Z}^{(0)}$ of an influence network $\mathbf{AW}$ is strongly connected, then the members will attain consensus.

He also generalized French's conclusion about unilateral connectivity. Networks exist that are *not unilateral* and that contain one or more actors who influence directly or indirectly all the actors. However, for any $\mathbf{Z}$ the strong condensation $\mathring{\mathbf{Z}}$ has one and only one *subset* of strong components from which paths of influence reach the members of all other components and to which there are no paths of influence; Harary (1959) refers to *each* of the strong components in such a subset as a *power subgroup*. Because there are no influences on the members of a power subgroup other than those among its members, each such subgroup is an independent subsystem. Hence, Harary forwards the more general conclusion that a sufficient condition of consensus is the presence of a unique power subgroup:

3 French and Harary make additional assumptions about the content of **W**; and some of their conclusions rest on these additional assumptions, which I do not deal with here.

> For $\mathbf{A} = \mathbf{I}$, if the adjacency matrix $\mathbf{Z}^{(0)}$ of an influence network $\mathbf{AW}$ has exactly one power subgroup, then the members of the network will attain consensus.

A unique power subgroup is the one and only component in $\mathring{\mathbf{Z}}$ that is not influenced by any other component and that has a direct or indirect influence on all the other components in $\mathring{\mathbf{Z}}$.

Reachability in an influence network indicates a flow of influence but nothing about the strength of that flow. When the influence network is a single strong component, we may conclude that every actor can influence every other actor, but there is no discrimination between the minor and major flows of influence among the actors in this component. In the case of multiple components, even the existence of a unique power subgroup does not necessarily imply that this subgroup has an important influence on actors in the other components. These limitations on the interpretation of the structure of an influence network arise in the general case of the influence process, where the weight of the endogenous interpersonal influences may vary among the actors (i.e., where $\mathbf{A} \neq \mathbf{I}$ and $\mathbf{Y}^{(t)} = \mathbf{AWY}^{(t-1)} + (\mathbf{I} - \mathbf{A})\mathbf{Y}^{(1)}$ for $t = 2, 3, \ldots$). In this general case, the pattern of interpersonal adjacencies no longer provides a secure basis for conclusions about equilibrium outcomes (e.g., the emergence and location of agreements).

However, there is an important special case of $\mathbf{A} \neq \mathbf{I}$ for which definite conclusions can be derived. The special case concerns a situation in which actors have either zero self-weights ($a_{ii} = 1$) or maximal self-weights ($a_{ii} = 0$), which is approximately the circumstance of the actors in each of the six science faculties; see Table 6.4. In such a situation, there will be a consensus if the actors in the latter subset (a) have identical initial opinions and (b) contain a unique power subgroup that can influence all actors in the former subset directly or indirectly. In effect, the influence process can be treated as if it were the special case of $\mathbf{A} = \mathbf{I}$, with the understanding that for each actor with a maximal self-weight, w_{ii} is not set to zero (as is required by the stipulation $w_{ii} = 1 - a_{ii}$), but instead w_{ii} is set to one. Hence, this special case is formally subsumed by Harary's analysis.

This formal analysis describes the conditions for a *strict* consensus. However, in the absence of a perfect satisfaction of the conditions of consensus, an approximate consensus may be produced by the influence process. To attain an approximate consensus, the connectivity conditions of consensus must be satisfied, so that influences can reach all actors with low self-weights ($a_{ii} \approx 1$), and the remaining actors with large self-weights ($a_{ii} \approx 0$) must be located in the same region of social space.

9.2 Structure of Direct Interpersonal Influences

In Chapter 8, I described the structure of interpersonal attachments. The relationship between the structure of interpersonal attachments and the structure of interpersonal influences is somewhat subtle. First, we must distinguish between direct and total (or net) interpersonal influences. Total interpersonal influences arise from the flows of influence that, in turn, arise from the repetitive response of actors to the changing opinions of significant others; these total effects are only weakly constrained by the underlying structure of interpersonal attachments. I deal with total interpersonal effects in Chapter 10. Second, although the structure of interpersonal attachments provides opportunities for direct (unmediated) interpersonal influences, the strength of such an influence upon an actor is a function of an *interaction* between the self-weight (centrality) of the actor and the relative weight of the significant other. Hence, the direct (unmediated) interpersonal influence of actor j on actor i (a) will be *weak* to the extent that either the self-weight of actor i is large or the relative weight of actor j as a significant other for actor i is slight and (b) will be *strong* to the extent that the self-weight of actor i is slight and the relative weight of actor j as a significant other for actor i is large. A high probability of an interpersonal attachment from actor i to actor j does *not* necessarily indicate a strong direct interpersonal influence from actor j to actor i, nor does a low (nonzero) probability of such an attachment necessarily indicate a weak influence. In short, although interpersonal attachments are the foundations of the influence system, a description of these foundations does not describe the superstructure of interpersonal influences that is constructed upon them.

Formally, the direct interpersonal influences of actors are given by the coefficients in the matrix **AW**. At each point in time the weight of the interpersonal effect of actor j on actor i is $a_{ii}w_{ij}$ in

$$y_i^{(t)} = a_{ii}w_{ii}y_i^{(t-1)} + \sum_{j \neq 1} a_{ii}w_{ij}y_j^{(t-1)} + (1 - a_{ii})y_i^{(1)} \tag{9.2}$$

[Eq. (2.5)], where $0 \leq \{a_{ii}, w_{ij}\} \leq 1$, $w_{ii} = 1 - a_{ii}$, and $\sum_j w_{ij} = 1$; and this weight, in turn, is a function of the centrality of actor i (c_i) and probability of actor i's attachment to actor j (c_{ij})

$$a_{ii}w_{ij} = (1 - c_i)\frac{c_{ij}}{\sum_k c_{ik}} \tag{9.3}$$

[Eq. (6.14–6.15)]. Because this formulation entails an equation of an actor's centrality and self-weight, $1 - c_i = (1 - w_{ii})^2$, it can be said that actors with sufficiently high structural centrality are *heavyweights* and are not susceptible to interpersonal influence regardless of their interpersonal attachments. Because $c_{ij/}\sum_k c_{ik} = w_{ij/}\sum_k w_{ik}$ for $i \neq \{j, k\}$ [Eq. (4.11)], and because all of the direct effects on actor i sum to 1,

$$a_{ii}w_{ii} + \sum_{j \neq i} a_{ii}w_{ij} + (1 - a_{ii}) = 1 \tag{9.4}$$

[Eq. (2.8)], it is the *relative weight* of actor j in the bundle of actor i's attachments and influences that allows actor j to be a significant other for actor i, rather than the absolute strength or intensity of their relationship.

To describe the pattern of direct *interpersonal* effects among social positions, a blockmodel of **AW** can be utilized and a reduced image of the interpositional effects can be described in terms of the mean aggregate influence *upon* an actor in a position-cluster of the members of another position-cluster. To obtain the effect of position-cluster B on A, the effects of the actors in position-cluster B on the actors in position-cluster A are summed and this sum is divided by the number of actors in position-cluster A. Because the largest possible aggregated effect of the members of cluster B on cluster A is equal to the number of members in cluster A, the derived statistic also is a measure of the extent to which the effect of a cluster approaches its maximum possible value.

These blockmodels of direct influence are reported in the Appendix, and Figures 9.1–9.6 (which are based on them) describe the effects among the position-clusters. In each of the science faculties, the position-clusters are embedded in a dense fabric of weak to moderate effects; i.e., there are few clusters between which there is no influence. The strongest effects are organized in a center–periphery pattern. In certain science faculties, the center consists of a single cluster, and in other faculties, the center contains multiple clusters. The central clusters are not subject to strong influences, and the effects that radiate from them include all the peripheral clusters.

In Chicago Physical Science (Figure 9.1), the central position-clusters are Clusters 5 (Chemistry, Physics) and 6 (Physics, Astronomy & Astrophysics); both clusters have substantial within-cluster effects and Cluster 6 has the largest such effect of any of the clusters in the system. Apart from the mutual influence of these two clusters, they more strongly affect than are affected by the other clusters in the system. These other clusters are divided into two subsets between which the influences are weak or absent; one of these subsets consists of Mathematics, Statistics, and Geophysical Science clusters (1, 2, 3, 4, and 10), and the other subset consists of Chemistry and Astronomy & Astrophysics clusters (7, 8, and 9). The central clusters influence both of the subsets, and each other. This net-

Figure 9.1. Chicago Physical Science blockmodel image of influence system (mean direct effects within and among position-clusters).

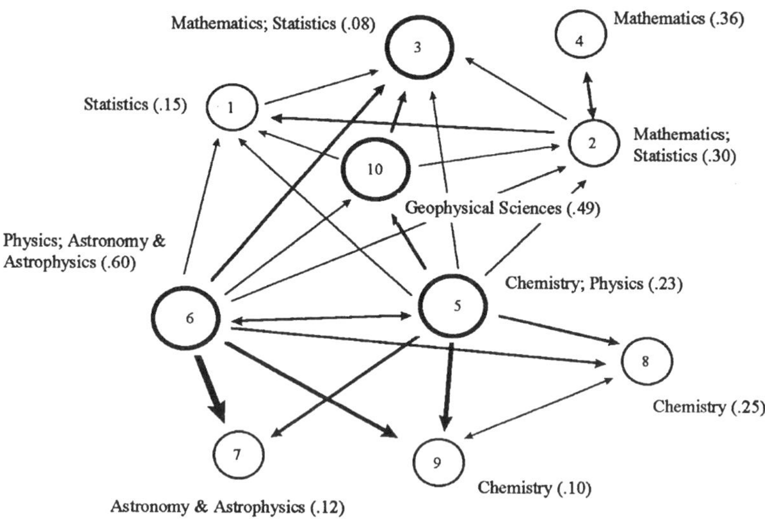

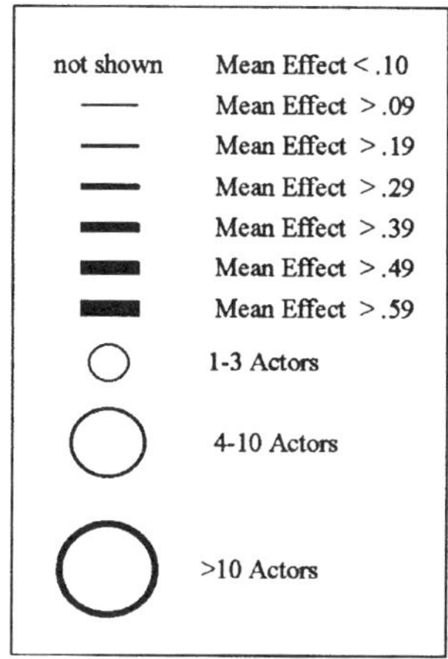

Figure 9.2. Chicago Biological Science blockmodel image of influence system (mean direct effects within and among position-clusters).

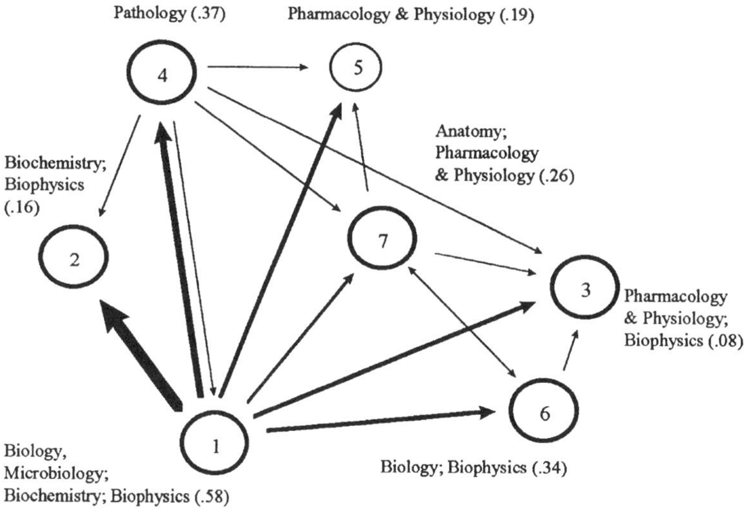

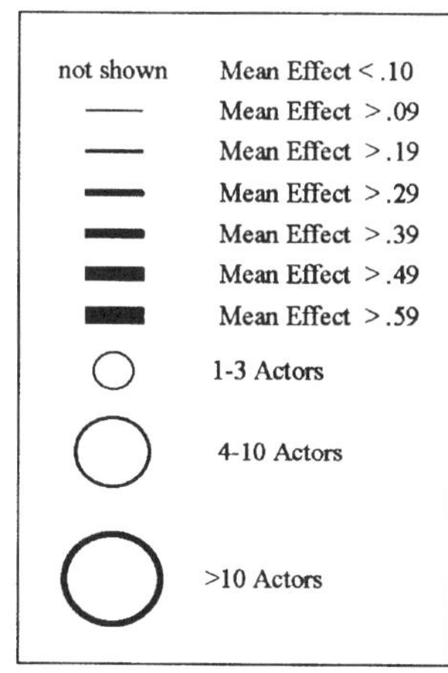

Figure 9.3. Chicago Social Science blockmodel image of influence system (mean direct effects within and among position-clusters).

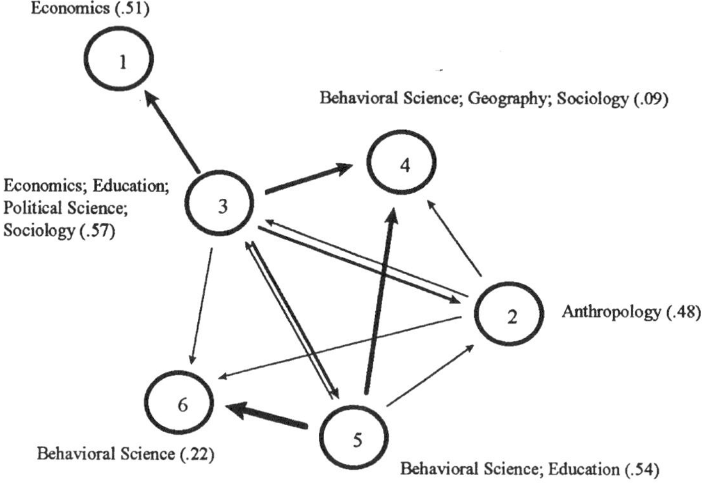

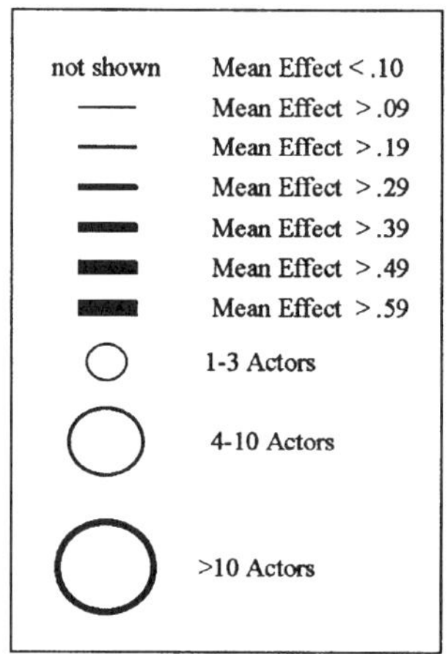

Figure 9.4. Columbia Physical Science blockmodel image of influence system (mean direct effects within and among position-clusters).

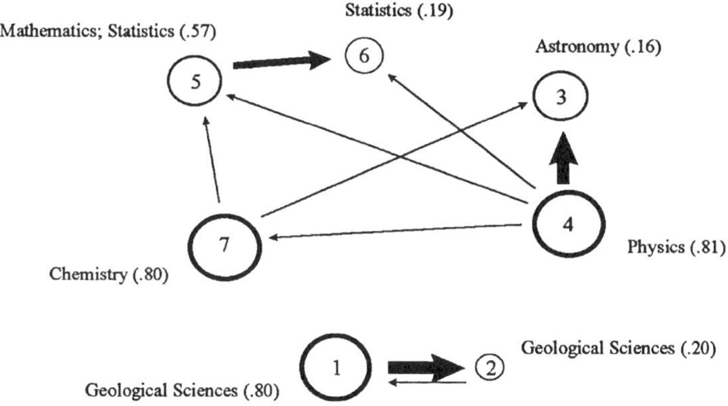

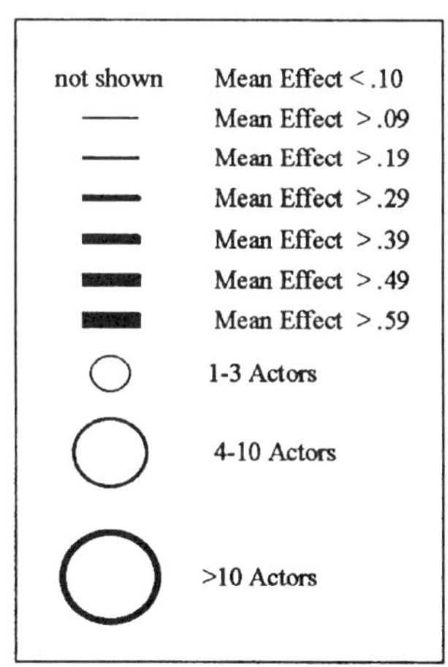

Figure 9.5. Columbia Biological Science blockmodel image of influence system (mean direct effects within and among position-clusters).

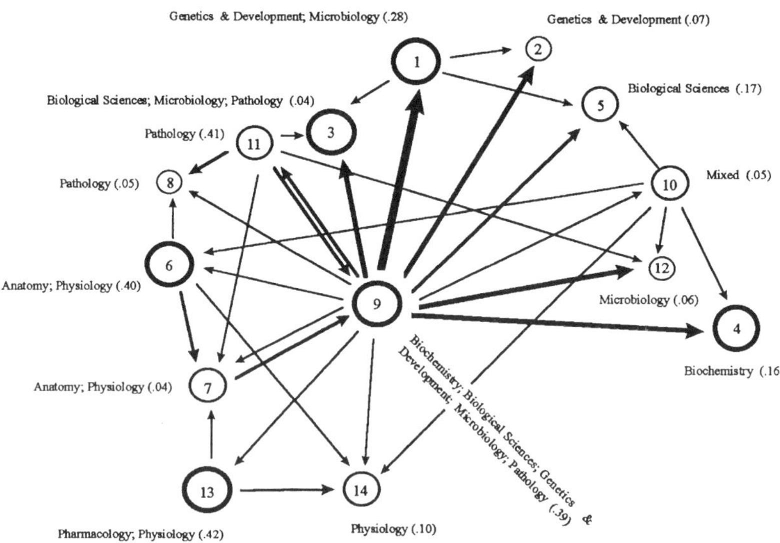

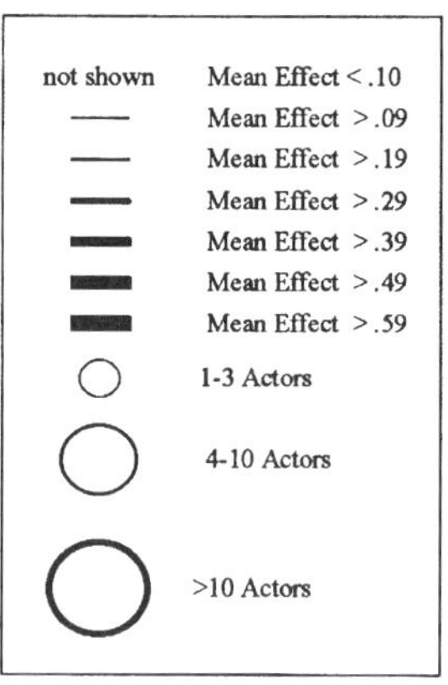

Figure 9.6. Columbia Social Science blockmodel image of influence system (mean direct effects within and among position-clusters).

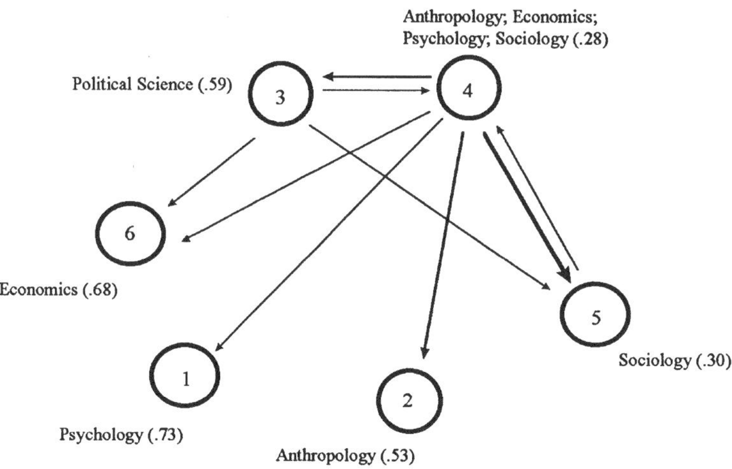

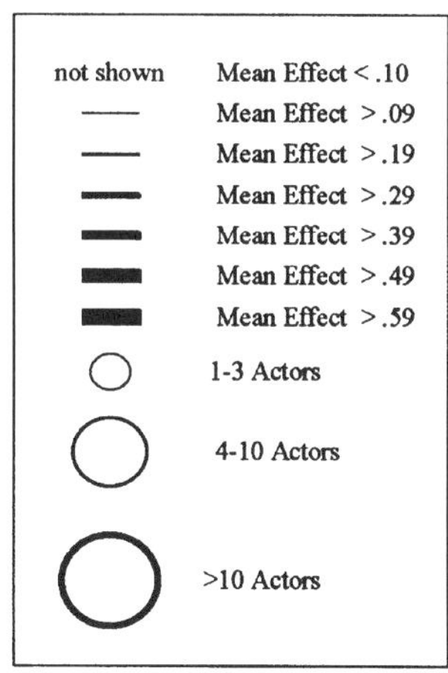

work image of the influence system is unilaterally connected, and Clusters 5 and 6 are *point bases* from which flows of influence reach all the other clusters in the system.

In Chicago Biological Science (Figure 9.2), Cluster 1 (Biology, Microbiology, Biochemistry, Biophysics) is the central cluster. It radiates effects to all the other clusters. Cluster 4 (Pathology) also radiates effects (including one to Cluster 1), but these effects are less substantial than those from Cluster 1. Both Clusters 1 and 4 have substantial within-cluster effects, and Cluster 1 has the largest such effect of any of the clusters in the system. This network image of the influence system is unilaterally connected, and Clusters 1 and 4 are *point bases* from which flows of influence reach all the other clusters in the system.

In Chicago Social Science (Figure 9.3), the situation is more complex. Cluster 3 (Economics, Education, Political Science, Sociology) and Cluster 5 (Education, Behavioral Science) radiate effects and appear to be most central. Three of the clusters are clearly peripheral with respect to their effects on other clusters: Cluster 1 (Economics), Cluster 4 (Behavioral Science, Geography, Sociology), and Cluster 6 (Behavioral Science). However, Cluster 2 (Anthropology) also radiates effects (including an effect on Cluster 1). This network image of the influence system is unilaterally connected, and Clusters 2, 3, and 5 are each *point bases* from which flows of influence reach all the other clusters in the system. These three clusters also have substantial within-cluster effects, but so does the peripheral Cluster 1 (Economics). Hence, the likely outcomes of this system are less obvious than those of the Physical and Biological Sciences.

In Columbia Physical Science (Figure 9.4), the network image of the influence system is disconnected; however, the system is connected on the basis of the weaker effects (not shown). The Geological Sciences (Clusters 1 and 2) form one subnet, and the remaining clusters form a unilaterally connected subnet in which Cluster 4 (Physics) is a *point basis* from which influence radiates to each of the other clusters. Although Cluster 4 has a substantial within-cluster effect, so do Clusters 5 and 7, which are members of the same subnet. There are no point bases in the image of this system, from which flows of influence reach all the other clusters in the system.

In Columbia Biological Science (Figure 9.5), Cluster 9 (Biochemistry, Biological Sciences, Genetics & Development, Microbiology, Pathology) is the central cluster, and it radiates effects to all the other clusters. The network image of the influence system is unilaterally connected, and Cluster 9 is a *point basis* from which flows of influence reach all the other clusters in the system. Cluster 9 has a substantial within-cluster effect, but so do Clusters 1, 6, 11, and 13. In this system, Clusters 6, 7,

11, and 13 are also point bases; however, they all depend on Cluster 9 for their reachability.

In Columbia Social Science (Figure 9.6), Cluster 4 (Anthropology, Economics, Psychology, Sociology) radiates effects to all the other clusters. Clusters 3 (Anthropology) and 5 (Sociology) have effects on Cluster 4 and, via these effects, also influence all of the clusters in the system. All of the clusters have substantial within-cluster effects. Clusters 3, 4, and 5 are *point bases* however, Clusters 3 and 5 depend on Cluster 4 for their reachability.

9.3 Reduction of Social Distance

I now present evidence that shows that in five of the six faculties of science, the influence system produces a massive convergence of actors to a particular region of the social space. The exception is Columbia Physical Science (Figure 9.4), where there is a convergence to two different regions.

Evidence on the extent and pattern of the convergence of actors to a single region of social space is obtained with a hierarchical analysis of the equilibrium distances $\Delta_{ij}^{(\infty)}$ among the actors. The equilibrium distance $\Delta_{ij}^{(\infty)}$ between two actors is

$$\Delta_{ij}^{(\infty)} = \Big[\sum_{k=1}^{K} (y_{ik}^{(\infty)} - y_{jk}^{(\infty)})^2\Big]^{1/2} \tag{9.5}$$

where $\mathbf{Y}^{(\infty)} = [y_{ik}^{(\infty)}]$ are the coordinates of the equilibrium opinions obtained from

$$\mathbf{Y}^{(\infty)} = (\mathbf{I} - \mathbf{AW})^{-1} (\mathbf{I} - \mathbf{A})\mathbf{Y}^{(1)} \tag{9.6}$$

[Eq. (2.11)]. The foundations of this equation and its three components – **A**, **W**, and $\mathbf{Y}^{(1)}$ – have been described in the previous chapters.

At Chicago in the Physical, Biological, and Social Sciences, and at Columbia in the Biological and Social Sciences, the percentage reduction of initial distances

$$\frac{\left(\sum_i \sum_j \Delta_{ij}^{(1)}\right) - \left(\sum_i \sum_j \Delta_{ij}^{(\infty)}\right)}{\left(\sum_i \sum_j \Delta_{ij}^{(1)}\right)} \times 100 \qquad i \neq j \tag{9.7}$$

is in the range of 93–95%, and nearly the entire population of actors is situated at equilibrium within a tight social manifold where the maximum distance between any two actors is approximately 0.05:

> In Chicago Physical Science, the initial distances have been reduced at equilibrium by 95.1%, and 129 of the 141 faculty

members (91.5%) are situated in a single equilibrium manifold of diameter 0.030.

In Chicago Biological Science, the initial distances have been reduced at equilibrium by 95.3%, and 135 of the 142 faculty members (91.5%) are situated in a single equilibrium manifold of diameter 0.048.

In Chicago Social Science, the initial distances have been reduced at equilibrium by 98.2%, and 149 of the 153 faculty members (97.4%) are situated in a single equilibrium manifold of diameter 0.014.

In Columbia Biological Science, the initial distances have been reduced at equilibrium by 93.4%, and 143 of the 153 faculty members (93.5%) are situated in a single equilibrium manifold of diameter 0.054.

In Columbia Social Science, the initial distances have been reduced at equilibrium by 95.5%, and 148 of the 157 faculty members (94.3%) are situated in a single equilibrium manifold of diameter 0.051.

In each of these cases, the faculty members who are *not* located in the equilibrium manifold are heavyweights, whose opinions have not been substantially affected by the influence process (I develop this finding in Chapter 10).

The situation in the Physical Sciences at Columbia University is quite different from all of the above cases. Table 9.1 presents the results. Although the initial distances have been substantially reduced (82.2%), this percentage reduction is markedly less pronounced than in the other cases, and the hierarchical clustering of the equilibrium distances indicates a differentiation of three clusters. One of these clusters contains all of the astronomers, most of the physicists, all of the mathematicians, most of the statisticians, and one chemist; another cluster contains all of the chemists, and the rest of the physicists and statisticians; and the remaining cluster contains all of the geological scientists. The differentiation of the first two clusters is modest: actors have converged to a small region of the social space where the distance between them is at most 0.09, and they are modestly differentiated within this region. However, the cluster of geological scientists occupies a distinct region at equilibrium, within which most of its actors have converged into a tight manifold. Thus, in Columbia Physical Science there is *weak convergence* that is comprised of essentially two clusters, each of which separately converges to a small region of the social space, but which are separated by greater social distance than we found at The University of Chicago or at Columbia University in the Biological and Social Sciences. The cleavage

Table 9.1. *Hierarchical Cluster Analysis (Diameter Method) of Equilbrium Social Distance*

Columbia Physical Science

```
ALL CLUSTERS FUSED -- overall maximum distance     =     0.64545
Distance      Cluster members
-------------------------------------------------------------------
       .      2.3.9.8.2.4.3.5.6.1.5.1.3.4.4.5.6.7.1.1.2.2.6.8.6.8.7.1.3.7.5.9.1.2.9.3.5.6.8.1.1.2.6.7.3.7.6.9.2.5.1.5.3.6.4.8.3.2.5.2.1.1.1.9.4.6.1.9.7.7.2.8.3.4.1.4.9.8.9.3.
       .      ..5.5.2.7.4.1.8.8.0.1.0...8.0.2.7.5...7.4.0.6.1.5.7...0.7.6.4.3.4.5.8.0.5.0.6.0.5.3.3.4.6.1.2.2.9.6.0...9...2...2.1.0.6.6.8.3.4.9.1.1.9.3.0.2.0.3.1.0.3...3.1.4.
       .      ..................2...1......................................................3.....................5.............................................0...........
   0.00036    F-F.............................................................................................................................................................
   0.01047    F-F-F-F-A-F-F-F-F-F-F-F.E-E-D-E.A-F-A.D-B.E-E-E-E-E-E-E-E...E-D-D-E-D-D-D-D.A-F-F.F-F-A-F-A-A-A-F-F.......B-B-B-B-B-B-B-B-B-B-B-B-B.B-B-B...D-D-F-F-F...B-F...B-
   0.02033    F-F-F-F-A-F-F-F-F-F-F-F-E-E-D-E-A-F-A-D-B.E-E-E-E-E-E-E-E-F.E-D-D-E-D-D-D-D-A-F-F-F-F-A-F-A-A-A-F-F...B-B-B-B-B-B-B-B-B-B-B-B-B-B-B-B-B-B-B.D-D-F-F-F-F.B-F-D.B-
   0.03125    F-F-F-F-A-F-F-F-F-F-F-F-E-E-D-E-A-F-A-D-B.E-E-E-E-E-E-E-E-F-E-D-D-E-D-D-D-D-A-F-F-F-F-A-F-A-A-A-F-F...B-B-B-B-B-B-B-B-B-B-B-B-B-B-B-B-B-B-B.D-D-F-F-F-F.B-F-D-B-
   0.04792    F-F-F-F-A-F-F-F-F-F-F-F-E-E-D-E-A-F-A-D-B-E-E-E-E-E-E-E-E-F-E-D-D-E-D-D-D-D-A-F-F-F-F-A-F-A-A-A-F-F...B-B-B-B-B-B-B-B-B-B-B-B-B-B-B-B-B-B-B-D-D-F-F-F-F.B-F-D-B-
   0.05194    F-F-F-F-A-F-F-F-F-F-F-F-E-E-D-E-A-F-A-D-B-E-E-E-E-E-E-E-E-F-E-D-D-E-D-D-D-D-A-F-F-F-F-A-F-A-A-A-F-F...B-B-B-B-B-B-B-B-B-B-B-B-B-B-B-B-B-B-B-D-D-F-F-F-F-B-F-D-B-
   0.07786    F-F-F-F-A-F-F-F-F-F-F-F-E-E-D-E-A-F-A-D-B-E-E-E-E-E-E-E-E-F-E-D-D-E-D-D-D-D-A-F-F-F-F-A-F-A-A-A-F-F-B.B-B-B-B-B-B-B-B-B-B-B-B-B-B-B-B-B-B-B-D-D-F-F-F-F-B-F-D-B-
   0.08960    F-F-F-F-A-F-F-F-F-F-F-F-E-E-D-E-A-F-A-D-B-E-E-E-E-E-E-E-E-F-E-D-D-E-D-D-D-D-A-F-F-F-F-A-F-A-A-A-F-F-B-B-B-B-B-B-B-B-B-B-B-B-B-B-B-B-B-B-B-B-D-D-F-F-F-F-B-F-D-B-
   0.09604    F-F-F-F-A-F-F-F-F-F-F-F-E-E-D-E-A-F-A-D-B-E-E-E-E-E-E-E-E-F-E-D-D-E-D-D-D-D-A-F-F-F-F-A-F-A-A-A-F-F-B-B-B-B-B-B-B-B-B-B-B-B-B-B-B-B-B-B-B-B-D-D-F-F-F-F-B-F-D-B-
   0.12117    F-F-F-F-A-F-F-F-F-F-F-F-E-E-D-E-A-F-A-D-B-E-E-E-E-E-E-E-E-F-E-D-D-E-D-D-D-D-A-F-F-F-F-A-F-A-A-A-F-F-B-B-B-B-B-B-B-B-B-B-B-B-B-B-B-B-B-B-B-B-D-D-F-F-F-F-B-F-D-B-
   0.15410    F-F-F-F-A-F-F-F-F-F-F-F-E-E-D-E-A-F-A-D-B-E-E-E-E-E-E-E-E-F-E-D-D-E-D-D-D-D-A-F-F-F-F-A-F-A-A-A-F-F-B-B-B-B-B-B-B-B-B-B-B-B-B-B-B-B-B-B-B-B-D-D-F-F-F-F-B-F-D-B-
   0.18053    F-F-F-F-A-F-F-F-F-F-F-F-E-E-D-E-A-F-A-D-B-E-E-E-E-E-E-E-E-F-E-D-D-E-D-D-D-D-A-F-F-F-F-A-F-A-A-A-F-F-B-B-B-B-B-B-B-B-B-B-B-B-B-B-B-B-B-B-B-B-D-D-F-F-F-F-B-F-D-B-

              [                                                                                FIRST MANIFOLD

continued
-------------------------------------------------------------------
       .      7.5.6.7.4.3.7.8.2.8.4.4.5.1.7.8.9.9.8.4.1.9.1.6.5
       .      7.9.4.8...8.2.8.8.9.7.5.3.0.9.4.0.6.5.6.9.7.2.9.7
       .      ..........................4......................
   0.00036    .................................................
   0.01047    B...C-C-C-C-C-C.C-C.....C-C-C-C-C-C.....C-C......
   0.02033    B...C-C-C-C-C-C-C-C-C...C-C-C-C-C-C-C...C-C......
   0.03125    B...C-C-C-C-C-C-C-C-C-C.C-C-C-C-C-C-C...C-C......
   0.04792    B...C-C-C-C-C-C-C-C-C-C-C-C-C-C-C-C-C...C-C......
   0.05194    B...C-C-C-C-C-C-C-C-C-C-C-C-C-C-C-C-C...C-C......
   0.07786    B...C-C-C-C-C-C-C-C-C-C-C-C-C-C-C-C-C...C-C-C....
   0.08960    B...C-C-C-C-C-C-C-C-C-C-C-C-C-C-C-C-C...C-C-C....
   0.09604    B...C-C-C-C-C-C-C-C-C-C-C-C-C-C-C-C-C-C.C-C-C....
   0.12117    B...C-C-C-C-C-C-C-C-C-C-C-C-C-C-C-C-C-C-C-C-C....
   0.15410    B...C-C-C-C-C-C-C-C-C-C-C-C-C-C-C-C-C-C-C-C-C-C..
   0.18053    B-D.C-C-C-C-C-C-C-C-C-C-C-C-C-C-C-C-C-C-C-C-C-C..

                ]^[          SECOND MANIFOLD                   ]
```

A=Astronomy B=Chemistry C=Geological Sciences D=Statistics E=Mathematics F=Physics between the geologists and other physical scientists at Columbia is most likely the result of the ecological organization of this community: most of the Geological Science faculty is located off the main campus. However, the differentiation within the other part of this community, which is located on the main campus, also is more pronounced than we found in the other faculties of science.

9.4 Equilibrium Destinations

In five of the science faculties there is a single equilibrium manifold that contains all but a few actors. In Columbia Physical Science there are two equilibrium manifolds, which I have labeled "First" and "Second" in Table 9.1. Because of the substantial convergence of actors, the *centroid* of the positions of actors in each of the equilibrium manifolds can be used to locate these manifolds in social space. The centroid is the point in social space with coordinates that are the mean values of the equilibrium coordinates of the members of the manifold. In the *k*th dimension of the social space, the coordinate of the centroid of the n_m members of the *m*th manifold, consisting of the subset of the actors H, is

$$\tilde{y}_{mk}^{(\infty)} = \frac{\sum_{h \in H} y_{hk}^{(\infty)}}{n_m} \tag{9.8}$$

The centroid of a particular equilibrium manifold may or may not be close to the social position (initial opinion) of any actor; it may be a compromise position that was not initially represented by any of the actors. However, if the centroid does happen to be in the vicinity of a social position, then the content of the equilibrium position of the members of the manifold can be identified with that neighboring social position.[4]

To locate the equilibrium manifolds in social space, we require a measure of distance between a manifold's centroid and the initial position of each actor:

4 In Chapter 10, I will show that the content of equilibrium manifolds can sometimes also be described in terms of the proportionate contributions of different actors (or social positions) to the equilibrium opinions. The method that I describe in the present chapter does not assume a simple partitioning of the contributions of social positions. When the net contributions to equilibrium opinions are distributed among many heterogeneous sources, and the consensus cannot be described in terms of the net contributions of a few social positions, the consensus can occur near one of the initial positions of the actors.

$$\Delta_{mi} = \left[\sum_{k=1}^{K} (y_{mk}^{(\infty)} - y_{ik}^{(1)})^2\right]^{1/2} \tag{9.9}$$

The findings are presented in Table 9.2. For each manifold, the table lists those actors whose initial positions are within a given distance from the centroid of the manifold. Of particular interest is the existence of one or more actors who are in the *immediate neighborhood* of the centroid. Hence, I have listed only actors whose initial positions are no more than 0.20 distant from the centroid of the equilibrium manifold.

With the exception of Columbia Physical Science, in each of the science faculties, the faculty members have converged to regions of the social space that are located near the initial positions of a subset of actors. Hence, in most cases it is possible to characterize the expected content of the agreements that are produced. For this analysis, it will be useful to recall the findings that were presented in Chapter 7, Table 7.2, on the memberships of the position-clusters.

In Chicago Physical Science, the actors converge to a region that is occupied by members of Position-Cluster 5, which is a multidisciplinary group of chemists and physicists, and Position-Cluster 6, which is a multidisciplinary group of physicists, astrophysicists, and astronomers. Recall that these clusters radiated direct effects to the other clusters in this influence system and had effects on each another (Figure 9.1). Of the twenty-five actors who are less than 0.150 distant from the centroid of the equilibrium manifold, twenty are members of The Enrico Fermi Institute; and of the seven actors who are within 0.10 of the centroid, six are members of this institute (including the actor whose initial position in social space is closest to the centroid).

In Chicago Biological Science, the actors converge to a region that is most closely represented by certain positions in Position-Clusters 1 and 4. Cluster 1 is occupied by a multidisciplinary group of biologists, microbiologists, biochemists, and biophysicists; and Cluster 4 is occupied by pathologists. These two clusters, especially Cluster 1, radiated direct effects to the other clusters in this influence system, and had effects on each other (Figure 9.2).

In Chicago Social Science, actors converge to a region in the vicinity of certain positions within Position-Cluster 3, which is occupied by a multidisciplinary group of faculty in Economics, Education, Political Science, and Sociology. Of the seven actors who are 0.10 distant from the centroid of the equilibrium manifold, six have primary or secondary affiliations with Sociology. Hence, the cross-pressure between Clusters 3 and 5 (Figure 9.3) is resolved in favor of Cluster 3.

In Columbia Biological Science, the actors converge to a region that

Table 9.2. *Distance of Actors' Initial Social Positions from the Centroid of an Equilibrium Social Manifold*

Distance	Actor and cluster identifications (clusters are in parentheses)						
	Chicago Physical Science	Chicago Biological Science	Chicago Social Science	Columbia Physical Science #1	Columbia Physical Science #2	Columbia Biological Science	Columbia Social Science
0.000–0.050	22(5)	.	.	.	.	.	.
0.050–0.100	32(6), 18(5), 51(6), 4(6), 29(6), 2(5)	61(1), 116(1), 7(4), 48(4), 131(4), 135(4)	2(3), 62(3), 63(3), 132(3), 23(3), 34(3), 53(3)	.	.	92(9)	13(4), 5(4), 9(4), 44(4)
0.100–0.150	23(6), 38(6), 73(6), 84(6), 93(6), 115(5), 126(5), 133(6), 55(6), 39(5), 113(6), 135(6), 19(5), 21(6), 56(6), 107(6), 122(6), 35(6)	77(4), 138(4), 24(4), 42(1), 50(4), 99(4), 111(4), 117(4), 33(4), 59(1), 5(1), 23(4), 18(1)	37(1), 55(1), 89(1), 99(3), 6(3), 29(3), 95(3), 127(3), 151(3), 131(4), 46(3), 117(3), 135(1), 12(1), 153(3)	.	.	5(9), 46(9), 68(9)	97(4), 110(4), 145(5), 8(4), 92(5), 107(4), 30(5), 42(5), 48(5), 58(4), 157(4), 51(3), 60(4), 128(5), 156(5), 12(5), 35(4)
0.150–0.200	101(6), 118(6), 124(6), 132(6), 114(6), 98(5), 34(6), 109(6), 50(6), 57(6)	11(1), 32(1), 64(1), 66(4), 120(1), 34(4), 40(4), 58(4), 93(4), 115(1), 30(1), 37(1), 75(1), 88(1), 95(1)	38(1), 133(3), 146(4), 5(3), 9(4), 24(3), 52(1), 73(3), 76(3), 85(1), 104(1), 113(4), 81(3), 101(3), 107(3), 4(3), 20(3), 50(1), 59(3), 67(3), 108(3), 126(1)	62(3), 27(3), 36(4)	85(1)	9(4), 8(4), 39(9), 84(10), 12(11), 36(9), 78(9)	37(4), 96(4), 139(5), 149(5), 3(3), 64(5), 90(5), 134(5), 78(5), 79(2), 147(4)

is most closely represented by the positions in Position-Cluster 9, which is a multidisciplinary group of biochemists, biologists, geneticists, microbiologists, and pathologists. The four faculty members whose initial positions are closest to the centroid of the equilibrium manifold are three geneticists and a microbiologist. The convergence to Cluster 9 is not surprising given the pattern of effects that radiate from this cluster (Figure 9.5).

Finally, in Columbia Social Science, the actors converge to a region that is most closely represented by the positions in Position-Cluster 4, which is a multidisciplinary group of anthropologists, economists, psychologists, and sociologists. The four faculty members whose initial positions are closest to the centroid of the equilibrium manifold are three sociologists and an anthropologist. The convergence to Cluster 4 is not surprising given the pattern of effects that radiate from this cluster (Figure 9.6).

The situation is more complex in the Physical Sciences at Columbia. Unlike the other science faculties, there are *two* destination manifolds. Furthermore, unlike the other science faculties, the equilibrium manifolds do not occupy regions that are in the vicinity of the initial position of any actor. This outcome is surprising, because it would have been reasonable to suppose (from Figure 9.4) that the First Manifold would be in the vicinity of the initial positions of one or more members of Cluster 4 and that the Second Manifold would be in the vicinity of the initial opinions of one or more members of Cluster 1. These results underscore the limitations of efforts to derive *systemic implications* from an inspection of simplified images of social structure. Although the implications are sometimes obvious, they are not always so; therefore, it is best to base these implications on formal analysis.

9.5 Concluding Remarks

Differentiated social structures are composed of social positions arrayed in multidimensional space, and the social distance between these social positions indicates the expected difference of opinion between actors who occupy different positions. The actors who occupy these social positions also are situated in a network of interpersonal influences. Flows of interpersonal influence allow the influence of actors, and the social positions they occupy, to ramify throughout the population and for agreements to emerge among actors in different social positions. The social space defines the domain within which such agreements are formed; if actors' opinions are transformed by the stipulated social influence process, then the transformed opinions must lie somewhere within this social space.

My analysis has shown that the social influence process, even in a highly differentiated social structure, can produce a convergence of opinion to particular regions of the social space. In some cases, the opinions have converged to locations that are proximate to the initial opinions of certain actors; hence, the agreements that are formed will tend to reflect the preferences of the occupants of these positions. In other cases, the agreements occupy locations that are not in the vicinity of any of the social positions of the actors; a more general method must be employed to characterize the content of such compromise agreements. In the next chapter I describe this method, which is based on the net relative contributions of particular actors and their social positions to equilibrium opinions.

The present analysis has served to define, in rough fashion, the *content* of the equilibrium outcomes of the influence system. Because of the multidisciplinary character of the clusters to which actors have converged, there is a strong suggestion of a dominant coalition that determines the equilibrium opinions of these science faculties; however, we must be careful in asserting that influence. Strictly, the evidence points to the content of the equilibrium opinions and *not* the influence of the actors who occupy these positions. The destinations of actors could arise as a compromise settlement from cross-pressures, rather than from the influence of those actors whose opinions closely reflect the content of the settlement. I now turn to an analysis of these influences.

9.6 Appendix: Mean Influence of Position-Clusters

Chicago Physical Science

	1	2	3	4	5	6	7	8	9	10
1	0.15	0.20	0.08	0.04	0.16	0.14	0.05	0.05	0.02	0.12
2	0.05	0.30	0.07	0.10	0.13	0.15	0.04	0.04	0.02	0.10
3	0.04	0.10	0.08	0.06	0.18	0.20	0.07	0.04	0.03	0.21
4	0.03	0.29	0.08	0.36	0.09	0.07	0.01	0.02	0.01	0.04
5	0.00	0.01	0.00	0.00	0.23	0.27	0.02	0.04	0.04	0.05
6	0.00	0.01	0.00	0.00	0.21	0.60	0.03	0.01	0.02	0.02
7	0.01	0.03	0.03	0.01	0.24	0.43	0.12	0.03	0.03	0.08
8	0.01	0.03	0.01	0.00	0.24	0.23	0.03	0.25	0.10	0.09
9	0.01	0.02	0.01	0.01	0.32	0.33	0.04	0.11	0.10	0.06
10	0.01	0.03	0.03	0.00	0.20	0.15	0.03	0.04	0.02	0.49

Chicago Biological Science

	1	2	3	4	5	6	7
1	0.58	0.08	0.01	0.10	0.02	0.03	0.02
2	0.60	0.16	0.04	0.11	0.03	0.04	0.03
3	0.38	0.09	0.08	0.15	0.08	0.11	0.11
4	0.40	0.06	0.03	0.37	0.06	0.03	0.05
5	0.34	0.05	0.08	0.17	0.19	0.05	0.12
6	0.33	0.03	0.05	0.06	0.03	0.34	0.15
7	0.28	0.03	0.07	0.11	0.08	0.18	0.26

Chicago Social Science

	1	2	3	4	5	6
1	0.51	0.07	0.31	0.03	0.07	0.02
2	0.04	0.48	0.29	0.04	0.12	0.03
3	0.07	0.12	0.57	0.05	0.11	0.01
4	0.06	0.11	0.36	0.09	0.30	0.03
5	0.03	0.08	0.20	0.08	0.54	0.07
6	0.04	0.13	0.12	0.05	0.44	0.22

Columbia Physical Science

	1	2	3	4	5	6	7
1	0.80	0.10	0.00	0.02	0.00	0.01	0.02
2	0.61	0.20	0.00	0.02	0.00	0.00	0.04
3	0.03	0.00	0.16	0.66	0.02	0.03	0.10
4	0.03	0.01	0.03	0.81	0.01	0.00	0.08
5	0.01	0.01	0.02	0.19	0.57	0.08	0.12
6	0.09	0.03	0.04	0.14	0.41	0.19	0.08
7	0.03	0.01	0.00	0.13	0.02	0.00	0.80

Columbia Biological Science

	1	2	3	4	5	6	7	8	9	10	11	12	13	14
1	0.28	0.02	0.02	0.03	0.02	0.02	0.00	0.00	0.45	0.05	0.04	0.02	0.03	0.01
2	0.14	0.07	0.07	0.05	0.03	0.05	0.01	0.01	0.32	0.09	0.06	0.02	0.06	0.02
3	0.10	0.03	0.04	0.07	0.04	0.06	0.02	0.01	0.33	0.07	0.11	0.03	0.08	0.02
4	0.04	0.01	0.01	0.16	0.02	0.07	0.01	0.01	0.39	0.11	0.04	0.01	0.08	0.03
5	0.11	0.01	0.04	0.06	0.17	0.07	0.01	0.00	0.27	0.12	0.04	0.01	0.06	0.03
6	0.02	0.01	0.01	0.04	0.02	0.40	0.05	0.00	0.14	0.11	0.06	0.01	0.08	0.05
7	0.04	0.01	0.02	0.06	0.02	0.22	0.04	0.00	0.20	0.06	0.10	0.02	0.18	0.04
8	0.04	0.04	0.03	0.04	0.02	0.13	0.02	0.05	0.17	0.06	0.27	0.03	0.07	0.02
9	0.09	0.01	0.01	0.08	0.01	0.03	0.01	0.00	0.39	0.07	0.04	0.01	0.03	0.01
10	0.01	0.00	0.00	0.06	0.01	0.05	0.01	0.00	0.14	0.05	0.01	0.00	0.04	0.02
11	0.04	0.01	0.03	0.03	0.01	0.07	0.02	0.01	0.21	0.06	0.41	0.03	0.06	0.01
12	0.08	0.01	0.05	0.06	0.01	0.03	0.01	0.00	0.31	0.10	0.18	0.06	0.08	0.01
13	0.02	0.01	0.01	0.05	0.01	0.07	0.04	0.00	0.16	0.09	0.05	0.02	0.42	0.05
14	0.02	0.01	0.01	0.08	0.03	0.18	0.03	0.00	0.15	0.15	0.03	0.01	0.20	0.10

Columbia Social Science

	1	2	3	4	5	6
1	0.73	0.05	0.03	0.13	0.03	0.02
2	0.08	0.53	0.09	0.21	0.05	0.04
3	0.02	0.04	0.59	0.25	0.04	0.06
4	0.05	0.04	0.13	0.28	0.11	0.03
5	0.07	0.07	0.13	0.37	0.30	0.06
6	0.02	0.03	0.12	0.12	0.03	0.68

10

Influence of Actors and Social Positions

Abstract: This chapter concludes my analysis of the influence system. I analyze the relative contributions of actors and their social positions to defining the content of the settled opinions of actors. I also develop and support an argument about the emergence of social dominance in macro-structures.

The equilibrium destinations of actors are a consequence of the system of interpersonal influences. If actors have converged to a region in which a particular subset of social positions is located, it is not necessarily the case that the actors in these positions are the most influential actors in the system and that they have determined this outcome. To be sure, if a particular actor has a dominant influence, then all actors' opinions will converge to the position of this actor. However, it also is possible that actors may converge to the location of an actor who is not an influential actor as a *compromise* position; in such a case, the actor to whose position other actors have converged represents the equilibrium consensus, but he or she is not an important determiner of the consensus. Moreover, in more complex circumstances (e.g., Columbia Physical Science) the destinations of actors may converge to a region in social space that is not in the vicinity of any occupied social position.

I now analyze the relative contributions of actors (and their social positions) in defining the content of the settled opinions of actors. In this assessment of the systemic implications of the influence system, the units of analysis are both individual actors and social positions (or position-clusters) that are occupied by actors. The distinction can be important. Individual actors, and therefore the social positions that they represent, may be highly influential. However, it also may be the case that no single actor in a social position is highly influential, while the social position (or cluster of proximate positions) has a large influence on other actors via the aggregation of influences of those actors who occupy the position.

The network of interpersonal influences that is involved in the opinion-formation process is described by **AW**, a $N \times N$ matrix of direct (unmediated) influences. The influence process generates flows of interpersonal influence, as well as a set of net or total interpersonal effects that are based on these flows. These total effects are a derived feature of the influence system, and are described by **V**:

$$\mathbf{V} = (\mathbf{I} - \mathbf{AW})^{-1} (\mathbf{I} - \mathbf{A}) \tag{10.1}$$

a $N \times N$ matrix of reduced-form coefficients that transform initial into equilibrium opinions

$$\mathbf{Y}^{(\infty)} = \mathbf{VY}^{(1)} \tag{10.2}$$

[Eqs. (2.11) and (2.15)]. As with **W**, the coefficients in **V** are nonnegative $(0 \leq v_{ij} \leq 1)$ and each row of coefficients sums to unity $\left(\sum_j v_{ij} = 1\right)$. Hence, an entry in **V** gives the *relative weight* of the initial opinion of actor j in determining the settled opinion of actor i. To get an image of the pattern of direct interpersonal influences among the social positions, we must concentrate on **AW**. To get an image of systemic implications of the influence system, we must concentrate on **V**.

10.1 Effects of Social Positions

To obtain an image of the macro-structure of influence among social positions, I employ the position-clusters that describe the major cleavages in these communities. If the members of each position-cluster have converged to approximately the same location in social space, then the total effects of actors upon them will be similar; hence, the sums of the total effects upon each actor in these position-clusters also will be similar. Moreover, to the extent that the members of a position-cluster have the same initial opinion, the sum of the total effects of the position-cluster indicates the combined relative weight of the opinion that is identified with the position. Thus, to indicate the pattern of influences of some position-cluster B upon another position-cluster A, I sum the total effects of the actors in B upon the actors in A and divide the sum by the number of actors in A. This procedure gives the relative total effect of each position-cluster. The results (reported below) confirm that the destinations to which the actors in these communities have converged are in the region of position-clusters that are occupied by subsets of actors who are collectively the most influential.

The Chicago Physical Science community converged to a region of social space occupied by certain members of Position-Clusters 5 and 6. The blockmodel of the total effects of the position-clusters is:

0.000	0.000	0.000	0.000	0.643	0.357	0.000	0.000	0.000	0.000
0.000	0.000	0.000	0.000	0.639	0.361	0.000	0.000	0.000	0.000
0.000	0.000	0.000	0.000	0.664	0.336	0.000	0.000	0.000	0.000
0.000	0.000	0.000	0.000	0.644	0.356	0.000	0.000	0.000	0.000
0.000	0.000	0.000	0.000	0.763	0.237	0.000	0.000	0.000	0.000
0.000	0.000	0.000	0.000	0.542	0.458	0.000	0.000	0.000	0.000
0.000	0.000	0.000	0.000	0.637	0.363	0.000	0.000	0.000	0.000
0.000	0.000	0.000	0.000	0.632	0.368	0.000	0.000	0.000	0.000
0.000	0.000	0.000	0.000	0.638	0.362	0.000	0.000	0.000	0.000
0.000	0.000	0.000	0.000	0.677	0.323	0.000	0.000	0.000	0.000

This blockmodel clearly shows that Clusters 5 and 6 determine the content of the equilibrium opinions, and that Cluster 5 is the more influential of the two clusters.

In Chicago Biological Science, the actors converge to a region that is most closely represented by certain positions in Position-Clusters 1 and 4. The blockmodel of the total effects of the position-clusters is:

1.000	0.000	0.000	0.000	0.000	0.000	0.000
1.000	0.000	0.000	0.000	0.000	0.000	0.000
1.000	0.000	0.000	0.000	0.000	0.000	0.000
1.000	0.000	0.000	0.000	0.000	0.000	0.000
1.000	0.000	0.000	0.000	0.000	0.000	0.000
1.000	0.000	0.000	0.000	0.000	0.000	0.000
1.000	0.000	0.000	0.000	0.000	0.000	0.000

This blockmodel shows that Cluster 1 has determined the content of the equilibrium opinions.

In Chicago Social Science, actors converge to a region in the vicinity of certain positions within Position-Cluster 3. The blockmodel of the total effects of the position-clusters is:

0.001	0.002	0.794	0.199	0.004	0.000
0.001	0.002	0.786	0.207	0.004	0.000
0.001	0.001	0.804	0.190	0.004	0.000
0.000	0.001	0.730	0.264	0.004	0.000
0.001	0.002	0.772	0.221	0.005	0.000
0.001	0.002	0.773	0.220	0.005	0.000

This blockmodel shows that Cluster 3 mainly determines the content of the equilibrium opinions. Here, the surprise is that Cluster 4, which appeared to be peripheral in the image of the structure of direct effects, emerges as a position that has modest effects on the consensus.

In the Physical Sciences at Columbia, there are two equilibrium manifolds that do not occupy regions in the vicinity of the initial position of any actor. The blockmodel of the total effects of the position-clusters is consistent with this result:

0.612	0.147	0.000	0.214	0.000	0.000	0.027
0.518	0.270	0.000	0.188	0.000	0.000	0.023
0.273	0.078	0.000	0.594	0.000	0.000	0.055
0.267	0.078	0.000	0.604	0.000	0.000	0.051
0.263	0.081	0.000	0.594	0.000	0.000	0.062
0.303	0.093	0.000	0.548	0.000	0.000	0.555
0.291	0.090	0.000	0.531	0.000	0.000	0.087

Most of the total effects are distributed between Clusters 1 and 4, but there also are nontrivial effects from Clusters 2 and 7. The pattern of the total effects of Clusters 1 and 2 differs from the pattern of effects for Cluster 4; in these patterns there are effects that span the cleavage in the social space of this faculty. Hence, the two parts of the social structure are pulled into regions that are occupied by neither.

In Columbia Biological Science, the actors converge to a region that is most closely represented by the positions in Position-Cluster 9, which is a multidisciplinary group of biochemists, biologists, geneticists, microbiologists, and pathologists. The blockmodel of the total effects of the position-clusters is:

0.000	0.000	0.000	0.000	0.000	0.001	0.000	0.000	0.691	0.307	0.000	0.000	0.000	0.000
0.000	0.000	0.000	0.000	0.000	0.001	0.000	0.000	0.636	0.363	0.000	0.000	0.000	0.000
0.000	0.000	0.000	0.000	0.000	0.001	0.000	0.000	0.645	0.354	0.000	0.000	0.000	0.000
0.000	0.000	0.000	0.001	0.000	0.001	0.000	0.000	0.640	0.358	0.000	0.000	0.000	0.000
0.000	0.000	0.000	0.000	0.000	0.001	0.000	0.000	0.603	0.396	0.000	0.000	0.000	0.000
0.000	0.000	0.000	0.000	0.000	0.003	0.000	0.000	0.571	0.425	0.000	0.000	0.000	0.000
0.000	0.000	0.000	0.000	0.000	0.002	0.000	0.000	0.611	0.386	0.000	0.000	0.000	0.000
0.000	0.000	0.000	0.000	0.000	0.002	0.000	0.000	0.608	0.389	0.000	0.000	0.000	0.000
0.000	0.000	0.000	0.000	0.000	0.001	0.000	0.000	0.748	0.251	0.000	0.000	0.000	0.000
0.000	0.000	0.000	0.000	0.000	0.000	0.000	0.000	0.249	0.750	0.000	0.000	0.000	0.000
0.000	0.000	0.000	0.000	0.000	0.002	0.000	0.000	0.627	0.371	0.000	0.000	0.000	0.000
0.000	0.000	0.000	0.000	0.000	0.001	0.000	0.000	0.642	0.357	0.000	0.000	0.000	0.000
0.000	0.000	0.000	0.000	0.000	0.001	0.000	0.000	0.600	0.398	0.000	0.000	0.000	0.000
0.000	0.000	0.000	0.000	0.000	0.002	0.000	0.000	0.559	0.439	0.000	0.000	0.000	0.000

The blockmodel of total effects indicate that Cluster 9 is highly influential and that Cluster 10 also has a substantial influence in determining the equilibrium opinions of the actors: Cluster 10 appeared as highly central in the network of interpersonal attachments, but did not appear central in the structure of the influence network. Hence, the importance of this cluster stems from its radiation of *weak* effects to all the other clusters on the social space.

Finally, in Columbia Social Science, the actors converge to a region that is most closely represented by the positions in Position-Cluster 4, which is a multidisciplinary group of anthropologists, economists, psychologists, and sociologists. The blockmodel of the total effects of the position-clusters indicates that Cluster 4 almost entirely determines the equilibrium opinions in this faculty:

0.034	0.012	0.000	0.954	0.000	0.000
0.013	0.020	0.000	0.966	0.000	0.000
0.010	0.010	0.000	0.979	0.000	0.001
0.008	0.007	0.000	0.985	0.000	0.000
0.012	0.011	0.000	0.976	0.000	0.001
0.012	0.010	0.000	0.976	0.000	0.002

If influence is evenly distributed among the population of actors in a social space, then the effect of a particular position-cluster will depend on the *number* of occupants of the cluster, because the influences of a cluster are accumulated across all the actors who are members of the cluster. However, size is neither a necessary nor a sufficient condition of influential positions. Some positions may be influential because many small influences have been aggregated. Other positions may be influential because of a single important actor or small subset of important actors who occupy the position. Large clusters may contain no influential members.

10.2 Influences among Actors

We can dig deeper into the foundations of the macro-structure of social influence by examining the extent to which the effects of a position-cluster are based on a subset of the members of that position. If the members of a position-cluster are structurally equivalent, then each member will make an identical contribution to the effect of the position-cluster. However, position-clusters are likely to contain actors who differ in their interpersonal influences, and therefore a refined analysis of individual-level influences is useful. What is remarkable and satisfying about this shift in the level of analysis is that it is based on the intimate linkage between individual and positional effects; i.e., the effects of one position-cluster on another cluster are conveyed by individuals and their interpersonal influences. Thus, the analysis of the organization of the influence of a position-cluster follows straightforwardly from the analysis of the macro-structure of social influence. Of particular interest is the distribution of influence among actors within those position-clusters (dominant coalitions) that have large effects on the settled opinions of actors.

For an analysis of the influences of actors who are situated in an influential position-cluster, it is important to divide the influences into (a) within-cluster influences on other members of the cluster and (b) between-cluster influences on members of other clusters. This division is important because (even when a consensus is produced) an actor's within-cluster total effects may differ from the actor's between-cluster total effects.

10.2.1 The Effects of Influential Position-Clusters

First, consider an influential cluster's between-cluster effects. If a consensus has been produced, then a single vector of interpersonal weights $\bar{v} = \{\bar{v}_1, \bar{v}_2, \bar{v}_3, \ldots, \bar{v}_k\}$ will describe all of the total effects of the actors in the dominant position-cluster on actors in other clusters; for instance, each of the between-cluster effects of actor i in $\mathbf{V}$ (i.e., those that concern the effect of actor i on other actors who are not members of i's cluster) will be approximately equal to $\bar{v}_i$. This homogeneity of individual effects is not a necessary outcome of an influence system, but when such homogeneity occurs, each actor will have a certain relative weight in determining the consensus that is formed, and it becomes possible to analyze interpersonal influence as if it were an individual attribute.

Table 10.1 presents the average total effect of each actor j of the influential position-cluster(s) on actors who are in a different cluster than j. Elsewhere, I have discussed this measure as *total effects centrality* (Friedkin 1991), but I did not restrict it to a subset of the actors in an influence system, as I do now. The Between-Cluster Total Effect Centrality of actor j (BTEC) is defined as the average total effect of actor j on the $N - n_j$ actors who are not members of j's position-cluster P_j

$$c_{\mathrm{BTEC}(j)} = \frac{\sum v_{ij}}{N - n_j} \tag{10.3}$$

If actor j is the sole occupant of the position-cluster then $N - n_j = N - 1$, and the measure is simply TEC (Friedkin 1991). The measure indicates the relative contribution of each member of a position-cluster to the cluster's impact on actors in other clusters.

The findings in Table 10.1 show that the influence of actors in the influential position-clusters is highly stratified, and that the cluster's influence is typically based on a fraction of the occupants of the cluster.

Table 10.1. *Rank-Order of Total Effects Centralities among Actors in the Influential Position-Clusters on Actors in Other Position-Clusters*

Chicago Physical Science				Chicago Biological Science		Chicago Social Science					
Cluster 5 $n = 18$		Cluster 6 $n = 39$		Cluster 1 $n = 42$		Cluster 3 $n = 47$		Cluster 4 $n = 11$		Cluster 1 $n = 20$	
Actor	TEC	Actor	TEC	Actor	TEC	Actor	TEC	Actor	TEC	Actor	TEC
98	.107	29	.077	78	.164	23	.276	130	.212	69	.161
22	.102	23	.076	116	.157	62	.257			12	.056
18	.099	21	.074	5	.156	117	.246			97	.023
115	.096	51	.070	18	.141	5	.002			19	.022
19	.095	124	.031	42	.139					47	.012
126	.078	113	.013	120	.127					28	.003
2	.073	55	.005	115	.095					89	.003
		73	.002	30	.015						
				32	.005						
				37	.002						

Columbia Physical Science				Columbia Biological Science				Chicago Social Science	
Cluster 2 $n = 2$		Cluster 4 $n = 28$		Cluster 9 $n = 24$		Cluster 10 $n = 5$		Cluster 4 $n = 19$	
Actor	TEC	Actor	TEC	Actor	TEC	Actor	TEC	Actor	TEC
46	.077	57	.524	68	.13	130	.164	44	.167
45	.009	76	.015	92	.128	70	.107	5	.161
		15	.006	36	.100	84	.105	17	.138
		56	.005	5	.098			97	.123
		29	.005	96	.081			58	.105
		36	.002	39	.049			13	.096
		71	.002	117	.023			35	.085
		82	.001	10	.008			8	.082
				45	.003			60	.010
				86	.001			96	.004

Note: Only total effect centralities greater than 0.001 are shown.

These findings also show that the impact of an influential cluster is usually an aggregated outcome of the occurrence of multiple influential actors in the cluster.

10.2.2 The Internal Organization of Influential Position-Clusters

I now consider the pattern of interpersonal influences *within* the influential position-clusters – the internal organization of the dominant coalitions. In each of the influential clusters, there is a center–periphery pattern in which influence is concentrated on a small fraction of the members. Further, the social organization is oligarchical in the sense that the self-weights of the most influential actors are close to the theoretical maximum values for such weights. The central actors are strongly attached to their preferences; however, these preferences are quite similar to those of the other central actors because they occupy a similar region in social space. Hence, the influence of these central actors on other actors (both near and far from them in social space) is *aggregated* and produces a consistent and powerful effect of the position-cluster of which they are members.

I will describe the internal social organization of the influential position-clusters with a submatrix of **V** that gives the total effect of actor j on actor i for each ordered pair of actors who are members of an influential position cluster. If there is more than one influential position-cluster, then internal organization of the combined clusters will be presented. To better convey the pattern of these total effects, the coefficients have been replaced with symbols:

*	$0 \leq v_{ij} \leq 0.024$
A	$0.025 \leq v_{ij} \leq 0.074$
B	$0.075 \leq v_{ij} \leq 0.124$
C	$0.125 \leq v_{ij} \leq 0.174$
.	
.	
.	
S	$0.875 \leq v_{ij} \leq 0.924$
T	$0.925 \leq v_{ij} \leq 0.974$
U	$0.975 \leq v_{ij} \leq 1$

In Chicago Physical Science, the submatrix of total effects among members of the influential position-clusters (i.e., Clusters 5 and 6) is:

```
ID
↓  CLUS
   ↓ TEC
     ↓      Total Effects Matrix
            ↓
 98 5 0.11  U********************************************************
 22 5 0.10  *U*******************************************************
 18 5 0.10  **U******************************************************
115 5 0.10  ***T*****************************************************
 19 5 0.10  ****U****************************************************
126 5 0.08  *****T***************************************************
  2 5 0.07  ******R**************************************************
 39 5 0.00  CCCCBBB***********CCCCB**********************************
 54 5 0.00  CCCCCCB***********CCCCB**********************************
 42 5 0.00  CCCCCCB***********CCCCB**********************************
 12 5 0.00  CCCCCCB***********CCCBB**********************************
 87 5 0.00  CCCCCCC***********BCCCB**********************************
 90 5 0.00  CCCCCBB***********CCCBB**********************************
104 5 0.00  CCCCCCB***********CCCCB**********************************
 63 5 0.00  CCCCCCC***********CBCBB**********************************
106 5 0.00  CCCCCCB***********CCCCB**********************************
130 5 0.00  CCCCCBB***********CCCBB**********************************
 92 5 0.00  CCCCCCC***********CBCBB**********************************
 29 6 0.08  ******************T**************************************
 23 6 0.08  *******************R*************************************
 21 6 0.07  ********************R************************************
 51 6 0.07  *********************R***********************************
124 6 0.03  BBBBBBB***********BBBBI**********************************
113 6 0.01  CCCCBBB***********BBBBBE*********************************
 55 6 0.01  CCCCCBB***********CCBBB*B********************************
 73 6 0.00  CCCCCBB***********CCCCB**B*******************************
133 6 0.00  CCCCCCB***********CCCCB**********************************
  4 6 0.00  CCCCCCB***********CCCCB**********************************
 35 6 0.00  CCCCCBB***********CCCCB**********************************
 32 6 0.00  CCCCCCB***********CCCCB**********************************
 93 6 0.00  CCCCCCB***********CCCCB**********************************
 84 6 0.00  CCCCCCB***********CCCCB**********************************
                   .                .
                   .                .
                   .                .
Essentially the same pattern of effects occurs for the remaining 25
members of Cluster 6.
```

There are two influential clusters. In each cluster the most influential actors have large self-weights (R, S, T, or U), and are negligibly influenced by any other actor. The heavyweights have relatively uniform modest effects (C or B) on the peripheral actors in the clusters. Finally, the peripheral actors in these clusters have negligible influences on each other. This is a classic center–periphery pattern, with the important qualification that the actors in the center (the heavyweights) do not influence each other. The submatrix of the social distances among the heavyweights indicates that they are modestly differentiated in social space:

	98	22	18	115	19	126	2	29	23	21	51	124
98	0											
22	0.323	0										
18	0.341	0.11	0									
115	0.155	0.188	0.224	0								
19	0.451	0.227	0.244	0.359	0							
126	0.463	0.173	0.187	0.343	0.127	0						
2	0.430	0.182	0.179	0.326	0.102	0.103	0					
29	0.435	0.187	0.189	0.293	0.360	0.256	0.305	0				
23	0.362	0.173	0.173	0.231	0.368	0.297	0.308	0.146	0			
21	0.415	0.180	0.225	0.276	0.365	0.280	0.324	0.124	0.117	0		
51	0.387	0.154	0.148	0.244	0.321	0.234	0.254	0.100	0.135	0.165	0	
124	0.389	0.196	0.215	0.256	0.383	0.308	0.321	0.155	0.069	0.112	0.139	0

Hence, the consensus that is produced does not simply reflect the similarities among the influential actors, but also reflects a potential *resolution* of the disagreements among them. Recall that all but twelve of the 141 actors are contained in an equilibrium manifold of diameter 0.030. The actors who are not contained in this tight region of consensus are the heavyweights.

In Chicago Biological Science, the submatrix of total effects among members of the influential Cluster 1 is:

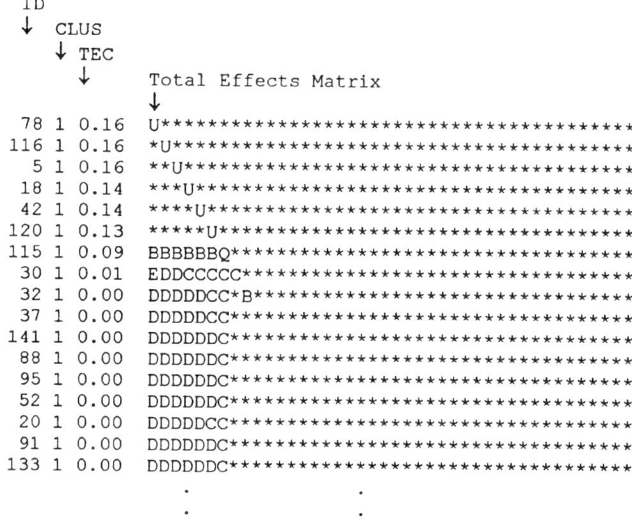

```
ID
↓  CLUS
   ↓ TEC
     ↓      Total Effects Matrix
            ↓
 78 1 0.16  U*****************************************
116 1 0.16  *U****************************************
  5 1 0.16  **U***************************************
 18 1 0.14  ***U**************************************
 42 1 0.14  ****U*************************************
120 1 0.13  *****U************************************
115 1 0.09  BBBBBBQ***********************************
 30 1 0.01  EDDCCCCC**********************************
 32 1 0.00  DDDDDCC*B*********************************
 37 1 0.00  DDDDDCC***********************************
141 1 0.00  DDDDDDC***********************************
 88 1 0.00  DDDDDDC***********************************
 95 1 0.00  DDDDDDC***********************************
 52 1 0.00  DDDDDDC***********************************
 20 1 0.00  DDDDDCC***********************************
 91 1 0.00  DDDDDDC***********************************
133 1 0.00  DDDDDDC***********************************
               .               .
               .               .
               .               .
Essentially the same pattern of effects occurs for the
remaining 25 members of Cluster 1.
```

There is a single influential cluster, and within this cluster there is a subset of six heavyweights who are not influenced by each other and who have uniform modest effects on the peripheral members of the cluster. The peripheral members of the cluster have negligible net effects on the consensus that is produced in this system. The submatrix of the social distances among the heavyweights indicates that they are modestly differentiated in social space:

	78	116	5	18	42	120	115
78	0						
116	0.472	0					
5	0.412	0.213	0				
18	0.435	0.377	0.367	0			
42	0.399	0.368	0.324	0.140	0		
120	0.428	0.473	0.340	0.252	0.233	0	
115	0.437	0.389	0.393	0.102	0.124	0.294	0

Again, the consensus that is produced does not simply reflect the similarities among the influential actors, but also reflects a compromise of the disagreements among them. Recall that all but seven of the 142 actors are contained in an equilibrium manifold of diameter 0.048. Here also, the actors who are not contained in this tight region of consensus are the heavyweights.

In Chicago Social Science, the submatrix of total effects among members of the influential Clusters 3 and 4 is:

```
ID
↓  CLUS
   ↓ TEC
     ↓     Total Effects Matrix
           ↓
 23 3 0.28 U*********************************************************
 62 3 0.26 *U********************************************************
117 3 0.25 **U*******************************************************
  5 3 0.00 FFF********************************************E**********
 59 3 0.00 FFF********************************************E**********
 76 3 0.00 FFF********************************************E**********
 53 3 0.00 FFF********************************************E**********
 29 3 0.00 FFF********************************************E**********
108 3 0.00 FFF********************************************E**********
               .              .
               .              . Essentially the same pattern continues
               .              . for the next 25 members of Cluster 3

 81 3 0.00 GFF********************************************E**********
 19 3 0.00 GFF********************************************E**********
151 3 0.00 GFF********************************************E**********
119 3 0.00 FFF********************************************E**********
147 3 0.00 GFF********************************************E**********
130 4 0.21 BBB********************************************R**********
  9 4 0.00 FFF********************************************E**********
106 4 0.00 FFF********************************************E**********
 27 4 0.00 GFF********************************************E**********
116 4 0.00 FFF********************************************E**********
 44 4 0.00 GFF********************************************E**********
 98 4 0.00 GFF********************************************E**********
146 4 0.00 GFF********************************************E**********
113 4 0.00 GFF********************************************E**********
131 4 0.00 GFF********************************************E**********
 58 4 0.00 GFF********************************************E**********
```

There are two influential clusters in this system. Cluster 3 is dominant, and within this cluster there is a subset of three heavyweights who are not influenced by each other and who have uniform modest effects on the peripheral members of both clusters. The influence of Cluster 4 is due to one actor, who also is influenced by the heavyweights in Cluster 3. The peripheral members of the cluster have negligible net effects on the consensus that is produced in this system. The submatrix of the social distances among the heavyweights indicates that they are modestly differentiated in social space:

	23	**62**	**117**	**130**
23	0			
62	0.141	0		
117	0.217	0.152	0	
130	0.323	0.301	0.329	0

Again, the consensus that is produced reflects a compromise of the positions of the influential actors. In this case, recall that all but four of the 153 actors are contained in an equilibrium manifold of diameter 0.014, and again the actors who are not contained in this tight region of consensus are the heavyweights.

In Columbia Physical Science, the submatrix of total effects among the members of the influential Clusters 1, 2, and 4 is:

```
ID
↓  CLUS
   ↓ TEC
     ↓      Total Effects Matrix
            ↓
 69 1 0.16  NB******************B*C***************************
 12 1 0.06  FHBB****************C*D***************************
 97 1 0.02  GCDB****************C*E***************************
 19 1 0.02  GCBD****************C*E***************************
 47 1 0.01  HCBBB***************D*E***************************
 28 1 0.00  HCBBB***************D*E***************************
 89 1 0.00  HCBBB***************D*E***************************
 96 1 0.00  HCBB****************D*E***************************
 84 1 0.00  HCBBB***************D*E***************************
 64 1 0.00  HCBBB***************D*E***************************
 79 1 0.00  HCBBB***************D*E***************************
 88 1 0.00  HCBBB***************D*E***************************
 78 1 0.00  HCBBB***************D*E***************************
 90 1 0.00  HCBBB***************D*E***************************
 38 1 0.00  HCBBB***************D*E***************************
 72 1 0.00  HCBBB***************D*E***************************
 53 1 0.00  HCBB****************D*E***************************
  4 1 0.00  HCBBB***************D*E***************************
104 1 0.00  HCBB****************D*E***************************
 85 1 0.00  GCBB****************D*F***************************
 46 2 0.08  GBBB****************H*D***************************
 45 2 0.01  ICBBB***************DBE***************************
 57 4 0.52  **********************U***************************
 76 4 0.01  DB******************B*LB**************************
 15 4 0.01  DB******************B*L***************************
 56 4 0.01  DB******************B*L***************************
 29 4 0.00  DB******************B*L***************************
 36 4 0.00  DB******************B*L***************************
 71 4 0.00  DB******************B*L***************************
 82 4 0.00  DB******************B*L***************************
                .                .
                .                .
                .                .
Essentially the same pattern of effects occurs for the
remaining 20 members of Cluster 4.
```

Influence is restricted to a subset of five actors in Cluster 1 and to two actors in Cluster 4. However, there is only one heavyweight in this system – actor 57 in Cluster 4 – and the effects of this actor are substantially larger for members of Cluster 4 than for the members of Clusters 1 and 2. Conversely, the effects of the most influential actor in Cluster 1 (actor 69) are substantially larger for members of Clusters 1 and 2 than for members of Cluster 4. Although there are mutual influences between the two main parts of this system, these influences are weak and the single heavyweight in the system does not have a structural basis for the production of consensus. The submatrix of the social distances among the influential actors indicates that they are modestly differentiated in social space:

	69	12	97	19	47	46	57
69	0						
12	0.455	0					
97	0.454	0.014	0				
19	0.453	0.012	0.022	0			
47	0.016	0.448	0.447	0.446	0		
46	0.429	0.457	0.458	0.452	0.436	0	
57	0.735	0.875	0.866	0.880	0.740	0.864	0

The social distances among the influential actors are larger on average in this faculty than in the other science faculties, and we have previously seen that no single region of consensus is produced. The single influential actor in Cluster 4 (i.e., actor 57) is separated widely in social space from all the other influential actors in the system, and the diameter of the equilibrium manifold containing the actors upon whom this actor's influence is concentrated is 0.078; although there has been a substantial reduction of opinion differences, the area of convergence has been shifted away from actor 57 as a consequence of other distant influential actors in the system. These other influential actors are concentrated in the Geological Science Clusters 1 and 2. Of the twenty-three members of these clusters, eighteen occupy a relatively tight social manifold of diameter 0.048 at equilibrium; the six actors who are outside this manifold are the influential geologists. Hence, in Geological Science, the organization is similar to the pattern of the other communities; however, this Geological Science consensus is unusual because it is not located in the vicinity of any of the positions of the influential geologists; its location has been affected by the combined weak forces of the other physical scientists whose positions are distant from those of the influential geologists.

In Columbia Biological Science, the submatrix of total effects among members of the influential Clusters 3 and 4 is:

```
ID
↓  CLUS
   ↓ TEC
     ↓      Total Effects Matrix
            ↓
 68 9 0.13  U****************************
 92 9 0.13  *U***************************
 36 9 0.10  **U**************************
  5 9 0.10  ***T*************************
 96 9 0.08  ****T************************
 39 9 0.05  BBBBBL******************BBB**
117 9 0.02  CCCCBBG*****************CBB**
 10 9 0.01  CCCCCB*D****************DCC**
 45 9 0.00  CCCCCBB*B***************DCC**
 86 9 0.00  CCCCCB******************DCC**
 66 9 0.00  CCCCCBB*****************DCC**
  4 9 0.00  DDCCCBB*****************DBC**
 79 9 0.00  DDCCCBB*****************DBC**
133 9 0.00  DDCCCBB*****************DCC**
 26 9 0.00  DDCCCBB*****************DCC**
153 9 0.00  DDCCCBB*****************DCC**
141 9 0.00  DDCCCBB*****************DCC**
 46 9 0.00  DDCCCBB*****************DCC**
 34 9 0.00  DDCCCBB*****************DCC**
 19 9 0.00  DDCCCB******************DCC**
 78 9 0.00  DDCCCB******************DCC**
 16 9 0.00  CCCCCB******************DCC**
 55 9 0.00  DDCCCBB*****************DCC**
 38 9 0.00  DDCCCB******************DCC**
130 10 0.16 ************************U****
 70 10 0.11 *************************U***
 84 10 0.10 **************************U**
113 10 0.00 DDCCBB******************DCC**
122 10 0.00 CCCCCB******************DCC**
```

There are two influential clusters. In each cluster the most influential actors have large self-weights (T or U), and these heavyweights have relatively uniform modest effects (B, C, or D) on the peripheral actors in the clusters. The peripheral actors in these clusters have negligible influences on each other. The consensus that is produced in this system is closely associated with the positions of certain heavyweights in Cluster 9, especially actor 92. The submatrix of the social distances among the influential actors indicates that they are modestly differentiated in social space:

	68	92	36	5	96	39	117	130	70	84
68	0									
92	0.199	0								
36	0.126	0.248	0							
5	0.207	0.141	0.204	0						
96	0.239	0.289	0.177	0.220	0					
39	0.222	0.293	0.139	0.229	0.207	0				
117	0.228	0.285	0.159	0.198	0.116	0.211	0			
130	0.388	0.218	0.452	0.335	0.483	0.489	0.482	0		
70	0.426	0.471	0.488	0.484	0.569	0.489	0.558	0.513	0	
84	0.379	0.297	0.408	0.309	0.468	0.395	0.458	0.313	0.342	0

In this case, recall that 143 of the 153 actors are contained in an equilibrium manifold of diameter 0.054; as in the other science faculties, the actors who are not contained in this tight region of consensus are the influential actors. Hence, the consensus that is produced reflects a compromise of the positions of influential actors; and the disproportionate influence of Cluster 4 in this system is due simply to the greater aggregated weight of the heavyweights who are situated in Cluster 9 than those who are situated in Cluster 10.

Finally, in Columbia Social Science, the submatrix of total effects among members of the influential Clusters 3 and 4 is:

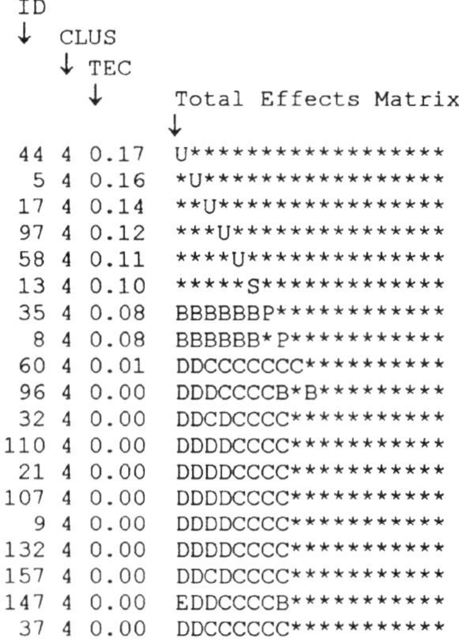

```
ID
↓  CLUS
   ↓ TEC
     ↓      Total Effects Matrix
            ↓
 44 4 0.17  U******************
  5 4 0.16  *U*****************
 17 4 0.14  **U****************
 97 4 0.12  ***U***************
 58 4 0.11  ****U**************
 13 4 0.10  *****S*************
 35 4 0.08  BBBBBBP************
  8 4 0.08  BBBBBB*P***********
 60 4 0.01  DDCCCCCCC**********
 96 4 0.00  DDDCCCCB*B*********
 32 4 0.00  DDCDCCCC***********
110 4 0.00  DDDDCCCC***********
 21 4 0.00  DDDDCCCC***********
107 4 0.00  DDDDCCCC***********
  9 4 0.00  DDDDCCCC***********
132 4 0.00  DDDDCCCC***********
157 4 0.00  DDCDCCCC***********
147 4 0.00  EDDCCCCB***********
 37 4 0.00  DDCCCCCC***********
```

There is a single influential cluster, and within this cluster influence is concentrated on a subset of eight actors; six of these actors are heavy-weights who are not influenced by each other and who have uniform modest effects on the peripheral members of the cluster. The peripheral members of the cluster have negligible net effects on the consensus that is produced in this system. The consensus that is produced in this system is most closely associated with the positions of the heavyweights 13, 5, and 44. The distances between the initial positions of the influential actors, i.e.,

	44	5	17	97	58	13	35	8
44	0							
5	0.194	0						
17	0.192	0.304	0					
97	0.226	0.224	0.309	0				
58	0.265	0.244	0.398	0.144	0			
13	0.251	0.262	0.360	0.121	0.081	0		
35	0.136	0.297	0.202	0.243	0.280	0.251	0	
8	0.253	0.231	0.388	0.182	0.103	0.103	0.278	0

indicate that they are modestly differentiated. Here 149 of the 157 actors are contained in an equilibrium manifold of diameter 0.066; as in the other science faculties, the eight actors who are not contained in this region of consensus are the influential actors.

10.3 Structural Foundations of Social Dominance

In a densely occupied region of social space, a large number of proximate actors can produce an unusually high level of interpersonal cohesion, and some or all of the occupants of such regions can possess unusually high indegrees with respect to their attachments. As a consequence of their high indegrees, the self-weights of actors will be near the theoretical maximum for such weights; these actors will be resistant to interpersonal influence and anchored on their initial preferences. High self-weight precludes a flow of influence to the actor; hence, a heavily self-weighted actor (a heavyweight) can be only a source of influence.

Heavyweights are not likely to be scattered throughout a social space, but are likely to be concentrated in a small number of regions. A high self-weight is a product of an *unusually* large number of received ties relative to the mean indegree of the population of actors. Therefore, a heavyweight is likely to emerge only from those regions of the occupied social space in which the probability of social ties among the occupants of the region is high and there are a large number of proximately located actors. A heavyweight is not likely to be based on attachments from actors in distant social positions, because the probability of social ties declines with social distance. Thus, high levels of cohesion among actors in proximate social positions is the most likely foundation for a heavyweight. Moreover, such highly cohesive regions are likely to contain one or more heavyweights who, by virtue of their near maximal self-weights, will be the originating points for many of the influence flows in the system.

Not all influence systems will have heavyweights, and when they occur they may be located in one or several regions of the social space. (a) If all the heavyweights in a population are located in a single region of the social space, and if the influence system produces numerous flows of influence from these heavyweights to other actors in the system, then the opinions of the population of actors are likely to converge toward the initial opinions of the heavyweights. Because of the proximate social positions of the heavyweights, a near consensus will be produced even though the interpersonal influences among the heavyweights are weak or nonexistent. (b) If heavyweights are located in several distant locations of the social space, then there will be competing influences on the actors who are not located in these positions, and the end product will be either a more differentiated pattern of equilibrium opinions or a consensus that is a compromise situated between the positions of the influentials.

In large-scale systems, the direct (unmediated) influences on each actor are not likely to be restricted to a few significant others, and the magnitudes of the direct interpersonal effects are likely to be small. To the extent that actors have many weak direct sources of influences upon them, a strong total effect of a particular actor (or social position) must be based on the *aggregation* of numerous sequences of interpersonal influences from the actor (or social position) to the other actors in the population. For the occurrence of strong total effects that encompass actors located in *distant* parts of the social space, the influence system must entail a large number of influence flows to those distant positions.

A segregated macro-structure is consistent with either a settled pattern of disagreement or consensus. Bridges allow flows of influence to reach all parts of the social structure, but do not imply that a consensus will be formed. Moreover, although connectivity among social positions is a necessary condition of consensus formation, it does not elucidate the structural basis and location of the dominant social positions toward which other actors' opinions tend to converge. To be sure, there are numerous structures of interpersonal influence that, on the basis of the social influence process described by Eq. (2.2), would produce a convergence of opinion to a particular social position. However, under the assumptions of the structural parameterization of the social influence theory (Chapter 4), the structure of the influence network is constrained by the pattern of social cohesion. My explanation of the emergence of social dominance takes this constraint into account.

10.4 Concluding Remarks

The pattern of influence in these faculties of science is hierarchical and markedly stratified. A special case of hierarchy occurs when the influence of the position-cluster is concentrated on a *single* actor. Another special case of hierarchy occurs when the influence of a position-cluster is concentrated on a larger subset of disagreeing actors, who form a consensus that determines the equilibrium opinions of the rest of the population. Neither of these special cases of hierarchy reflects the organization of influence in the communities under study, where the pattern of influence can be described as oligarchical. In these science faculties, the influence of a position-cluster is based on a subset of actors each of whom has a high self-weight ($w_{ii} \approx 1$); actors with such high self-weights are primarily anchored on their own initial opinions.[1] Such a constellation of heavyweights does not imply a lack of consensus. First, if the influential actors occupy a common position-cluster, then the equilibrium opinions of the population will converge to the general region that is occupied by the cluster. Second, the consensus that is produced in oligarchical structures will be a compromise position that reflects the relative contributions of influential actors; this position may or may not happen to be close to the initial positions of any of the influential actors.

This chapter has dealt with features of the macro-structure of interpersonal cohesion and influence which, in large-scale systems, allow the emergence of consensus and dominant social positions, toward which the opinions of numerous actors converge in a process of social influence. Influential actors, dominant social positions, and a consensus that reflects the preferences of these actors and positions have appeared in five of the six communities under study. In other types of communities, consensus and social dominance may not occur as often as they have in

1 N.B. This organization of influence does not imply an absence of interpersonal attachments among the heavyweights, only an absence of their susceptibility to influence.

these science faculties. As I have demonstrated with the analysis of Columbia Physical Science, the present theory also allows an analysis of the structural conditions under which consensus does *not* arise.

For instance, Heinz, Laumann, Nelson, and Salisbury (1993) document the occurrence of social spaces in policy arenas where dominant positions do not arise:

> Our findings reveal what appears to be a curious combination of structure and uncertainty in the social organization of interest representation. In many respects, the policy domains we have studied reflect a high degree of structure: the social characteristics and behaviors of both individual and organizational actors exhibit clear, sociologically interpretable patterns (Giddens 1984). One might expect such highly structured systems to produce relatively stable, predictable policy outcomes. Yet our analyses of a large set of policy events from 1977 to 1982 reveal considerable uncertainty in the policy-making process, both in terms of what items received serious consideration and in terms of who won and lost. (Heinz, Laumann, Nelson, and Salisbury 1993, p. 370)

They represent each of these policy domains as a three-dimensional social space in which social positions are arrayed on the surface of a sphere. The sphere has a "hollow core" in that no actors occupy positions near its center. Because the social ties are between actors who occupy proximate social positions, flows of influence occur on the surface of the sphere in long chains. In this setting, because the mediating social structure is weak, no dominant social positions emerge and the expected outcome of the influence system is a *settled pattern of disagreement.* Thus, social choice mechanisms (bargaining and politics) are by default the only available means of resolving the disputes and arriving at collective decisions. Because the effectiveness of the bargaining strategies of players is evidently not associated with their positions in social space, the outcome is uncertain – a more or less haphazard pattern of wins and losses among the competing actors.

11

Durkheim's Vision

Abstract. I return to Durkheim's vision of a sociology that would allow a transformation or social engineering of communities and organizations toward desirable states of unity and self-regulation. I discuss the promise of a structural social psychology in aiding the development of an operations-research approach to macro-sociology, and the relationship of formal and ethnographic work in delivering on this promise.

11.1 The Transformation of Social Space

In order to diminish anomy in the highly differentiated societies of the West, Durkheim proposed a revitalization of the corporations or guilds that were a prevalent form of occupational organization during the Middle Ages. Durkheim believed that a resurgence of guild associations would fulfill the largely unmet needs of social integration that emerged with the progress of differentiation. This view appears in various places in Durkheim's work, but most especially in *The Division of Labor in Society* (1933) and *Suicide* (1951), and in his lectures on professional ethics, *Professional Ethics and Civic Morals* (1958).

In *The Division of Labor* Durkheim asserts that the structural conditions of social integration have not appeared in most complexly differentiated social structures – not in the scientific community, nor in the marketplace, nor in the nation. He argued that a system of so-called corporate organizations would fulfill the conditions of societal integration that the division of labor has brought into being:

> If it is true that social functions spontaneously seek to adapt themselves to one another, provided they are regularly in relationship, nevertheless this mode of adaptation becomes a rule of conduct only if the group consecrates it with its authority. . . . A moral or juridical regulation . . . rests in a state of opinion, and all opinion is a collective thing, produced by collective elaboration. For anomy to end, there must then exist, or be

> formed, a group which can constitute the system of rules actually needed. . . . An occupational activity can be efficaciously regulated only by a group intimate enough with it to know its functioning, feel all its needs, and be able to follow all their variations. The only one that could answer all these conditions is the one formed by all the agents of the same industry, united and organized into a single body. This is what is called the corporation or occupational group. (Durkheim 1933, pp. 4–5)

> The absence of all corporative institutions creates . . . in the organization of people like ours, a void whose importance it is difficult to exaggerate. It is a whole system of organs necessary in the normal functioning of the common life which is wanting. Such a constitutive lack is evidently not a local evil, limited to a region of society; it is a malady . . . affecting all the organism. Consequently, the attempt to put an end to it cannot fail to produce the most far reaching consequences. It is the general health of the social body which is here at stake. (Durkheim 1933, p. 29)

In his other masterpiece, *Suicide,* Durkheim lays out a complementary theoretical context in which the significance of corporate organization might be seen. Rather than deducing the possible role of corporate organizations, as he had in *The Division of Labor* from a body of speculations about ideally integrative processes and conditions, in *Suicide* the possible role of corporate organization is inferred from data on suicide rates among different groups:

> We have shown that, while religion, the family and the nation are preservatives against egoistic suicide, the cause of this does not lie in the special sort of sentiments encouraged by each. Rather, they all owe this virtue to the general fact that they are societies and they possess it only in so far as they are well integrated societies; that is, without excess in one direction or the other. Quite a different group may, then, have the same effect, if it has the same cohesion. Besides the society of faith, of family and of politics, there is one other of which no mention has yet been made; that of all workers of the same sort, in association, all who cooperate in the same function, that is, the occupational group or corporation. (Durkhiem 1951, 371)

> The corporation has everything needed to give the individual a setting, to draw him out of his state of moral isolation; and faced by the actual inadequacy of the other groups, it alone can fulfill the indispensable office. (Durkheim 1951, pp. 378–9)

It is, finally, with an historical appreciation of corporate organizations that Durkheim underscores their significance. "In the past," he writes, "the corporation has proved that it could form a collective personality, jealous even excessively so, of its autonomy and its authority over its members; so there is no doubt of its capacity to be a moral environment for them" (1933, p. 378; also see Durkheim 1958). The agreements formed and enforced by corporate organization were not limited to occupational activity, but also penetrated into all aspects of their members' affairs. This penetration into various domains of social life underlies Durkheim's belief that occupational guilds are a potentially powerful basis for social integration that might promote the development of agreements on a spectrum of issues.

Durkheim is clear on what corporate organization ought to accomplish: It is to constitute the agreements that coordinate and control the activities of actors in a complexly differentiated population. Corporate organization should help maintain mutual understandings (concerned with belief, sentiment, trust, civility, procedure, and convention) within and across the differentiated parts of a social structure. Corporate organization, by maintaining these understandings, should foster the formation of the various technical and ad hoc agreements that are necessary to maintain the effective coordination and control of differentiated activities. Corporate organization ought also to foster a feeling of well-being among individuals by embedding them in a cohesive local setting or milieu, for society at the macro-level has ceased to exist except as a system of interdependencies and a body of vague sentiments and symbols.

However, Durkheim is vague on the form of corporate organization and the mechanisms by which it fosters the coordination and control of large-scale complexly differentiated populations. His discussions emphasize the development of *formal* decision-making bodies charged with the responsibility of regulating the activities of actors (Durkheim 1958). In his most concrete vision of this organization he describes a hierarchical subordination of regional associations to larger regional associations, governed ultimately by a legislative body that defines the rules of the system (Durkheim 1958, p. 37). Such a regulatory system is likely to be coercive if it is not constructed on a foundation of agreements; and it is not clear how the proposed formal system of regulation would generate such a foundation. Any such formal apparatus of hierarchical control is more likely to enforce the preferences of those regulators who happen to occupy positions of power in the apparatus, regardless of the degree of consensus on these preferences, than it is to create a consensus on these preferences.

Thus, Durkheim does not attend to voluntary noncoercive forms of social control, and his analysis of how social control is affected by informal social processes is weak. My contribution to this problem is a theory that focuses attention on certain key constructs and processes involved in the production of boundary-spanning interpersonal agreements. From the standpoint of this theory, it is the distribution of actors in social space that determines the gross features of the social structure. This theory does not deal with the transformation of social space, but it contributes to the study of such transformation (a) by directing attention to the important features of social structure that might be changed and (b) by allowing an assessment of the systemic implications of proposed or actual transformations of the social structure.

If Durkheim's essential argument is correct, i.e., that a guild system is likely to produce a cohesion that is the foundation of agreements among differentiated actors, then the present theory suggests that a guild system will have this effect only to the extent that it transforms social space. The antecedent condition of anomy is the absence of a ridge structure that would serve to reliably coordinate differentiated social positions. If anomy is to be reduced (as an inherent problem of social structure) via the development of formal or voluntary associations, then such a development must alter social space and produce a coherent ridge structure, i.e., a more or less ramifying social manifold in which all actors are joined via sequentially overlapping and densely populated regions of social space.

Is it reasonable to imagine that an array of formal and voluntary associations might alter social space and substantially reduce the structural foundations of anomy? Or must we rely on coercive mechanisms of social control to mitigate the absence of broadly shared agreements? Social science does not currently have an informed answer to these fundamental and important questions. In this vein of analysis, the work of McPherson and Ranger-Moore (1991) appears as a seminal effort to understand the role of voluntary associations in generating ridge structures. The emergence of voluntary associations is affected by the structure of social space, and when such associations come into being and affect actors' opinions and interpersonal ties, they also alter the structure of social space. Hence, a capacity to shape the structure of social space (to reduce conflicts between certain parts of the social structure) may depend on our understanding of the conditions under which those voluntary associations can be established and maintained that have substantial effects on ridge structures.

In short, I suggest that Durkheim's argument about corporate institutions might be usefully reconceptualized as a hypothesis within a larger theory about the origins and shape of social space. Such a theory would be concerned with the effects of social conditions and events on the definition of social space, the distribution of actors in this space, the configuration of social ties, and the influence network that joins social positions. The development of such a theory of structure, along with the development of a theory of the social influence process that is played out in the structure, should be viewed as two parts of a single coherent theoretical attack on Durkheim's problem.

11.2 Prospects for a Structural Social Psychology

What can structural social psychology contribute to the analysis of the structure of social space? While events and processes are affecting the distribution of actors in social space, it is the *influence network and process* that do the work of forming interpersonal agreements among the differentiated actors. The positions of actors in social space are the "start points" that define their predisposition on issues; their settled opinions on issues are "destination points" that may be some distance from these initial preferences. The systemic implications, or equilibrium outcomes, of a social structure are often not evident from the configuration of social distances and concrete interpersonal attachments among actors. These implications are sometimes revealed by a simple inspection of the structure of the influence network; however, it must be recognized that such implications rest on assumptions about the influence process. For instance, a production of consensus in networks where interpersonal influences are mediated effects (i.e., mainly based on flows of influence through intermediaries) depends on the repetitive monitoring and response of actors to the changing opinions of their significant others; without such repetitive monitoring and response no consensus would be formed. Thus, assumptions about social process govern the implications of social structure.

In influence networks with a complex structure, the systemic implications of the influence process can be understood only after a formal analysis has been conducted of the expected process of opinion formation among the actors; such analysis not only reveals the expected equilibrium destinations of actors but also, and more importantly, the contributions of distinct social positions, and the actors who occupy them, to these destinations. Thoughtful efforts to transform social space to achieve desired goals require a deep understanding of the actual mechanisms by which such transformations are likely to occur.

A structural social psychology that attends to the network of influences among actors represents an approach to the development of agreements that is not inconsistent with approaches that assume autonomous, self-interested actors. The structural social psychology that I have proposed is consistent with a viewpoint on actors as "strategic players" who attempt to increase their autonomy and influence by altering their bundle of interpersonal attachments (Burt 1992). Such "strategic players" are the close cousins of actors who, as part of an ongoing status-organizing process, seek to form and maintain ties with actors who are perceived to hold valued resources. Moreover, this structural social psychology is not inconsistent with the assumption that actors may hold fixed preferences and with the viewpoint that the conflicts among such actors can be resolved only via social choice mechanisms; the social influence process that I have described dovetails with the procedural mechanisms of voting that allow collective decision making in the absence of consensus.

However, the conceptual fit between the structural social psychology that I seek to advance and the rational choice approach to social action is not entirely comfortable. First, the idea that social space might be transformed via the actions of "strategic players" vastly inflates the abilities of such actors to acquire influence. Pursuing interpersonal attachments does not lead to autonomy and influence unless such attachments deliver resources to the "strategic player" that are perceived by others as being valuable. Influence is acquired by an actor to the extent that other actors seek and maintain ties with the actor; hence, if the ties a "strategic player" has pursued do not result in the acquisition of a basis of power, then the actor will not be influential. I suspect that there are many more "strategic players" than there are actors whose strategies to acquire influence actually pay off in achieved autonomy and influence.

Second, the idea that agreements among rational actors with fixed opinions provide a foundation for coordination and control vastly inflates the independent status of the bargaining and voting procedures that are involved in the production of such agreements. The idea that the strategic activities of rational actors provide a comprehensive explanation of norm formation is arguable; see Coleman's (1990) work along these lines. For instance, the mechanisms of logrolling and side payments logically do not apply to any situation that involves an important issue on which everyone has a strong interest and is unwilling to bargain. More fundamentally, such mechanisms are based on a foundation of mutual understandings entailing issues of trust and civility, legitimated procedures and authorities, and rights and privileges that is difficult to produce and maintain by social choice mechanisms. It is, for instance, difficult to legislate trust. Thus, Durkheim, in his lectures on professional ethics, dismisses the argument that unrestrained market activity is a sufficient basis of society (1958, p. 11), and he describes as a "strangely superficial notion" the idea that social control can be attributed to a set of activities, rather than to the fundamental agreements of belief and sentiment upon which the activities are maintained (1958, pp. 28–9).

The present structural theory of social influence describes in formal terms an interplay of social structure and process. Ironically, this work leads to an appreciation of qualitative ethnography as an adjunct to structural analysis. The outcomes of the social influence process that I have described are determined by the particular, more or less idiosyncratic, set of conditions under which the process occurs. The contextual conditions of the process are the structure of social space and the influence network that connects the actors in this space; and these conditions are shaped by numerous factors. For an understanding of the exact structure of a given social space and influence network, we not only must attend to the important bases of social differentiation and to the status characteristics of actors, but also may have to take into account unique local conditions (traditions, ecology, events) and individual personalities and animosities. Because the structure of social space and influence networks do not conform to standard templates, the analysis of an influence system is a form of descriptive ethnography – a network ethnography. There is a pressure to want to dig ever more deeply into the events and conditions that have shaped both the social space and influence networks. I have resisted this temptation, partly because I am not currently skilled at ethnographic inquiry, but also because my interest in the book focuses on the development of an approach to systems analysis that is based on a structural theory of social influence.

Jacob Moreno, the founder of sociometry, sought to develop social network analysis as a technology for improving the mental health of individuals, just as Durkheim sought to develop sociology so that it might inform efforts to reduce anomy. In this vein of social engineering, the present structural theory of social influence can be used to solve operations research problems – optimal structural changes that would enhance the production of consensus in a population or the power of certain social positions. This is a valuable direction in which to push the present work, because I suspect that it is the repetitive efforts to apply theory to concrete social problems that sustain theoretical advancements in a domain of problems. Any application of the present theory of social influence, which proposes a modification of social structure, requires a detailed ethnography of the targeted structure. It is not widely appreciated that a sophisticated application of operations research technology is typically based on a deep understanding of the constraints under which optimal solutions are obtained. These constraints deal not only with expense and practicality but also with values, sentiments, and conventions.

References

Abelson, Robert P. 1964. "Mathematical models of the distribution of attitudes under controversy." Pp. 142–60 in N. Frederiksen and H. Gulliksen (Eds.), *Contributions to Mathematical Psychology*. New York: Holt, Rinehart & Winston.

Alba, Richard D. 1982. "Taking stock of network analysis: A decade's results." *Research in the Sociology of Organizations* 1:39–74.

Alba, Richard D. and Charles Kadushin. 1976. "The intersection of social circles: A new measure of social proximity in networks." *Sociological Methods & Research* 5:77–102.

Allport, Gordon W. 1985. "The historical background of social psychology." Pp. 1–46 in G. Lindzey and E. Aronson (Eds.), *Handbook of Social Psychology, Vol. I*. New York: Random House.

Anselin, Luc. 1988. *Spatial Econometrics: Methods and Models*. Dordrecht, The Netherlands: Kluwer Academic Publishers.

Arabie, Phipps, Scott A. Boorman, and Paul R. Levitt. 1978. "Constructing blockmodels: How and why." *Journal of Mathematical Psychology* 17:21–63.

Asch, Solomon E. 1951. "Effects of group pressure upon the modification and distortion of judgement." Pp. 117–90 in M. H. Guetzkow (Ed.), *Groups, Leadership and Men*. Pittsburgh: Carnegie.

Asch, Solomon E. 1956. "Studies of independence and conformity: A minority of one against a unanimous majority." *Psychological Monographs* 70, no. 9, whole no. 416.

Berger, Joseph, Susan J. Rosenholtz, and Morris Zelditch. 1980. "Status organizing processes." *Annual Review of Sociology* 6:479–508.

Blau, Peter M. 1973. *The Organization of Academic Work*. New York: Wiley.

Blau, Peter M. 1974. "Parameters of social structure." *American Sociological Review* 39:615–35.

Blau, Peter M. 1977. *Inequality and Heterogeneity*. New York: Free Press.

Blau, Peter M. 1994. *Structural Contexts of Opportunities*. Chicago: University of Chicago Press.

Blau, Peter M. and Joseph E. Schwartz. 1984. *Crosscutting Social Circles*. Orlando, FL: Academic Press.

Boorman, Scott A. and Harrison C. White. 1976. "Social structure from multiple networks II: Role structures." *American Journal of Sociology* 81:1384–446.

Borg, I. and J. Lingoes. 1987. *Multidimensional Similarity Structure Analysis.* New York: Springer-Verlag.

Borgatti, Stephen and Martin Everett. 1992. "Notions of positions in social network analysis." Pp. 1–35 in P. V. Marsden (Ed.), *Sociological Methodology, Vol. 22.* Oxford: Basil Blackwell.

Bradbury, Malcolm, Bryan Heading, and Martin Hollis. 1972. "The man and the mask: A discussion of role-theory." Pp. 41–64 in J. A. Jackson (Ed.), *Role.* London: Cambridge University Press.

Brass, Daniel J. 1984. "Being in the right place: A structural analysis of individual influence in an organization." *Administrative Science Quarterly* 29:518–539.

Breiger, Ronald L. 1976. "Career attributes and network structure: A blockmodel study of a biomedical research specialty." *American Sociological Review* 41:117–35.

Breiger, Ronald L., Scott A. Boorman, and Phipps Arabie. 1975. "An algorithm for clustering relational data with applications to social network analysis and comparison with multidimensional scaling." *Journal of Mathematical Psychology* 12:328–83.

Burt, Ronald S. 1976. "Positions in networks." *Social Forces* 55:93–122.

Burt, Ronald S. 1982. *Toward a Structural Theory of Action.* New York: Academic Press.

Burt, Ronald S. 1987. "Social contagion and innovation: Cohesion versus structural equivalence." *American Journal of Sociology* 92:1287–335.

Burt, Ronald S. 1988. "Some properties of structural equivalence measures derived from sociometric choice data." *Social Networks* 10:1–28.

Burt, Ronald S. 1992. *Structural Holes: The Social Structure of Competition.* Cambridge, MA: Harvard University Press.

Camic, Charles and Yu Xie. 1994. "The statistical turn in American social science: Columbia University, 1890 to 1915." *American Sociological Review* 59:773–805.

Cartwright, Dorwin. 1965. "Influence, leadership, control." Pp. 1–47 in J. G. March (Ed.), *Handbook of Organizations.* Chicago: Rand-McNally.

Cartwright, Dorwin and Frank Harary. 1956. "Structural balance: A generalization of Heider's theory." *Psychological Review* 63:277–93.

Cole, Jonathan and Stephen Cole. 1973. *Social Stratification in Science.* Chicago: University of Chicago Press.

Cole, Stephen and Jonathan R. Cole. 1968. "Visibility and the structural bases of awareness of scientific research." *American Sociological Review* 33:397–413.

Coleman, James S. 1990. *Foundations of Social Theory.* Cambridge, MA: Harvard University Press.

Coombs, Clyde H. 1964. *A Theory of Data.* New York: Wiley.

Coser, Rose L. 1961. "Insulation from observability and types of social conformity." *American Sociological Review* 26:28–39.

Crane, Diana. 1972. *Invisible College: Diffusion of Knowledge in Scientific Communities.* Chicago: University of Chicago Press.

Crawford, Susan. 1970. *Informal Communication among Scientists in Sleep and*

Dream Research. Unpublished doctoral dissertation, University of Chicago.

Culliton, Barbara J. 1975. "XYY: Harvard Researcher Under Fire Stops Newborn Screening." *Science* 188:1284–5.

Dahrendorf, Ralf. 1959. *Class and Class Conflict in Industrial Society*. Stanford, CA: Stanford University Press.

Davis, James A. 1963. "Structural balance, mechanical solidarity, and interpersonal relations." *American Journal of Sociology* 68:444–62.

Davis, James A. 1967. "Clustering and structural balance in graphs." *Human Relations* 20:181–7.

Davis, James A. 1968. "Social structures and cognitive structures." Pp. 544–50 in R. Abelson, E. Aronson, W. McGuire, T. M. Newcomb, M. Rosenberg, and P. Tannenbaum (Eds.), *Theories of Cognitive Consistency: A Sourcebook*. Chicago: Rand-McNally.

Davis, James A. 1970. "Clustering and hierarchy in interpersonal relations: Testing two graph theoretical models on 742 sociomatrices." *American Sociological Review* 35:843–51.

Davis, James A. and Samuel Leinhardt. 1972. "The structure of positive interpersonal relations in small groups." Pp. 218–51 in J. Berger et al. (Eds.), *Sociological Theories in Progress, Vol. 2*. Boston: Houghton Mifflin.

Davis, James H. 1973. "Group decision and social interaction: A theory of social decision schemes." *Psychological Review* 80:97–125.

DeGroot, Morris H. 1974. "Reaching a consensus." *Journal of the American Statistical Association* 69:118–21.

Diener, E. 1980. "Deindividuation: The absence of self-awareness and self-regulation in group members." Pp. 209–42 in P. B. Paulus (Ed.), *Psychology of Group Influence*. Hillsdale, NJ: Lawrence Erlbaum.

Doreian, Patrick. 1981. "Estimating linear models with spatially distributed data." *Sociological Methodology* 1981:359–88.

Durkheim, Emile. 1933. *The Division of Labor in Society*. Translated by G. Simpson. New York: Free Press.

Durkheim, Emile. 1951. *Suicide*. Translated by J. A. Spaulding and G. Simpson. New York: Free Press.

Durkheim, Emile. 1958. *Professional Ethics and Civic Morals*. Translated by C. Brookfield. Glencoe, IL: The Free Press.

Ennis, James G. 1992. "The social organization of sociological knowledge: Modeling the intersection of specialties." *American Sociological Review* 57:259–65.

Erickson, Bonnie. 1988. "The relational basis of attitudes." Pp. 99–121 in B. Wellman and S. Berkowitz (Eds.), *Social Structures: A Network Approach*. New York: Cambridge University Press.

Festinger, Leon. 1950. "Informal social communication." *Psychological Review* 57:271–82.

Festinger, Leon. 1953. "An analysis of compliant behavior." Pp. 232–56 in M. Sherif and M. O. Wilson (Eds.), *Group Relations at the Crossroads*. New York: Harper.

Festinger, Leon. 1954. "A theory of social comparison processes." *Human Relations* 7:117–40.

Freeman, Linton C. 1979. "Centrality in social networks: conceptual clarification." *Social Networks* 1:215–39.
Freeman, Linton C. 1992. "The sociological concept of 'group': An empirical test of two models." *American Journal of Sociology* 98:152–66.
Freeman, Linton C., Douglas Roeder, and Robert R. Mulholland. 1980. "Centrality in social networks: II. Experimental results." *Social Networks* 2:119–41.
French, John R. P., Jr. 1956. "A formal theory of social power." *The Psychological Review* 63:181–94.
French, John R. P., Jr. and Bertram Raven. 1959. "The bases of social power." Pp. 150–67 in D. Cartwright (Ed.), *Studies of Social Power*. Ann Arbor, MI: Institute for Social Research.
French, John R. P., Jr. and Richard Synder. 1959. "Leadership and interpersonal power." Pp. 118–49 in D. Cartwright (Ed.), *Studies of Social Power*. Ann Arbor, MI: Institute for Social Research.
Friedkin, Noah E. 1978. "University social structure and social networks among scientists." *American Journal of Sociology* 83:1444–65.
Friedkin, Noah E. 1982. "Information flow through strong and weak ties in intraorganizational social networks." *Social Networks* 3:273–85.
Friedkin, Noah E. 1983. "Horizons of observability and limits of informal control in organizations." *Social Forces* 62:54–77.
Friedkin, Noah E. 1984. "Structural cohesion and equivalence explanations of social homogeneity." *Sociological Methods & Research* 12:235–61.
Friedkin, Noah E. 1986. "A formal theory of social power." *Journal of Mathematical Sociology* 12:103–26.
Friedkin, Noah E. 1990a. "A Guttman scale for the strength of an interpersonal tie." *Social Networks* 12:239–52.
Friedkin, Noah E. 1990b. "Social networks in structural equation models." *Social Psychology Quarterly* 53:316–28.
Friedkin, Noah E. 1991. "Theoretical foundations for centrality measures." *American Journal of Sociology* 96:1478–504.
Friedkin, Noah E. 1993. "Structural bases of interpersonal influence in groups: A longitudinal case study." *American Sociological Review* 58:861–72.
Friedkin, Noah E. and Karen S. Cook. 1990. "Peer group influence." *Sociological Methods & Research* 19:122–43.
Friedkin, Noah E. and Eugene C. Johnsen. 1990. "Social influence and opinions." *Journal of Mathematical Sociology* 15:193–205.
Friedkin, Noah E. and Eugene C. Johnsen. 1997. "Social positions in influence networks." *Social Networks* 19:209–22.
Giddens, Anthony. 1984. *The Constitution of Society: Outline of the Theory of Structuration*. Berkeley: University of California Press.
Goldberg, S. C. 1955. "Influence and leadership as a function of group structure." *Journal of Abnormal and Social Psychology* 51:119–22.
Gouldner, Alvin W. 1960. "The norm of reciprocity: A preliminary statement." *American Sociological Review* 25:161–78.
Granovetter, Mark S. 1973. "The strength of weak ties." *American Journal of Sociology* 78:1360–80.

Granovetter, Mark S. 1982. "The strength of weak ties: A network theory revisited." Pp. 105–30 in P. V. Marsden and N. Lin (Eds.), *Social Structure and Network Analysis*. Beverly Hills, CA: Sage.

Griffith, Belver C. and A. J. Miller. 1970. "Networks of informal communication among scientifically productive scientists." Pp. 125–40 in C. Nelson and D. Pollack (Eds.), *Communication among Scientists and Engineers*. Lexington, MA: D.C. Heath.

Griffith, Belver C. and Nicholas C. Mullins. 1972. "Coherent social groups in scientific change." *Science* 177:959–64.

Griffith, Belver C., M. S. Jahn, and A. J. Miller. 1971. "Informal contacts in science: A probabilistic model for communication processes." *Science* 17: 164–6.

Hall, Rupert. 1963. "Commentary by R. Hall." Pp. 361–81 in A. C. Crombie (Ed.), *Scientific Change*. London: Heinemann.

Hallinan, Maureen T. 1974. *The Structure of Positive Sentiment*. New York: Elsevier Scientific.

Harary, Frank. 1959. "A criterion for unanimity in French's theory of social power." Pp. 168–82 in D. Cartwright (Ed.), *Studies in Social Power*. Ann Arbor, MI: Institute for Social Research.

Harary, Frank, Robert Z. Norman, and Dorwin Cartwright. 1965. *Structural Models: An Introduction to the Theory of Directed Graphs*. New York: Wiley.

Haskins, Charles H. 1923. *The Rise of Universities*. New York: H. Holt and Company.

Hechter, Michael. 1987. *Principles of Group Solidarity*. Berkeley, CA: University of California Press.

Heider, Fritz. 1946. "Attitudes and cognitive organization." *Journal of Psychology* 21:107–12.

Heider, Fritz. 1958. *The Psychology of Interpersonal Relations*. New York: Wiley.

Heinz, John P. and Edward O. Laumann. 1982. *Chicago Lawyers: The Social Structure of the Bar*. New York: Russell Sage Foundation.

Heinz, John P., Edward O. Laumann, Robert L. Nelson, and Robert H. Salisbury. 1993. *The Hollow Core: Private Interests in National Policy Making*. Cambridge, MA: Harvard University Press.

Heiss, Jerold. 1981. "Social roles." Pp. 94–129 in M. Rosenberg and R. H. Turner (Eds.), *Social Psychology: Sociological Perspectives*. New York: Basic Books.

Holden, C. 1978. "ABASS: Social sciences carving a niche at the Academy." *Science* 199:1183–5.

Holland, Paul W. and Samuel Leinhardt. 1970. "A method for detecting structure in sociometric data." *American Journal of Sociology* 70:492–513.

Holland, Paul W. and Samuel Leinhardt. 1971. "Transitivity in structural models of small groups." *Comparative Group Studies* 2:107–24.

Holland, Paul W. and Samuel Leinhardt. 1973. "The structural implications of measurement error in sociometry." *Journal of Mathematical Sociology* 3: 85–111.

Holland, Paul W. and Samuel Leinhardt. 1976. "Local structure in social networks." Pp. 1–45 in David Heise (Ed.), *Sociological Methodology 1976*. San Fransisco: Jossey-Bass.

Horowitz, I. L. 1962. "Consensus, conflict and cooperation: A sociological inventory." *Social Forces* 41:177–88.

Janowitz, Morris. 1975. "Sociological theory and social control." *American Sociological Review* 81:82–108.

Johnsen, Eugene C. 1985. "Network macrostructure models for the Davis–Leinhardt set of empirical sociomatrices." *Social Networks* 7:203–24.

Johnsen, Eugene C. 1986. "Structure and process: Agreement models for friendship formation." *Social Networks* 8:257–306.

Johnsen, Eugene C. 1989. "The micro-macro connection: Exact structure and process." Pp. 169–201 in F. Roberts (Ed.), *Applications of Combinatorics and Graph Theory to the Biological and Social Sciences, Vol. 17*. New York: Springer-Verlag.

Kadushin, Charles. 1966. "The friends and supporters of psychotherapy: On social circles in urban life." *American Sociological Review* 31:786–802.

Kadushin, Charles. 1968. "Power, influence and social circles: A new methodology for studying opinion makers." *American Sociological Review* 33:685–99.

Kandel, Denise. 1978. "Homophily, selection, and socialization in adolescent friendships." *American Journal of Sociology* 84:427–36.

Knoke, David and Ronald S. Burt. 1983. "Prominence." Pp. 195–222 in R. S. Burt and M. J. Minor (Eds.), *Applied Network Analysis: A Methodological Introduction*. Beverly Hills: Sage.

Komarovsky, Mirra. 1973. "Presidential address: Some problems in role analysis." *American Sociological Review* 38:649–62.

Kruskal, J. B. 1964. "Multidimensional scaling by optimizing goodness of fit to a nonmetric hypothesis." *Psychometrika* 29:1–27.

Kuhn, Thomas S. 1962. *The Structure of Scientific Revolutions*. Chicago: University of Chicago Press.

Latane, Bibb. 1981. "The psychology of social impact." *American Psychologist* 36:343–56.

Laumann, Edward O. and David Knoke. 1986. "Network Theory." Pp. 83–107 in S. Lindenberg, J. Coleman, and S. Nowak (Eds.), *Approaches to Social Theory*. New York: Russell Sage.

Laumann, Edward O. and David Knoke. 1987. *The Organizational State: Social Choice in National Policy Domains*. Madison, WI: University of Wisconsin Press.

Laumann, Edward O. and Franz U. Pappi. 1976. *Networks of Collective Action: A Perspective on Community Influence Systems*. New York: Academic Press.

Lazer, David M. 1995. *Social Comparison Processes in Political Networks: The Case of Bureaucracy*. Unpublished doctoral dissertation, University of Michigan.

Lazarsfeld, Paul F. and Robert K. Merton. 1954. "Friendship as a social process." Pp. 18–66 in M. Berger, T. Abel, and C. H. Page (Eds.), *Freedom and Control in Modern Society*. Princeton, NJ: Van Nostrand.

Lewin, Kurt. 1948. *Resolving Social Conflicts*. New York: Harper.

Likert, Rensis. 1961. *New Patterns of Management*. New York: McGraw-Hill.

Luce, R. Duncan and Albert Perry. 1949. "A method of matrix analysis of group structure." *Psychometrika* 14:95–116.

MacRae, Duncan. 1960. "Direct factor analysis of sociometric data." *Sociometry* 23:360–71.

March, James G. 1957. "Measurement concepts in the theory of influence." *Journal of Politics* 19:202–26.

Marsden, Peter V. 1989. "Methods for the characterization of role structures in network analysis." Pp. 489–530 in L. C. Freeman, D. R. White, and A. K. Romney (Eds.), *Research Methods in Social Network Analysis*. Fairfax, VA: George Mason University Press.

Marsden, Peter V. and Noah E. Friedkin. 1993. "Network studies of social influence." *Sociological Methods & Research* 22:127–51.

McPherson, J. Miller and James R. Ranger-Moore. 1991. "Evolution on a dancing landscape: Organizations and networks in dynamic Blau space." *Social Forces* 70:19–42.

Mead, George H. 1925. "The genesis of self and social control." *International Journal of Ethics* 25:251–89.

Mead, George H. 1956. *George Herbert Mead: On Social Psychology*. Edited by Anselm Strauss. Chicago: University of Chicago Press.

Merton, Robert K. 1957. "The role-set: Problems in sociological theory." *British Journal of Sociology* 7:106–20.

Merton, Robert K. 1968. *Social Theory and Social Structure*. New York: Free Press.

Merton, Robert K. 1976. *Sociological Ambivalence*. New York: Free Press.

Merton, Robert K. and Elinor Barber. 1976. "Sociological ambivalence." Pp. 3–31 in R. K. Merton (Ed.), *Sociological Ambivalence and Other Essays*. New York: The Free Press.

Moscovici, Serge. 1985. "Social influence and conformity." Pp. 347–412 in G. Lindzey and E. Aronson (Eds.), *Handbook of Social Psychology, Vol. II*. New York: Random House.

Mulkay, Michael J., G. Nigel Gilbert, and Stephen Woolgar. 1975. "Problem areas and research networks in science." *Sociology* 9:187–203.

Naegele, Kaspar D. 1966. "Superintendency versus superintendents: A critical essay." *Harvard Educational Review* 30:372–93.

Newcomb, Theodore M. 1953. "An approach to the study of communicative acts." *Psychological Review* 60:393–404.

Newcomb, Theodore M. 1961. *The Acquaintance Process*. New York: Holt, Rinehart & Winston.

Newcomb, Theodore M. 1968. "Interpersonal balance." Pp. 28–51 in R. P. Abelson et al. (Eds.), *Theories of Cognitive Consistency: A Sourcebook*. Chicago: Rand-McNally.

Ouchi, G. 1977. "The relationship between organizational structure and organizational control." *Administrative Science Quarterly* 22:95–113.

Parsons, Talcott. 1937. *The Structure of Social Action.* New York: McGraw-Hill.

Pattison, Philippa. 1993. *Algebraic Models for Social Networks.* Cambridge, England: Cambridge University Press.

Pfeffer, Jeffrey. 1981. *Power in Organizations.* Boston: Pitman.

Pitts, Forrest R. 1979. "The medieval river trade network of Russia revisited." *Social Networks* 1:285–92.

Polanyi, Michael. 1962. "The republic of science: Its political and economic theory." *Minerva* 1:54–73.

Powell, Walter W. and Paul J. DiMaggio (Eds.). 1991. *The New Institutionalism in Organizational Analysis.* Chicago: University of Chicago Press.

Prentice-Dunn, Steven and Ronald W. Rogers. 1989. "Deindividuation and the self-regulation of behavior." Pp. 87–109 in P. B. Paulus (Ed.), *Psychology of Group Influence.* Hillsdale, NJ: Lawrence Erlbaum.

Price, D. and D. Beaver. 1966. "Collaboration in an invisible college." *American Psychologist* 21:1011–18.

Price, Derek J. de Solla. 1955. "The scientific foundation of science policy." *Nature* 206:233–8.

Rashdall, Hastings. 1936. *The Universities of Europe in the Middle Ages.* Oxford: The Clarendon Press.

Raven, Bertram H. 1965. "Social Influence and Power." Pp. 371–82 in I. D. Steiner and M. Fisbein (Eds.), *Current Studies in Social Psychology.* New York: Holt, Rinehart & Winston.

Schachter, S. 1951. "Deviation, rejection, and communication." *Journal of Abnormal and Social Psychology* 46:190–207.

Searle, John R. 1993. "Rationality and realism, what is at stake?" *Daedalus* Fall: 55–83.

Simmel, G. 1950. *The Sociology of Georg Simmel.* New York: Free Press.

Simmel, Georg. 1955. *Conflict and the Web of Group-Affiliations.* Translated by K. H. Wolff and Reinhard Bendix. Glencoe, IL: The Free Press.

Simon, Herbert A. 1953. "Notes on the observation and measurement of political power." *Journal of Politics* 15:500–16.

Simon, Herbert A. 1976. *Administrative Behavior: A Study of Decision-Making Processes in Administrative Organization,* 3rd ed. New York: Free Press.

Skolnick, Jerome H. and Joseph M. Woodworth. 1967. "Bureaucracy, information, and social control: A study of a morals detail." Pp. 99–136 in D. J. Bordua (Ed.), *The Police: Six Sociological Essays.* New York: Wiley.

Sneath, Peter H. A. and Robert R. Sokal. 1973. *Numerical Taxonomy.* San Francisco: W. H. Freeman.

Stasser, Garold, Norbert L. Kerr, and James H. Davis. 1980. "Influence processes in decision-making groups: A modeling approach." Pp. 431–77 in P. B. Paulus (Ed.), *Psychology of Group Influence.* Hillsdale, NJ: Lawrence Erlbaum.

Strang, David and John W. Meyer. 1993. "Institutional conditions for diffusion." *Theory and Society* 22:487–511.

Stryker, Sheldon and Anne Statham. 1985. "Symbolic interaction and role theory." Pp. 311–78 in G. Lindzey and E. Aronson (Eds.), *Handbook of Social Psychology, Vol. I* 3rd ed. New York: Random House.

Wallwork, Ernest. 1972. *Durkheim: Morality and Milieu.* Cambridge, MA: Harvard University Press.

Warren, Donald I. 1968. "Power, visibility, and conformity in formal organizations." *American Sociological Review* 33:951–70.

Wasserman, Stanley and Katherine Faust. 1994. *Social Network Analysis: Methods and Applications.* New York: Cambridge University Press.

White, Harrison C., Scott A. Boorman, and Ronald L. Breiger. 1976. "Social structure from multiple networks I: Blockmodels of roles and positions." *American Journal of Sociology* 81:730–81.

Wrong, Dennis H. 1961. "The oversocialized conception of man in modern sociology." *American Sociological Review* 26:183–93.

Wrong, Dennis H. 1994. *The Problem of Order: What Unites and Divides Society.* Cambridge, MA: Harvard University Press.

Author Index

Subject Index